WHAT'S HAPPENIN'?

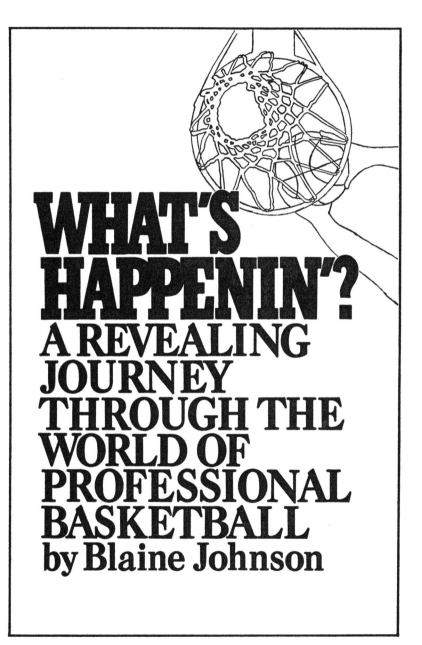

WHAT'S HAPPENIN'?
A REVEALING JOURNEY THROUGH THE WORLD OF PROFESSIONAL BASKETBALL
by Blaine Johnson

PRENTICE-HALL, INC., Englewood Cliffs, New Jersey

We acknowledge with thanks permission to quote portions from the following:

Newspaper articles reprinted courtesy of the Seattle *Post-Intelligencer*.

Wilt by Wilt Chamberlain and David Shaw. Copyright © 1973 by Wilt Chamberlain and David Shaw; reprinted by permission of Macmillan Publishing Co., Inc.

The Killer Instinct by Robert Cousy and John Devaney. Copyright © 1975 by Robert Cousy and John Devaney; reprinted by permission of Random House, Inc.

Basketball for the Player, the Fan and the Coach by "Red" Auerbach. Copyright © 1952, 1957, 1961, 1971, 1975 by Arnold Auerbach; reprinted by permission of Pocket Books, a Simon & Schuster division of Gulf & Western Corporation.

Material from column by Leonard Koppett in *The Sporting News.* Copyright © 1976 by The Sporting News.

What's Happenin'?: A Revealing Journey
Through the World of Professional Basketball
by Blaine Johnson

Printed in the United States of America
Prentice-Hall International, Inc., London
Prentice-Hall of Australia, Pty. Ltd., Sydney
Prentice-Hall of Canada, Ltd., Toronto
Prentice-Hall of India Private Ltd., New Delhi
Prentice-Hall of Japan, Inc., Tokyo
Prentice-Hall of Southeast Asia Pte. Ltd., Singapore
Whitehall Books Limited, Wellington, New Zealand
10 9 8 7 6 5 4 3 2 1

Library of Congress Cataloging in Publication Data
Johnson, Blaine,
    What's happenin'?
    1. Basketball—United States.   2. Johnson, Blaine.
3. Sportswriters—United States—Biography.
I. Title.
GV885.7.J63A35   796.32'3'0924 [B]   78-16719
ISBN 0-13-955120-4

For Ken and Ruth Johnson,
whose lessons of kindness and honesty
are all anyone could ask from parents,
and for Aaron, who is
everything one could hope for in a son.

Acknowledgments

In addition to the many pro basketball writers who shared their thoughts with me during the development of this book, I am especially grateful to Archie Satterfield, Scott Warmuth, Pat Detmer, Janet Miller, Mike Owens, Fred Brack, Merv Harris, and Steve Rudman for their assistance and guidance in the preparation of the material. Acknowledgment is also due to the players and coaches of the Sonics, as well as other individuals throughout the NBA, who became part of this story. Not all of them will applaud their role, but each represents a message which is vital.

CONTENTS

WHAT'S HAPPENIN'?

PROLOGUE

His voice is Monmouth Park tout, it's saaaaave-you-brothaaaa Savannah preacher and it's Shakespearean theater—all three riding on the spirit of ice cream man merriment. Zink makes 76ers games in the Philadelphia Spectrum a revival show. You are his from the time he brings the team out: "Heeeeeeeeearrrrrrrrr YOUR Philllllll-a-delfeeeeeeeeee-ah sev-UNNNNNNNNNNNN-teeeeeeeee SIXers."

McGinnis, Collins, there's the Doctor, Dawkins . . . here they come out onto the court, stars spangled in red, white and blue. And THE SONG. It starts with driving piano and follows with tambourine and voices full of gospel celebration. It's for the cause. Hallelujah. Hallelujah. "Clap your hands, evereeeeeeeebody, stomp your feeeet evereeeeeeebody. Heeer they come, Philadelphia Sevunteeeeesixers. On the run, stand up and see. . . ." It's strong. It fills the arena. The dunk line is going. Clap your hands, clap your hands. Doctah throw it off the glass, catch, twist, STUFF. "Heeer they come, Philadelphia, this is the year . . . ten, nine, eight, seventeeeeeesixers." Put your hands together, chil-ren. Cheer. Give me all your cares. Rejoice. "Clap your hands, Philadelpheeeeea, stomp your feet, stand up and cheer. Seventeeesixers."

You're loose. The dunk line is done. David Zinkoff, in his midsixties, the Philadelphia public address announcer since it all began back in 1946, a little man, hunches over his microphone playing up the crowd in a routine he never tires of. He's introducing Seattle. ". . . gawd, Pep-per-dine, Den-nus JOHNNN-sun. And HEEEER are your SON-nick star-tuhs. For-wud, Awl-CORN Ayy-n-mmm, Willie NORRRRR-wud, centuh, Nawth Car-ro-LINAH, Tommy Bur-LESS-sun . . ." Zink's into his rhythm. Nothing has happened yet. They haven't even played the National Anthem and you're bouncing your knee and tapping your hands. And you're sweating a little. "And NOW, the star-tuhs for YOUR Sev-un-TEE-Six-ers. Indeeee-ana, Numbah Thir-tah, Ge-ooooorg Mc-GINNNN-us . . ." Clap your hands, stomp your feet. The organist works in a salute, filling any audio holes left by eighteen thousand voices, hands, feet. "Mass-ah-chew-sus, Numbah Six, Ju-leeeeeus ERRRRRRR-ving. Al-baneeee State, Numbah Yo-leven, CALD-well JOOOONE-zzz . . ."

During the game, Zink punctuates every play, his voice climbing above the roar of the crowd after a spectacular dunk—putting on the frosting, making the play complete. Collins steals the ball, taps it ahead to McGinnis. This man of bull-power and racehorse grace comes up the right side in full flight. Erving, the floating sparrow, fills the wing. Omigod, it's the Doctah and McGinnis two-on-one. What the hell are

1

they going to DO? McGinnis thunders in. He takes off. The defensive man commits himself to the block. The ball is lobbed high over the basket. Erving's hands come out of the sky, controlling and thrusting the ball down at the hoop in a flash move. STUFFFFFF city. And out of the roar of the crowd, Zink's voice rides like an eagle, "ERRRRRRRR-ving from Mc-GINNNNNNNN-us."

When Zinkoff isn't being dramatic, he's cutesy. "Heard of Buffalo. Ta-ewwwwwwww for Mac-ka-dooooooooo. Spensaaaaaaaaaaw HAY-wud. Seeeee-uls shoooooooooo-ting thaaaaaaaaaaaa-reeeeeeee for TA-ewwwwwwwww. COLLLL-ins, by George. Bib-BEE in for FREEEEEEE. DUNNNNNNNK by DAWWWWW-kins." He has a hundred of them and even he has to wince at himself on some far-fetched occasions. But his genius is most evident when the 76ers are coming from off the pace late in a game. His voice rises, his inflections are like hits of Johnnie Walker. He has the crowd on a string. You let him take you away as you would give yourself to the revival tent evangelist. When it's over you feel totally fulfilled, yet in a way, used.

Initially I enjoyed being in the emotional clutches of Zinkoff. Eventually, though, I came to envy him. For he is the only creative person in all of pro basketball free of a role that can become muddled by conflicting perspectives. His job does not require him to deal with pro basketball in a manner that breeds the frustrations of making value judgments as well as analyzing personalities and events in the process of interpreting the significance of all that comes down in an NBA season. There are other positions and individuals who also do not demand this approach. But only Zinkoff's personality has attained such a colorful expression in a role so clearly open to the pursuit of fun. As anyone involved in sports understands, fun is what sports must be or something has gone wrong. This journey through an NBA season reveals how the rest of us, the reporters, the players and coaches, are caught in roles that so often deny that unobstructed pursuit of fun. It is left then to the fans to freely choose how they want to react in this world of pro basketball. That reaction, it will be discovered, is based on less than the full picture of what's happenin'.

1

Launching a Journey

Like the sun rising over a mountain, the aura is of brightness. It is springtime's sprouting possibilities. It just happens to fall in the autumn in the NBA. The optimism of a new job, a new home. The reverie of a new lover—well, it may not be that great—but this is the theme of enthusiasm that permeates all attached to the start of a new season in sports. It is a new lease on life where limitations and restrictive realities are shoved into the corners. The latter will eventually crowd hopes and unfounded aspirations. But, as training camp opens, everyone believes this is the year they will accomplish their full potential and maybe, somehow, go beyond.

Every player is convinced he can perform all the little things in his game with a greater proficiency than he has managed before. The aging vet shoves back time, trying to marry the skills learned to the health of yesterday. The knowledge came while the body was going, but this will be the year when the two will combine for the maximum product. The rookie comes with dreams of achieving a life-style in pro basketball for which he can imagine no acceptable alternative. He is desperate to show all he can do, or thinks he can do.

The coach seeks the blend, the revisions, that will bring cohesiveness among all these personalities and egos. Perhaps this will be the season his search for that seemingly magical string that ties it all together will be realized, allowing the team to contend for that ever-elusive excellence, a championship.

For the writer, for myself, at the beginning of this NBA season, it is a time of stimulation. There are the new faces and the fresh quotes of budding goals. There are the new match-ups and conflicts on the court. Old wounds and frictioned relationships are given a new start. The essence of sport is the unpredictability of events. The new season is a clean slate stretched out for the next nine months. In the time it takes to create a human being, life's full spectrum of drama can be developed—some of it that will be almost immediately forgotten, some that will be recorded in prose and statistics that will then be studied for as long as anyone cares about pro basketball.

There is no time as vivacious in a whole season, not even in the energy of a late-season playoff drive. And I was pumped. Pumped up and ready to go. In ten years in various aspects of sports journalism, I had never felt the enthusiasm I now felt. One season in the NBA covering the Sonics for the Seattle *Post-Intelligencer* had been like an appetizer, but there were so many rough spots: getting to know people, making contacts throughout the league and among the nation's major media. Now I would cruise.

My editor, a solid journalist named John Owen, brought up the probability our staff would be rotating beats every three or four years. It is a common enough practice with many sports departments—bringing a new mind with fresh eyes to a beat. But I felt as though someone were stealing my house to advocate such a thing. "No way. It takes at least three years to really establish yourself in a pro sport, to get comfortable, to become known so that people can trust you and know that you are a good man. It takes time to get fully into it. And when I do, I don't want to leave it. Of all the sports, basketball is the most entertaining, the atmosphere the most intimate, the personalities the most colorful. You can rotate all the other beats, but I want pro basketball till I retire. And that's at least thirty years down the line." Being recently divorced, I didn't even mind marrying myself to a job that required so much time and thought, often at the expense of big chunks of personal life. Except for too many days away from my ten-year-old son, Aaron, I was willing to devote the abundance of time required of the job.

It is important to understand what I was envisioning: I had been sufficiently encouraged in my inaugural season covering the Seattle SuperSonics that it could be one big happy family—where the players and the coaches and various management figures around the league would know I was tuned into their world. I didn't want to simply sit in judgment of their actions. We could be partners in an endeavor. Sure I might have to level criticism at times, but it would be fairly applied. By the nature of the world in which we worked, lived in a sense, we needed each other. There could be mutual respect, a camaraderie. Why not make it as comfortable as possible for each other? I was determined that it could be accomplished. Bold optimism was dominate in my approach to the new season at hand. I was convinced I was on the threshhold of establishing what would be a utopian role as a reporter. The pursuit of a long shot perhaps, but they do come in occasionally.

The soft glow of autumn sunshine was left beyond closed doors the morning the Sonics opened their training camp for the 1976–77 season in a windowless gym on the Seattle University campus. Nearly two dozen athletes clad in yellow sweat gear were sprawled across one end of the court as I walked in on the first session of drills. TV cameramen and photographers poked into the faces of the athletes for "mood shots"—heavy on the perspiration and grimaces. There were as many journalists on hand as there were athletes. Among them were newspaper columnists and radio and television reporters who would periodically look in on the Sonics during the season, but always from a distance. There were reporters who covered for the wire services and area papers, but only at home games. There were only three of us who traveled regularly with the team and therefore were full characters in the Sonic entourage that moved through a season. Radio broadcaster Bob Blackburn was one of the trio, but he was hired by the club and therefore was not in the role of true objectivity as a reporter. That left myself and Greg Heberlein, the pro basketball writer for the Seattle *Times* and thus my chief journalistic competition in the coverage of the Sonics.

Most of the press crew ringed the court, clutching notepads and sipping coffee from Styrofoam cups, smoking and exchanging wisecracks—all in contrast to the intensity felt by those they watched. Heberlein and I leaned against a wall, apart from the rest, and talked quietly. Both of us were in our early thirties and had developed a fairly expressive rapport as we spent the previous year, the first covering pro basketball for each of us, sharing the many road hours. It felt somehow strange after so much time together during the season to have not visited all summer. He was relating how the end of the previous season had left him emotionally devastated.

"I didn't realize how I had gotten on such a high level and when the season was over it was like a tremendous crash to come back to earth," the scholarly-appearing Heberlein explained quietly. "The tension in dealing with all these egos and the constant fear of getting beat on a story by you and trying to figure out just what's happening with the team all the time just built up over the months. You know something, I didn't realize how high I got on myself. Friends keep coming up and saying, 'Boy, you've got the greatest job in the world,' and guys in the office keep telling you what a great job you're doing and fans come up and tell you how much they like reading your stuff and every day you've got the lead story. And all the while you're flying all over the country first-class, sitting next to Bill Russell and talking to Kareem Abdul-Jabbar in the locker room. You get to thinking you're really somebody special. And when the season was over I just spun right off the end of the table. I mean I was really in bad shape for a while. I couldn't sleep, couldn't eat. I can't let that happen to me again and I've promised myself I won't get so emotionally involved again this year. I've got to keep my feet on the ground."

I confessed that I thought I had it pretty bad just because it took until July before I could get Russ's face out of my dreams. I knew, too, it wouldn't be long before the full cast would again be dancing in front of me night and day. That was part of the reason I was so interested on this morning to see who would eventually be selected to fill that cast for this season.

The leading role was already settled, of course. That belonged to Russell, beginning his fourth campaign as coach and general manager of the Sonics. Russell, the legendary heart of the great Celtics' dynasty. Eleven championships in thirteen years—in sports, that said it all. Now he stood on the sideline, stroking a few doughnut crumbs from his beard. It wasn't only his 6'9" size, but a face that so often seemed to mask over his emotions, that gave him a commanding image. He was clad in a black Greek fisherman's cap, a Sonic T-shirt, Levi's and sneakers.

His cousin, Bob Hopkins, was an inch taller than Russell. He was also Russell's assistant coach. Some said he was the basketball brains behind the Sonics. Some said that wasn't anything to brag about considering the club's tendency for undisciplined execution on the court. The polished, precise Celtics of Russell's era they weren't—but they had made the playoffs the previous two years.

There was reason to believe this might be the season Seattle would put on some of those Celtic airs. It was mainly up to Tommy Burleson, the 7'2" center Russell was supposed to make into his own image when he drafted him out of North Carolina State two years earlier. Things had looked very promising in Tall Tommy's rookie season. But coming off knee surgery the next year, Burleson had proven to be just one tall disappointment. Everyone was certain this season, his third as a pro, would tell just what sort of goods he stood for.

Hopkins, wearing green coaching shorts and a yellow perforated mesh shirt, fiddled with a whistle hanging from his neck as he paced among the players, who were prone for leg extensions. Trainer Frank Furtado, his beefy body clad in green—shirt, pants and shoes—led the drills. Fred Brown, wearing a brown knit shirt, brown slacks and loafers without socks, leaned back in a chair, his smooth features relaxed, his neatly trimmed Afro barely touching the wall.

"Why aren't you out there?" a reporter asked of Brown, who had slipped quietly into the gym and was now being discovered by some of the media.

Brown, who was starting his sixth NBA season, had been the league's fifth leading scorer the previous year with a 23.1 average. He was among the purest of shooters. His delicate shooting touch pretty well matched his attitude toward hard-nosed play. Smooth in his style and appearance, the 6'3" guard could be exasperatingly sly in his dealings with the press. Getting a straight answer out of him had proven to be one of the bigger challenges of my initial year's coverage of the Sonics. I had learned to be equally indirect with him, to spar and slide words around mischievously.

"I'm a holdout," he answered.

Heberlein perked up, asking, "Is that right?"

"Greg, come on, don't you believe I'd tell you the truth?" Brown answered, with his own special quiet laugh, which can seem to be mocking the partner in conversation.

Heberlein, right on a deadline for the *Times* afternoon editions, slipped out the door. He hadn't counted on getting this big a story out of the camp's opening. He went to a phone to call Bob Mussehl, attorney for Brown, Slick Watts and Spencer Haywood. Working for a morning paper, I didn't have a deadline to worry about for twelve hours, so I just sat on the floor next to Brown and tried to ease some information out of him as the first of the body-banging scrimmages got under way on court.

"What's really wrong?" I asked. "You hurt?"

"Don't you believe me, Blaine?" Brown asked, coy, enjoying the upperhand.

"No, because you just signed a three-year contract last year," I said.

"Well, I can renegotiate it, can't I?" he said.

"I imagine. What are you asking for?"

Brown got tired of the game and said, "Naw, I've got a groin pull."

"How long you going to be out?"

"Don't know, have to play it day by day," he stated, his eyes studying the court, where Burleson had just bowled over LaRue Martin with an inhospitable elbow.

Later, Heberlein returned and Brown found out that his holdout story had been pursued. "Can you believe that?" Brown asked me, sneering at Heberlein. "He called Mussehl. And Mussehl isn't my agent. He just does some papers for me. So don't be calling him about me," Brown continued to Heberlein, who, fuming, just stood looking out at the court. "I can't believe you did that, Greg. Can you believe that, Blaine?" I shrugged my shoulders. I hadn't believed the holdout story, but then I hadn't been under deadline pressure. Admittedly Heberlein looked like a sucker, but that's the price you so often pay if you're going to be a thorough reporter.

Mystery, more than mischievousness, surrounded the absence of Mike Green—the man who had the media drooling over the possibilities of a war of the post as he battled with Burleson for center supremacy. Green—the Sonics' No. 1 draft choice out of Louisiana Tech in 1973 who had hassled over contract details with Russell and opted for the ABA. Russell had said anyone 6′10″ and 185 pounds was too thin to play in the NBA, anyway. But, three years later, a summer's scramble for rights by Sonics owner Sam Schulman had finally brought Green into the Sonic net. Green was still piqued at Russell's comments of three years previous and he had snapped at reporters during the press conference called to introduce him to Seattle.

"What's your waist size?" a beer-barrel-bodied reported had asked.

"What's *yours*?" Green had shot back. And so on.

I had caught up with Green in the Sonics office after the conference. Looking for a means of establishing a line of communication with this lean—and seemingly mean—lad in a thirties gangster-style suit and a massive diamond ring, I tried to pursue a discussion of the ABA. It was my preseason prognosis that none of the four ABA teams coming into the NBA—Denver, Indiana, San Antonio and the New York Nets—had the depth to be competitive over the long season. I related this in so many words to Green.

"What do you think the NBA is, heaven?"

"No," I explained. "But I just don't think the ABA will be there for any division titles for a couple of years."

"Man, you ever seen Denver play?"

"Nope."

"Well, I'll tell you what," Green continued in a half-friendly, half-cockycool voice. "I'll lay two to one at least one ABA team wins a division title."

"All right," I said. This was great. I was getting into a dialogue that could be played with all season and I was going to take some of this rich man's money besides. No point in being too greedy. "How about forty against twenty?"

"Anything you want, sport."

So where was our aggressive, snipping Mike Green on this first morning of camp? Was he indeed the flake that had been reported? "He's absent due to personal problems," Russell explained, inviting and cooperating with no further discussion of the matter other than to say, "He'll be here tonight."

That took care of two thirds of the "hue-crew," in Brown and Green. The other, Leonard Gray, was bouncing people around on the court with zeal. Besides the bids of new recruits and the collision of match-ups for certain berths on the team, training camp is always marked with the big concern over a player's ability to rebound from major surgery. Gray, who at 6'7", 255, would put strain on steel, had torn his knee up just before the end of the previous season, doing it in the most absurdly unlikely manner possible—while *getting up* from the court after falling during a practice.

Now he was moving well, cutting and pushing himself into the thick of it. He roared into the hoop on fast breaks. He stopped and shot what always seemed like such a soft jumper from such a powerful body. He was the most imposing figure out there, although Burleson had beefed up 18 pounds from the end of the previous season to 256. Burleson now had some prowess in his presence. There was another "upright freezer" out there. A free agent named Collis Temple, 6'8", 220. He was everywhere. He was flying and diving and hungry as hell to make this ball club.

"There's no one in captivity mentally tougher than Collis Temple," Hopkins enthused, grinning as bodies bounced off one another very much in the sort of scene he thinks basketball should provide.

Suddenly there was a shove from Gray and an elbow flashed back by Temple. Everyone seemed to tense. Gray moved in on Temple, who put up his fists. Russell came out of his chair, "All right, all right." Still scowling at Temple, Gray dropped his hands. Temple held his hands up in an expression of innocence.

"I'm just followin' the leader. I'm just followin' the leader. I didn't do anything he didn't."

Reporters looked at each other. Hmmmmmm, someone to stand up to *Mister* Gray. Russell couldn't hide a smile.

The players ground away for nearly three hours. Then they shuffled off to the locker room, dismissed until the evening session six hours later. The reporters scurried up to Russell, notebooks poised. I was struck with the image of puppies scooting up to the feed dish. Russell served up a few cackles and a few quotes. "Yes, everyone seems in pretty good shape. No, I'm not disturbed that Mike Green isn't here. Yes, it's a wide-open battle at all positions. No, I didn't think Dennis Johnson looked lost. Yes, Leonard and Frank Oleynick looked pretty mobile—but you see you can't really tell about injuries until a player has to perform under the pressure of fatigue in a game." His catch line for this camp was: "This team will pick itself."

Russell was closing the doors on the evening sessions, which particularly hindered me because I was not going to get anything new for the morning edition whatever happened—and the Lord only knew what might happen when Green showed up to challenge Burleson and Temple and Gray got at it again. I headed off to the locker room for a feature interview with Temple, who had played at Louisiana State and failed in a couple of bids with ABA teams the previous year. He said he'd passed up law school to try another shot at the pros.

On the second day of camp, Green strolled into the gym at the very end of the morning drills, wearing a baseball cap sideways a la Alfalfa of Spanky and Our Gang. He took a ball and went to the far end of the gym and started shooting soft little jumpers. I went out onto the court and tried to establish a dialogue. He didn't want to discuss why he was late for camp, or much of anything for that matter. I asked him what Russell had told him about the center position.

"I haven't had three words with him. I assume it's a wide-open situation. It is in my mind."

He was still shooting, bouncing the ball and wheeling to his left and right. Bank shots, jump fall-aways. Little hooks. I decided to chase the ABA bit again.

"I'll bet you none of the ABA teams even make the playoffs," I announced—not being terribly confident, but feeling I'd already stolen some bucks from him on the division title bet.

He laughed. Sometimes Green comes across as a swaggering, slippery jive street freak. When he laughs like he was now, he seems more like a little boy, happy, innocent, almost huggable. He gave me my ten dollars against his twenty on that one. He went upstairs to the locker room where the players lingered in various states of undress. He came across Burleson, exchanged a brief greeting and hung around, getting a line on future teammates.

I brought out a picture taken at the previous day's practice. It showed Mike Bantom, who had been run down by Burleson, being pulled back to his feet by Russell. Some of the vets immediately got on Bantom, "Oh, is that your daddy helping you up? Is that your daddy, Michael? Look, his daddy's helping him." One got the impression Russell wasn't held in the same sort of reverence he had commanded during his first camp three years earlier. For the rookies who had come here now with that same reverence, these were derisive words and plainly puzzling. They didn't speak, but looked at each other as if to say, "Am I missing something?"

The next morning found Green and Burleson intact. No wars behind closed doors, apparently. Play was sluggish, everyone tired from two full days of toil. Russell called the bodies into a cluster at midcourt. He explained later: "I just wanted to remind them there are twenty-three guys here and only twelve are going to stick. I wanted to introduce a little stress into the situation and see who can handle it."

Russell's "games" frequently focus on individuals—often employing the word "boy." He once expressed very explicitly what he thinks of the word "boy." "No Negro man likes to be called 'boy.' We are men . . . not boys. Not some dumb backwoods slave . . . the connotation of 'boy' to the Negro is of servitude . . . of being less than a man."

Temple walked along the sideline near the end of the session.

"Come here, boy," called Russell.

Temple looked at Russell, mustering a slight smile. "My daddy told me to always respect my elders, sir. Just as long as they didn't ask too much or mean no harm." He didn't say, "So don't call me boy," but he meant it.

Then the show moved back behind closed doors.

Closed doors on some training camp drills are customary with some NBA coaches, but Russell and the Knicks' Red Holzman were the only ones to deny reporters access to regular season practices. Russell's banishing of the press developed from an incident I had with him in Boston in the middle of the previous year. The team was having a shooting practice in Boston Garden and since I needed something for a column, I decided this would be the best chance to catch a couple of the players without risking waking them or just not being able to find them in their hotel rooms. Nationally, most beat reporters attend team practices and file some sort of report. It had not been a practice for Seattle writers to schedule that sort of coverage, although my predecessor, Don Fair, used to catch most of them during his seven years on the beat—a work freak with unchallengeable determination to let nothing pass without his notice. It had a lot to do with why he was repeatedly named Washington's Sportswriter of the Year.

It had been a week or so since I'd been to a practice when I walked into the Garden along with Zaid Abdul-Aziz. The players, having thrown coats and scarves, hats and gloves, onto the courtside table, were involved in games of 21 while Russell leaned on the table. He spotted the two of us coming in. "What the fuck are you doing here?" he challenged, not viciously. I thought he was talking to Abdul-Aziz, because he was late. But Abdul-Aziz went out onto the court and Russell stood staring down at me.

Cheap shot, I thought. Here he is standing in the scuffy sports palace he had immortalized. A dozen (give or take one) World Championship banners dangling in the rafters and the guy who put them up there is asking me what I'm doing here. It felt kind of like Jesus meeting you in the church of your choice and telling you to go out front and guard the parking lot.

"What do you mean?" I asked Russell. "You told me in Salt Lake on the very first exhibition road trip that I could come to any practices I wanted and that if an occasion came up that you didn't want the press around, you'd tell me."

"I said that?" Russell asked. "Well, you aren't going to hold that against me, are you?" Which kind of reminded me of the question "Have you stopped beating your wife?" We kicked the matter around for another minute, then he said, "There are two main reasons why I don't like people (including reporters) at my practices. One is that guys tend to hot-dog it if there's anyone around to show off to. And that's when guys get hurt.

"Also, if I chew someone out he's more apt to listen to what I'm saying if there isn't anyone else except the team there. If he's in front of an outsider, he gets embarrassed and resents me for it."

It made sense. But as things developed over the next year and a half, it also provided a nice escape for embarrassing questions like, "Where's so and so?" and "Where were you?" and "How bad is so and so's ankle, which he just turned in practice?" and "Why aren't you guys practicing again today?" and "What started the fight?" and "Why don't you work on things you keep saying you're going to after all those losses?" Convenient not to have the press around.

No reporters in Seattle chose to challenge Russell on the matter. As reporters from other papers and national publications discovered, when Russell says he doesn't want you around, you can't get anywhere by challenging him. He just turns on a cold stare and walks away, refusing to discuss anything with the reporter—then, or later when he tries for an interview.

During the previous spring when Phoenix had humiliated Seattle in the first round of the Western Conference playoffs, Russell had become extremely reticent. His comments became increasingly innocuous. He seemed to have drawn way back inside of himself—to almost be out of anything but the most superficial of contact with those around him. He didn't even travel on the same flights with the team during the latter stages of the playoffs.

But he returned four months later from the Montreal Olympics as a refreshed man. His role as commentator for the TV coverage of the Games' basketball tournament had restored his ego. The drive across Canada had put some fresh breezes into his sails. He was having fun again. I encountered him one afternoon in his office. He sat behind his large desk, a large color photo of his first Sonic team on the wall behind him. The dark wood paneling and rust-colored carpet and the stereo and the soft leather couch all served to give the room the feeling of a fashionable den. The three-by-six-foot montage that hung on one wall depicted scenes of his career as a player. There were plaques and honorary degrees and several other large color photographs of himself which had been on the covers of national magazines. On the front of the desk sat a plaque which read "Experience Don't Mean Shit—Bill Russell."

His experiences and his ability to relate them, intermixed with his provocative and/or humorous observations, meant national celebrity status. Still he maintained a sense of mystique by carefully covering his motives and perspectives on things that might give people an unobstructed view of him. Since coming to Seattle he had declined to sit down for an extensive interview. I asked him for one and he granted it. The discussion came upon the matter of spoiled athletes, those who had come into easy money before ever having to prove themselves, thanks to the bidding war between the ABA and NBA.

I had asked: "Is it humanly possible to be real hungry when a player has been given a huge salary from day one?"

Russell: "Tommy Burleson is one of the few guys who, with prodding, not a lot but with prodding, is going to do his job, and the amount of money means nothing to him. Another guy is Bill Walton, I don't think you'll find another player in the league who works harder when he's healthy. He makes a lot of money and he started out making a lot. I think Kareem would be a superstar if he was making fifty thousand a year—because he takes pride in what he's doing."

"Do you think within the past decade the public has become disenchanted with players because of their big salaries—especially those who didn't have to work their way up?"

Russell: "I think the press has a lot to do with it. A writer sits there and says to himself, 'That son of a bitch is making a hundred thousand a year and he ain't doing his job. I work hard at mine. Why's he getting away with it?' "

"When talents like Spencer Haywood and John Brisker can't be used on your team, does this give you a feeling of frustration in what you've done as a coach?"

Russell: "No. I really don't want to get into it because there's only one player since I've been in pro basketball that I've said something bad about and that was Wilt. I don't want to come down on these guys now. I've been in pro basketball seventeen years as a player and a coach and I've been out of the playoffs once—that's not bad. In team games that's the only goal you can have. I don't think those guys understand that. They don't put a scoreboard up at the end of the court that says Number Five got seven points and Number Twenty got thirty-one. It just says that one team got a hundred and two points and the other got ninety. Until you come to grips with that realistically and do the things to make sure your team has the most points at the end of the game, you don't understand the principle of the game."

"How do you look back on your career as a player?"

Russell: "Sometimes I forget about the way I played. Then I'll come across a picture in a magazine or something that will show me playing and it'll make me feel good. I like to look back and say, 'Yeah, I played professional basketball and I was good.' I loved it. I enjoyed it. The older you get, the more of your life becomes memories. I'm glad that I don't look back and say, 'I played pro ball and I made a hundred thousand or four hundred thousand a year.' If that's all it meant, that would be sad. I was proud of what I did."

"What is important to you right now?"

Russell: "I'm proud of my accomplishments as a player. I'm especially proud of my accomplishments here. I'm not finished and like I say, success is a journey. I want to win a championship, of course."

"Why?"

Russell: "Because that's what the game is all about, winning. That shows that you're doing things right. And almost as important, or in some ways just as important, I want to make this franchise a financially successful operation."

"Does it bother you that some segments of Seattle's society are critical of your not taking a more active part in community affairs and making more speaking appearances?"

Russell: "No, it doesn't. I try to accept people for what they are and I hope they'll do the same for me. I guess this sounds kind of silly, but I'm basically a shy person. Now, I'm a single man, yet I find it very, very difficult to approach a woman and say, 'Let's go out' or 'I'd like to talk to you.'

"I never know what people are going to say to me. I don't think I'm overly friendly or unfriendly. What I try to do more than anything else in the world is not bother anybody. And I don't want anybody bothering me."

That was hardly a philosophy compatible with his role as a public figure, yet Russell was making more money than any of his NBA managerial counterparts, was certainly the most celebrated and there was no doubt—as the season began—he was captain of his ship.

2

In Search of the Brass Ring

Despite his ability to tidal-wave a room with his laugh, Russell was basically stoical in his rapport with the community. Even those of us who were more intimately involved as players and reporters traveling in his company so often felt Russell to be untouchable. That left the role of "The Fans' Main Man" to Slick Watts, Seattle's Love Child. He was a man-child of uncontrolled enthusiasm. His emotions spilled all over anyone who came near him—and most importantly, he let everyone feel they were welcome. He was a hustler, on the court in aggression, off the court in cunning, but he was huggable.

Watts had the credentials to be a storybook figure. When there seem to be limitations to what positive thinking can produce, a Watts comes along to force you to remember there are those who successfully grab for the brass ring. He mocks attempts at simple definition. However, you believe if you can understand what is emanating from such a special personality, you will know the wonders of hero worship, willpower and emotional relationships.

It is nearly impossible not to be fascinated by Watts. He is a living legend—in the "now" sense. He may not be celebrated when he is through with his accomplishments, as is a Russell or an Elgin Baylor or a Wilt Chamberlain. Yet he creates an atmosphere of awe. It isn't simply the feat, but the energy, the runaway self-esteem. His scrambling, make-mayhem ways on the court are a direct reflection of his quick and agile physical skills. Probably no one in the league can match his sense of showmanship and self-designed dramatics. His bald head, which sports a "cocked-halo" headband on the court, highlights his appearance of distinction. But it was much deeper than a shiny pate.

As this season was beginning, Watts was launching his fourth pro campaign. He was coming off a season in which he became the first NBAer to reign as league champion in both steals and assists. By a vote of the coaches, he had been named to the all-defensive team. He had been selected as the Citizenship Award winner by the nation's pro basketball writers. In his own supercharged way, Watts was gobbling enough life for a dozen men. And it was impossible not to sense an accompanying doom behind the dazzle of his daily exuberance—as if something would have to eventually give, break down, be atoned for. But now he had a headband wrapped around his world.

The details of his path to the pros are colorful and at the same time provide an insight into the life of the black child in the rural South, from which many of today's NBA performers emerged. It is also the account of how one develops the hunger to accomplish in such a competitive environment as the NBA and how littered the path is with obstacles that keep many others from ever making it. The style in which he imparts his story also signals Watts's genius for wit and entertainment:

"I been playin' all sports since I was about four. I was always small, but my uncle and my brother were the stars and they made sure I got to play. I couldn't really play no defense or anything like that, but I used to run behind people and steal balls—leave my man and just cause chaos for the other team. I guess I developed that as a kind of style. When I was in the sixth grade I had to transfer to Rolling Fork High 'cause my school was destroyed. I went out for the junior high team. My brother and my uncle were stars on the varsity in high school and my sister and my auntie were the stars on the girls' team. And my daddy played on a Sunday baseball team—he could hit a baseball a mile. My coach told me I was too small. I went home. I was depressed. But I kept comin' around every day and I got on by bein' the little water person on the bench. That spring the baseball coach told me I was too small, but after the season started, the little shortstop, Burns, got hurt and I got to play. I got started then and by the time I finished school it seemed I had been around forever. When we used to play other places people would boo me and say, 'He shouldn't be playin'. He's too old. He's older than my daddy. Boo.'

"I got my bald head when I was in the seventh grade. I caught a hook-and-go pass playin' football and a cat named Green and a cat named Duckins hit me and my helmet flew off and it was wet and I did the splits and cracked my head and it was kind of like a legend happenin'. My hair got a patch of bald and so I decided to shave it all off. People used to come to see us play in high school because I was bald. I was like an outcast. I was depressed sometimes, but my daddy said, 'All great men are made different.' When I got to the ninth grade, my brother was a senior and my uncle, Freddie—one of the best ballplayers in the world, one of the most versatile athletes I ever seen walk on God's earth—had graduated. Coach called me over and said, 'Duck, you got to get ready to be a leader now, so start working on your defense and passing.' They called me Duck then 'cause when I was littler I was real quick and my grandfather was real fast on his feet and he used to get behind me to whup me sometime, but he could never catch me. He used to run me all over, through the fields. Never catch me. He was faster than I was, but I'd wait until he got next to me, then I'd duck between his legs or cut back and make him trip. He just chased me for his entertainment. He was about fifty then, but he could run.

"My mother always taught us, whatever we had to be proud of it. The things we didn't have, we didn't miss. Now when I look back, we was poor. But then I thought I was gifted. We had clean clothes. My mama and daddy had to hustle to get it. We thought it was easy. But they did it for us. We always ate. Mama says now, it was hard times. If somebody threw me down and got me grass-stained, I'd have to fight, 'cause Mamma whupped me when I came home with my clothes stained. My mamma used to want me to wear jeans. But then I thought jeans was a disgrace. At school they used to talk about ya', 'ain't got nothin' but jeans.' But now jeans is the thing. Mamma used to say ain't nothin' wrong with jeans and khakis if they is clean. But I got me a job cleanin' up a grain elevator so I could buy my own clothes. I was happy though. Me and this guy used to play basketball by the moonlight up on this hill. Fella named Carl Frazier and I used to play about two hundred games a week. He'd be Wilt and I'd be Russell, or sometimes it would be the other way 'round. We had a rim with a gunnysack on it for a net.

"Rolling Fork, Mississippi, had about two thousand people. It was a rural area spread along the road, 'bout fifty miles south of Jackson. My father was known as a brave man. Everybody knew he was a nice fella and that he would compromise. But don't abuse none of his privileges and his privileges was his kids and his wife. My daddy had a big temper. He used to hunt. He was known for his use of guns. Just don't step on none of his property and the people he loved. Back then the police used to sometimes make you get out of the car. 'Spit out you gum, take off you hat and wanna whup ya.' They stop me and say, 'You Ivory's boy, right?' I say, 'Yes, sir.' They say, 'You be slowin' that thing down there, boy,' and they let me go 'cause they know how my daddy was. He was very emotional, cry in a minute. But he used to tell the police, 'You all know my chillin'. Don't ever harm them or I'll be layin' in the grass to kill ya.' He always taught me don't fight unless you mean to do harm.

"We never did go outside the area, like up to Jackson or other places where we wasn't known. We always stuck around where we had roots. I went to my first zoo when I was sixteen years old. You didn't get a chance to do all those things then. Played ball at night, went to school in the day and ate good, had friends. For my little old round world, that was all I needed. When I was young and in high school I was about five-eleven, hundred thirty-two pounds, nothin' but thin and balls, smallest guy on our team. But I could run all day. I used to run eight miles up the highway to see this little girl friend named Barbara Berry after practice. Then I'd run back home before Mamma got home so she wouldn't whup me.

"When we played tough teams, coach would say, 'Duck, you gotta go your way.' I was cocky and I could get sixty, seventy points a game if we needed 'em. When I was a senior our coach was L. C. Thigpin. He had a philosophy—'up it' he used to say. That's the only strategy he had, bring it down and 'up it.' Freddie didn't make it in college. He knew he was good, but he didn't take no type of advice from nobody. He'd go into the gym and shoot twenty in a row in front of the coach and then say, 'You need me, but I won't come to none of your practices.' So the scouts didn't come around much because the only fella they had tried didn't work out.

"I went off to a mostly white school. The dean of students at this junior college got on us for dating white girls, but I tried to look past the hurt and make them feel ashamed for the way they was treatin' us. My daddy taught me you can deal with a situation by rebelling and gettin' killed or you can handle it by dealin' with it and showin' others their weakness. I was at this school, Henderson Junior College in Arkansas, for about a week and I said, 'I'm lonely. I got to get away from here.' Bob Hopkins was coachin' at Alcorn A&M. He wanted me. They had won about twenty-seven in a row, but they was a young team and I wanted to start somewhere as a freshman. I saw Drake lose to UCLA for the national championship on TV and I wanted to go to Drake. But when I got there my grades wasn't good enough. I wanted to give it up, but my daddy said. 'Wherever you go, you gonna have problems. Stick it out.'

"So I went to Grandview J.C. in Iowa. I stayed there a year. I got into a lot of trouble. I was the type of fella that didn't want to go to school and knew I couldn't go home and tell my mamma I had quit. She'da had a fit. My daddy would have wanted to kill me. I used to do crazy things and try to get thrown out. But no matter what happened they wouldn't do it. I said, 'I did it,' and they'd say, 'No, Shine'—they called me Shine then—'you too good, you didn't do it.' I pulled the fire alarm. They wouldn't believe me. I said, 'Oh my God, I can't even get *thrown* out of school.' So I settled down and learned to enjoy myself and learn about life. We went to the nationals and lost to Bob McAdoo's team. He shot that same ol' long jumper from the corner. It was cold and snowy up there in Iowa. I called Coach Hopkins, who had moved down at Xavier in New Orleans, and said, 'It's cold up here and I want to come to your school.' He said, 'I don't know why you went way up there, anyway. Come on down.'

"I worked on a golf course during the summer up there in Iowa and they gave me four hundred dollars for a plane ticket, thinking I was coming back to school, but I didn't show up no more. I got down there at Xavier like on about August 15 and I had this big ol' wide hat on my head when I walked into the cafeteria. People say, 'Now, what in the hell is *that*?' Coach Hopkins say, 'He can play basketball.' I was kind of small and they just all kind of looked at me and was all kind of freaked out, just checkin' me out. Some people was tryin' to talk me down. I went into the cafeteria the next day and got up on a chair and said, 'I know you all checkin' me out. But give me four months and this going to be my school.' I was crazy, but in about three months' time everybody there was my people. I could go up to the financial aids office and get what I wanted. Other kids had to wait in line, they just let me in up front. Girls wouldn't even give no party on campus until I got there. It was about two thousand people and we all dug each other. I wasn't bigity, I just got in line kind of sweet so I wouldn't step on nobody's feelin's.

"Coach Hopkins didn't want me scorin', but I still would put in some shots that would scare myself. It just was the way I felt about the game. Coach Hopkins changed me and took some of my love for the game away. He was tryin' to make me have control and play tough defense. My daddy called and said, 'Don't let him upset you. Be a man.' He always said it ain't a question of who is right or wrong, but a question of what position you is in. If someone is over you and he tell you to do something, if it ain't nothin' to hurt you or kill you, do it. I learned to steal balls so I could stay in the limelight. I couldn't get no scorin' on offense, but he couldn't stop me from gettin' layups on defense. It's like the fans in Seattle now. They know I don't have to score to be good. Anybody that knows basketball anywhere in the country that watches me play knows that.

"When I didn't get drafted, I gave up. I figured it was all politics. I said, well that's it, I'm going to be a teacher. I started swinging toward Deborah more. She had been the girl who was strong and never got upset. I needed someone to lean on when I thought I wasn't going to be in the pros. So, I said, 'Mamma, I'm gonna get married.'

"My mamma said, 'You gonna get married? Is the girl pregnant?'

"No, Mom, I'm just gettin' married. My daddy said, 'Well, boy, you know how I told you about a man being a fool to get married.' So I got married. And Coach Hopkins came to my wedding and that's when I found out he liked me. I thought he didn't like me. We went through three years cussin' each other out and then he drove two hundred miles to be at my wedding. Coach Hopkins didn't do things like that and that really freaked me out.

"Hop and I called Russ in Seattle and tried to get him to give me a tryout.

"Russ said, 'Boy, can you play?'

"I said, 'Yes, sir, I can play.'

"He said, 'You know you're very little. You gonna have to bring your game.'

"I said, 'I can play.'

"So he sent me a ticket and I sold all my furniture, called up all my friends and said, 'I ain't comin' back.' They all said, 'You be back, you too small.'

"I was layin' up in bed one night thinkin' about what Coach Russell was sayin' in the papers about how he was gonna bring a bat and a carrot to camp and if you can't run you better walk to the unemployment office. And I could envision myself in Seattle—ain't never been there yet or even heard about it, but I could see myself there.

"Now, I had a slipped disk or something. I couldn't even put on my shoes sometimes. In college they used to call me 'Soft Behind' because I used to walk around with a pillow instead of books because I couldn't sit on nothing hard. Doc said I inherited it from my father. When I was seventeen years old I used to lay up in bed and cry it hurt so bad sometimes.

"So Hop and I got on the bird and came to Seattle. And when I got there I looked up at the mountain and the rain and I called my ma and said, 'Ma, this is pretty country up here. Just like God made it for me. It's lovely even when it's raining.' And my daddy said, 'We be prayin' for you.'

"On the first day of rookie camp I went into the gym and I seen all these big ol' fellas and Coach Russell sittin' up there and laughing at everybody and sayin' they couldn't play. Being a free agent you didn't get much of a look. Then Russell would say, 'Come here, boy, you get out there and play with those draftees.' At first he was giving me a look just because of Hoppy and trying to be nice.

"Hoppy said, 'You gotta shot. These fellas are all for themselves.' I kept on my game, scored a little, passed, stole the ball. The newspapers started writing a little about me: 'Who's this little bald-headed fella out there taking the ball away from everybody?'

"After the final rookie camp scrimmage, the fans gave me a big hand and we went into the dressing room and Russell came in and all the rookies were just sittin' there with their heads down. And Russell said, 'Anybody gonna read to see who gonna stay for the vets' camp?' Silence. So he says, 'Harold Fox.' Then he named that other jumpin' boy from South Carolina, can't remember his name. 'And Slick Watts.'

"I said, 'Whew, that's a trip.'

"I called my daddy and said, 'Well, I got past the first round. He invited me back.' And my daddy said, 'We praying for you.' And so we went to picture day and I got me a green headband and they give me a little suit with Number Thirteen on it. I signed a contract, but it was just to make sure I wouldn't sue them if I got hurt in camp. Didn't say nothing about giving me no money. One down and eight days to go.

"We got all loaded up for the bus up to Port Angeles. And I was just sittin' in the back of the bus waitin' to leave in front of the Sonic office and all these veterans drove up in their Cadillacs and their Mercedes-Benzes and they had on their bad leather suits and their wives and girl friends was all kissin' them good-bye and I was just sittin' there all alone. I'll never forget that.

"The first day of camp Russ is out there really exercising all of us, trying to see who has heart. You have to show heart or you're gone. Man, he was workin' us. Russ came up to me and he said, 'Boy, you can't touch your toes?' Man, my back was killing me so bad that day I paid this little boy to put on my socks. But when he said touch my toes, God or somebody just gave me the strength to endure the pain. I mean, pain shot all up my legs and across my back and I was just shuddering it hurt so bad. But I got down. He said, 'Yeah, I see you can touch your toes, boy.' He was just grinnin'. I might have paralyzed myself, but I had to do it.

"I left every practice walkin' like a snail. Just fall into bed. I was so beat I didn't eat or nothing, just fall into bed till they drug you back out for more.

"I laid in bed one night and I said, 'God, it ain't worth this much.' And I called my daddy and I said, 'Basketball is not worth this, Daddy.' But he said to stick with it.

"Me and Dick Gibbs looked better than anyone else in camp. We was hustling and diving on the floor and stealin' balls. On about the third or fourth day we had this scrimmage and I was takin' all of them. I was scoring on Fred Brown and Dick Snyder and all of 'em.

"Russ says, 'Who's checkin' you, boy?'

"I shouted back, 'Nobody, sir!'

"And Hop was standin' out there tellin' Russ, 'I told you this boy could play. I told you this boy could play.' And the papers were writing about me and Russ said, 'He is the best-looking guard I've got out there right now. I don't like to be enthused about things like that.' Russ said that in the paper. 'But he's the best-lookin' guard we got out there. I don't know how long he's gonna last, though.' I kept scratchin'.

"Then the sixth day of camp he came to me with another contract. Said, 'Sign this, boy, you a pro ball player.' I was the only rookie to make it. He gave me fifteen hundred bucks. I sent it all home to Mom and Dad. I came back the next day and asked him for some more. He said, 'You a free agent, boy.' I said, 'But I can play, sir.' He said, 'I'll tell you what I'm gonna do. I'll give you more than I give most people. I'll give you twenty-five thousand.' So I got twenty-three thousand a year and the bonus.

"I looked pretty good through exhibition season and then the regular season started and he called me one day and I went for a ride in his car and he said, 'Boy, you gonna be all right. In four years, you'll be ready.'

"I said to myself, 'Oh, man, you just don't know.' "

"After camp, Russell set me down for about thirty games. I didn't get no playin' time. Best thing that ever happened to us, losin'. I got to go out there and it was fun for the fans. They didn't have nothin' else to cheer for. They enjoyed watchin' someone out there doin' the best he knew how and divin' on the floor and creatin' excitement. When things was goin' bad, they started chantin', 'We want Slick. We want Slick.' I remember he put me in against Portland and I shot a fadeaway fallin' out of bounds. I got my confidence from that one shot. Then it was December the first, 1973. We was playin' Atlanta. He put in the paper, 'Watts might start.' Russ said, 'I'm tired of this no pass, no teamwork team. He's four years away, but we can't wait on him. Gotta try him now.' Started me against Pistol Pete. I block three of his shots, got twenty-one points, nine rebounds and fourteen assists. I was doin' things Jerry West and Dave Bing did. Not some guy named Slick. Russ figured I was playin' over my head. I had a big game a couple days later in Chicago, and afterward Reverend Jesse Jackson came to me and said, 'You a leader. One day Russ gonna let you have it. You a leader.' I started about nineteen games in a row and they started writin' about me bein' Rookie of the Year. Sayin' wouldn't it be nice for a free agent to take it all.

"I was just a little ol' walk-on and I didn't know what was happenin'. The veterans would say to me on the road, 'Come on, rook, I'm gonna feed you tonight.' But all of a sudden when I started gettin' all that publicity, some of them stopped talkin' to me, stopped smilin' at me, stopped takin' me to dinner. Said I was big time. I became a loner. I was gettin' all the headlines: "What Slick Means to the Sonics. Watts Does It Again. Watts Does This and Watts Does That.' Woody said, 'You gotta keep your head out of them papers.'

"I had learned to let nobody beat me down, though. When I was fifteen years old, I came late to baseball practice and the coach, Jerome Williams, he was a good college player but his coach broke him down and he tried to break me down the same way, didn't do nothin' until the next day. Then, durin' an assembly he made me roll on the floor. He thought I wouldn't do it. That I would quit. I just rolled. He had a lot of scars and I just had to see past what he was doing and not let him make me quit. It was just like when Woody came to town that first time after he got traded to the Knicks. He needed the support of the people. He's got a lot of scars, he's been hurt. Doesn't know who he is. He needed the support of the press and so when he came to town he had to stir up something to let everybody know he mattered. Coaches have turned me away, told me I was too small. People always tellin' me I can't play. So now I can put up with anything.

"Russ is the man and he done paid his dues. He's suffered from abuse and he's suffered in agony in his life. When you've taken a lot of agony and abuse, God steps in and shines you light. I think that's what he's doin' for Russ and I think that's what he's doin' for me. Most all men who make things out of their life go through it. Russ didn't have no heaven when he was in Boston and he didn't have no heaven when he was winnin' all those championships. But the man has a right to be respected. I know there are more kids in Seattle that are attached to me than there are to Russ. But I'd be a fool to think I'm more important than he is, because this man done paid his dues. It takes a price to win eleven championships. That's a lot of rings, man. And if you think about how hard it is for us now, compare eleven championship rings with the way we are scufflin' and you know he's been places we ain't and paid a price to get there. I think he likes me in his own way. He doesn't like to show his own emotions. Like in that win when we came back against Detroit in the last thirty-four seconds when I stole the ball three times and hit the shot that won it at the buzzer. He wanted to hug somebody so bad, so he just hugged himself and jumped around. He's very emotional. But he doesn't like to give anything to anybody, because he might get hurt.

"That three-year no-cut contract I signed for this year made me feel like I had made it, that I was appreciated. Bob Mussehl, my lawyer, and Deborah, my wife, wanted me to ask for more. But Russ told me to sign. He could have made me sit if I didn't. Maybe he doesn't know what I can do. He left my name off the All-Star ballot last year. I think he thinks I'm tryin' to go off on him when I ain't. But he's the man and I respect him for what he's been through. Basketball is a beautiful game, beauty and expression are what it means to me, but Russ wants discipline and he should get it. We are gettin' paid to do what the man says. I feel lucky kids want to be around me and want my autograph. I just try to be to other people the way I want them to be to me. If I had gone up to John Havlicek, say he's my idol, and asked him for an autograph and he says, 'Get lost,' I would be crushed for life. I can't do that to kids who look up to me. This team could be better, we didn't go very far in the playoffs this last year, but sometimes I get tears in my eyes about how tight this team is."

That was the way he saw the world on the eve of this season, which would prove to be so much different from what we envisioned in our individual and collective search for the brass ring.

3

Removing the Rain Clouds

Anticipation is the appetizer for sports fans. Whether it is the emergence of a potentially important performer onto the scene or a shot on the way to the hoop, the anticipation of what might happen is almost as enjoyable as the resulting performance. The anticipation is especially keen among those who are desperate for an improved reality—as in the case of a team that is flat on its back and looking for a savior. That precisely was the circumstance when Bill Walton was drafted No. 1 by Portland in 1975. Three-time collegiate player of the year at UCLA, Walton seemed destined to have the greatest instant impact on the NBA since Abdul-Jabbar had preceded him into the league half a decade earlier.

Alas, sometimes the greater the anticipation, the more solid the disappointment. While Watts popped out of nowhere like a seventy-five-degree day in the middle of a midwestern winter, Walton came up like a rainstorm on a long-planned picnic.

After two injury-marred NBA campaigns, the storm clouds were still overhead, but there were a lot a changes in the Blazers' camp as I encountered Walton after the first exhibition game of the season. Seattle had dispatched Golden State in a thriller to open the doubleheader at Portland. I had stayed to catch the second game between Portland and Los Angeles while the Sonics flew back home. The Blazers had come up with a dramatic dose of confidence. Maurice Lucas—6'9", 220 pounds, a new face from the ABA whose reputation and presence ranged in the realm of power, a pugilist in one corner and a polished pearl of jump shots and graceful rebounds in the other—had made the big play. He had taken the ball at the top of the key with ten seconds left. The score was tied. The lane was cleared except for Abdul-Jabbar. Lucas accelerated on two mighty strides, rose and stuffed over Jabbar—fouling out the Laker chief, winning the game.

Walton had twice checked Abdul-Jabbar's fabled Sky Hook, chasing the ball down after the second block and firing a picture full-court pass to Lionel Hollins for a layup. I couldn't help but sense this would be the year Walton would dance on the mountaintop—not as the hippie guru or cultural guerrilla he had come to be in the eyes of the national media, but as challenger to Abdul-Jabbar as the ultimate player in basketball. Walton was anticipating all this was going to be part of this season's chase that October night.

As I walked across the locker room toward him, Walton's eyes were flashing. A kaleidoscope of happiness, eagerness and conquer-the-world aggressiveness radiated off his sweat-coated cheeks and went after every living being in the Portland locker room. It was an attitude that inundated the Blazers, flowing from Walton because his will dominates all those who allow themselves to be opened by him. It was an attitude that was priming a pump that would write headlines for a season and colorful chapters for pro basketball's history.

He rolled his eyes toward Lucas, who was bent forward untying his shoes in the dressing booth next to Walton's. He cocked his jaw in an expression that said, "Isn't he *something*?" Walton looked like a ten-year-old who had just unwrapped his Christmas bike and was thinking of all the wonderful adventures they would take together. The Blazers had a new coach in Jack Ramsay, half a roster of new faces, and Walton was sparkling in full good health. He wanted to win all the marbles; to be challenged all the way would be even finer. In that locker room scene, Walton and his teammates weren't just another team dreaming of climbing all the way over the next nine months to the title. They were planning on it.

After he had showered, given the press a dab of his time, if not a great deal of commentary, rushed the necessary icing of his tender knees and made plans to meet Lucas and Herm Gilliam at a restaurant, we headed into the dripping Portland night in his jeepster. Bouncing along, the noise of the vehicle's doorless ways and a country and western tape made conversation inconvenient. I thought back to his first days as a pro, the first contact I had with him, and all the changes he had gone through—within himself and as a public subject.

He had come into the NBA as the first choice in the draft and coveted as the answer to the demands of so many different factions—almost none of which he satisfied initially. He was supposed to be the "Great White Hope." He was supposed to give Portland the immediate prowess that "Black Panther nigger Jabbar" had given Milwaukee four years earlier. Portland fans were particularly insistent on this because the Blazers kept doing so terribly and getting the very top picks in the collegiate draft and striking out—especially on center LaRue Martin, picked No. 1 ahead of Bob McAdoo and Julius Erving in 1972. Walton—so quick and active and aggressive in college—was supposed to be the ticket to the top.

Instead, he turned out to be everything sports fans couldn't handle—political radical, unshaven, long-haired, wouldn't eat meat, refused to cooperate with reporters, wouldn't sign autographs, wouldn't make public appearances. He wore lumberjack shirts and logging boots. He drove a jeep and lived in a custom-built $100,000 A-frame with a girl he wasn't married to and was constantly in the company of other socially outrageous individuals, such as sports activist Jack Scott and his wife, Micki. He said the FBI was . . . oh, he said a lot of things that were uncharacteristically candid for the sports world to begin with and bordered on mental irrationality by the time a lot of probably biased media got through with them.

He wouldn't even let the Blazers list him as a seven-footer. Forget the press release hype—he said he was 6'11", and no more. A nature lover nurtured on the gentle sunny days and soft evenings of Southern California, Walton couldn't adjust to the cold and damp Portland winter. His head was full of uptight and out-of-sight thoughts. No one had been able to sit down with him and get a full study on the guy. Barely two months into his rookie season he had already caused all this fuss. I saw him as a challenge sitting just down the freeway.

I had sent a letter care of Portland forward Barry Clemens, with whom I had played in a Seattle summer league, outlining how I wanted to do the piece as the cover story for the first issue of *Young Athlete*, a youth-oriented magazine we were getting off the ground in Seattle. I explained to Walton that I would let him see the piece before it went into print. I disliked having to submit to this practice, but I felt it was my only shot with Walton. I felt this way he would have more trust in what was being expressed and how it would read.

Clemens got the word back to me that Walton would do the interview. It took weeks of calling his house, usually getting a recording that greeted the caller with the sound of a galloping calliope, and after fifteen seconds or so said to leave a message. Finally, I got a connection and an agreement to meet him after practice in Portland. He was nursing a foot injury and was already setting a Red Cross pace that would keep him on the sidelines two thirds of his first season.

We had the locker room to ourselves, except for occasional interruptions in the form of high-pitched singing and nonsensical jive by Sidney Wicks. Walton spoke haltingly, sometimes leaving thoughts uncompleted. He refused to discuss at least a third of the questions posed, saying, "Uh, I don't want to talk about that." For the hour that we sat in the locker room he rubbed a knotted red lump on the top of his arch with chunks of ice. It was a trial in human exchange. I could move with no more confidence in my questioning than a blind man can have running through a forest. It was clumsy, exasperatingly trying. The only thing that made it tolerable was that it was more than anyone else was getting.

I had asked him how he felt about the criticism of his nonconformist attitudes. "It's hard to get ideas across, especially ones that are contrary or different to the majority. People tend to put a person down if he doesn't fit into the mold, so to speak. I think values and life-styles are pretty structured in our society. People should be more confident of their own abilities to make decisions and live the life they think is important instead of just following the images set down by advertising and so on."

Here I was, sitting with a twenty-two-year-old whose ability to play basketball had put him on a stage where anything he said about anything was of interest to the public. No one interviews the world's greatest diesel mechanic as to his opinions on social reform. Yet there is something in fans and their relationship with their sports heroes that has them demanding to know the players—and yet giving themselves to them. The public regards an athlete as an authority figure, and the greater the player's ability, the more authority he is granted. Hence the power of endorsements and the influence of the athlete's philosophies and opinions. If it had been someone other than the league's No. 1 draft choice spouting off about the FBI and such, the nation wouldn't have taken much heed when Bill Walton talked.

As that initial Walton interview continued, I agonized over the sheets of questions I had prepared, trying to get a feeling for which of

25

them would be answered. I began to fear that the next one that brought an "I don't want to talk about that" might end the whole interview. One time I asked him, "What *do* you think is worthwhile talking about?"

"I feel I have to be as honest as I can in the areas I feel are worth talking about. I like to talk about anything that helps me learn. But I don't like to get into particulars about books I've read, because there isn't any one thing that stands out. I'd hate to have someone run and grab a certain book thinking that this is what makes Bill Walton think the way he does. I like to study all sides of things so that when it comes to making a decision I feel I have prepared myself with the knowledge to make a proper one. I like to make choices out of knowledge, rather than emotion."

Actually, emotion seems to have been strongly at play in Walton's behavior and attitudes during his early rounds as a pro. These were emotions of a youth outraged at the ample amount of things in the world capable of inspiring outrage. He had drawn the spotlight onto himself with a lot of spectacular criticism of social status quo. He was speaking from a social consciousness that had been stirred up at UCLA—which represented an atmosphere, well, as Los Angeles *Times* columnist Jim Murray once wrote: ". . . let's just say God would need a parking pass same as everyone else, or there'd be a stern editorial in the daily paper."

When I went back over the tape, there were a lot of rough spots— an awkward, sometimes stuttering speech pattern. He had a tendency to pause, sometimes in midsentence. His voice was nasal, while softly fuzzy. When he granted several TV interviews the following year, many viewers deemed him to be another dumb jock. But there were some things of substance in our taped conversation and I had gone there to collect his thoughts and attitudes, not give him an A in public speaking. Sadly, the whole thing went for naught, at least initially. It was probably a very appropriate statement on just what Bill Walton was midway through his rookie season when *Young Athlete* decided "he was too controversial" and dropped the story. And I left the magazine.

There were a couple of "How ya doin'?" encounters as our paths passed in airports and locker rooms during the next season—his second in the league. Plenty was being written *about* Walton, having another injury-marred campaign, but no one was really hearing from *him*. He was agreeable to another interview, which we set up the morning following a visit by the Sonics to Portland. I met him at a restaurant, where he waded through a meal with gauze packed in his nose—that courtesy of a Burleson elbow the previous evening.

His hair was still shoulder length, his dress still lumberjack readiness, but his words were smoother, his thoughts more collected, his manner warmer—though still not particularly blessed with humor. He bristled at a question I posed regarding the amount of food he was eating. He would discuss his increase in weight and frustrations at never being able to get into top shape because of injuries and his vegetarianism. ("I've been into natural foods since I was a junior at UCLA. Meat is full of poisons. The human body is not designed to digest meat. It's full of acids and toxins that just tear up the body. What you put into your body is going to have a big effect on what you are. If you put junk into it, you become garbage. I hate to see the influence of TV commercials and ads in other media that tell people certain foods are good for you when they are not. Aging is a disease and people in this country age way too fast because of the way they live.") He said he was getting more comfortable with the Pacific Northwest climate and the people of Portland. "The people here have become more relaxed about seeing me around and are seeing me as a human being rather than some performer."

As he answered questions around gulps of breakfast, I wondered to what extent my own attitudes were influencing my pursuit of this interview. Certainly there was the ego of landing the "In-depth Walton Interview," but the fact he was expressing some values that I shared inspired me all the more to get them out in public. It is impossible for a reporter not to be influenced by his own prejudices and causes. It isn't supposed to interfere with the product, with the message imparted by an individual, but if a reporter is anything but a robot it is unavoidable.

"I just wish people would be a little more demanding of their consciousness and try to think things out rather than just following an idol in his beliefs. I think hero worship contributes to the establishment of a class system in this country. Actually, all over the world people believe others are better than they are and they forget that everyone has his strengths and weaknesses. People should take pride in what they do best. You can appreciate what someone else can accomplish, but that doesn't necessarily make him better than you all around."

He had sold the A-frame and was living in a rambling older home close to downtown Portland. After he finished eating we drove up to his place. His nose began to bleed. He lay down on a couch, but it wouldn't stop. I left for the airport as Micki drove him to the hospital, where it was discovered his nose was broken.

He was still regarded as very much an outcast by most sports fans. And to many who didn't disdain him as he mocked the expectations of the traditionalists, he was at least a mystery. His rough-hewn appearance and ruggedly independent philosophies posed a national curiosity which had only been poked at in a couple of national magazine articles. The *Post-Intelligencer* ran the piece under the headline "Walton Marches to a Different Drummer." Associated Press picked it up and moved it nationally.

That visit, compared to the original one, had allowed me to become more aware of his personality, to see something of his mind beyond just rhetoric. It was as though pieces of a puzzle had begun to give hints to the whole, providing a fuller image. Still, while I had written more than had been written elsewhere about him, I didn't feel I had seen the full person. It struck me as to how much shallowness there is in personality journalism—just a few images, some stereotyping for quick reference and a couple of wang-bang quotes is the best most of us can do as reporters. Many writers are weak in their abilities of perception and communication. But the public's demand to know its entertainers often creates a clash between the writer and the athlete—the one digging ruthlessly and the other trying to defend himself.

As this, his third NBA season, was beginning, Walton had come through the bottom of the valley and was moving up the mountain. He was adjusting to the life of being a pro basketball superstar, and the added pressures of being a public commodity, a renegade at that. If he had thought about escaping the game when he was injured and awash in charges of being "a dirty commie, unwashed carrot-topped rat," he seemed anxious only to make up for lost time now. His values were still dear to him, contrary to the norm and important to discuss—but not so much in public. He was involved in helping the American Indian Movement and other social crusades, but his mind was eager, enthusiastic to put together a grand basketball season.

Now, an exhibition game into his third season, we trucked through Portland's rain-washed streets. The restaurant of scheduled rendezvous was closed. Two stops later we had given up on finding Gilliam or Lucas and entered a Greek restaurant.

The manager knew of Walton's vegetarianism and filled the table with some very good food, which went down while a band of musicians, just off a Greek freighter, played some very loud music. Around the hammering music, Walton's enthusiasm for what the club had accomplished in training camp spilled out. He was excited by such newcomers as Gilliam, a guard acquired from Seattle; Lucas, a veteran of the ABA; Moses Malone, a high school phenom who had done some amazing things in the ABA; and Dave Twardzik, a spunky little guard also from the ABA. He liked Ramsay's drive and disciplined determination, his demand for excellence. "We're going to be good. I mean, we are going to be good." Walton glowed, his face broken out in full grin.

Over the beer and around the thundering music, Walton reflected on how good it felt to be healthy. "I haven't been able to play my game yet in the pros. I go up against guys who I know I should be able to do certain things against and I haven't been in top shape or I've been injured so I couldn't. It got depressing when I couldn't play my game. I wasn't having any fun."

That's probably the hardest part of Walton for people to understand. He likes his wealth, but once commented, "Unless a person is just totally unable to earn the amount of money they need to get by on, most people are going to do the types of things they enjoy most, regardless of how much money they have." Call it "utopian hippie bullshit" or whatever you like. But Walton is motivated by the pursuit of good friends, good health and mental growth. He doesn't like things that interfere with that. Simple. He can't stand to play at less than his full abilities, because he plays to achieve satisfaction within himself—not just to draw a paycheck or to slap out a win.

I asked him what his NBA goals were. "Only each player knows how good he is. There are different ratings to determine who is best at each position and who is down the line. But, basically, if you're satisfied with your effort, that's all that is important. The material rewards, the honors that come along with success, are just a small part of the personal satisfaction you get when you know you've done your best."

A few days after that Greek restaurant encounter, Walton was in Seattle for another exhibition game. We sat in his hotel room, watching a UCLA–Ohio State football game, and talked about the life of an NBAer of his stature and what it is like to have the media coming at you every waking, and often sleeping, moment.

A biography of Muhammad Ali lay on the bed. He watched the TV game without sound, expressing fuller thoughts than he had even a few nights earlier. I wondered if it was just his comfort with me or just a steady coming out with the public in general. I asked him if he was becoming more comfortable with the press as a whole and if he thought a lot of the hassles with the media had been an outgrowth of his isolation from reporters while he was at UCLA.

"Coach Wooden wouldn't allow reporters into the locker room. Some players chose to speak to reporters, others, like myself, chose not to. You'd go out in the hallway or in another room to meet them if you wanted. I didn't understand the press very well then. I was like seventeen or eighteen years old and I just wanted to play basketball, go to school, party with my friends. I didn't want people asking me questions and then having my answers written down in the paper the next day. Coach Wooden provided the excuse so that I didn't have to. Until you know a reporter a little, you don't know where they're coming from. When a reporter asks a question he has certain biases and attitudes which are going to affect how he writes what you say."

"Do you get the feeling sometimes that a reporter has the story written and he's just trying to get you to fill in the blanks?"

"That happens sometimes. That's one of the unfortunate things about being written about so much. A lot of people have preconceived ideas."

UCLA scored on a long pass and Walton reached for the sound, turned it up to hear the details and turned it back down. "Helluva play. Look at this." He nodded at the rerun showing a wide receiver diving across the screen. Walton slapped his hands with enthusiasm, settled back with his hands behind his head and propped his shoeless feet back on the bed next to the Ali book.

"What drew you into cooperating with the press?"

"When people asked me a question I tried to give them an honest answer. When you become a professional athlete you assume certain responsibilities and part of that is dealing with the press and public, as long as you feel it is constructive."

"What role does the press have in pro basketball?"

"They keep the fans informed. The good reporters do more than just say who scored at what time. The good reporters look at situations and say this happened because of this. This team is a good team for these reasons. This team played a bad game for these reasons. And there are other reporters who just say, 'He got ten points and ten rebounds'—no insight is provided for the fan."

"Do you think reporters seek quotes and comments from coaches and players to protect their own lack of knowledge about what is going on in the game?"

"Well, one comment on that is that I think that is prevalent in our society. A lot of people are not qualified for the position they are in. It covers all people, not just sportswriters. The fans are a lot more sophisticated now and they want to know about the people they are watching play. I think Muhammad Ali had a lot to do with bringing that about. He's such a lively personality, the fans picked up on that a lot. There are people who never watch boxing who are followers of him. A lot of that has to do with the fact he is a terrific athlete, but also he is attractive because he has such a lively personality, an interesting, unique personality.

"There are certain reporters that you know you can't say anything to except that it was really a good game and both sides played well. And there are others who you can say more to. You know them better and they understand what you are talking about. Most guys realize there are a lot of pretty ordinary games and the reporters can't always have a lot of interesting questions to ask. There's always six or seven guys on the team who never get asked any questions. But there are a lot of questions that there just isn't anything intelligent to say. And I don't like to give one-liners that much."

"Don't you think that there's a basic problem just in the very nature of sports journalism, singling certain things out for emphasis?"

"I'm not sure I follow you."

"Well, let's say a game is like a full-length film clip. You could liken an interview or a conversation the same way. You have this whole conversation on a long strip of film. Then you take scissors and clip out a frame here and a couple more there and no matter how literally you re-create those in print, the fact is that there is a magnification of those words or statements. And if you clip out a couple of plays from a game, or one player's performance, it is being emphasized by the ignoring of all the rest. That's what sometimes makes a reporter look so shallow in his story—he's been forced to create such a contrast by spotlighting some things and acting like the rest didn't exist."

"I can see how that happens, and probably there isn't any way to avoid that generally," added Walton. "But you still get situations where a reporter doesn't really look at the whole thing objectively. He might just decide on certain words that support his bias."

I asked him how he draws the line on the unending parade of requests for radio and TV, magazine and newspaper interviews.

"I try to limit it to certain guys that I know. Reporters started coming around when I was about seventeen and I've just decided to stick to the guys who I know where they're coming from. I don't expect writers to always write nice things about me. They've got to write what they see. I don't like writers because they write something nice about me. I like them because they write intelligent things. I cooperate with people I respect and know are going to do an intelligent and meaningful job. I don't enjoy just putting words into some TV microphone. I like to do things that have some meaning with people I know and understand."

The phone rang. It was former UCLA teammate Jamaal Wilkes.

"I like this life," Walton said as he hung up a minute later. "It's nice during the exhibition season to get around and see all your friends and the other players. The hotels and the games, the going around the country and seeing people, hey, it's all right."

He was ready to go meet Wilkes for lunch. He stretched, ran long fingers through his hair, which closely matches the color of iron left out in the rain. It had been trimmed back to a mod shag just below his ears, after having become shoulder length in ponytail proportion during his first two years as a pro. His beard was a shadow of its former bushy self. By season's end Walton cropped his hair exceedingly, exposing his ears in a portrait reminiscent of the craggy-faced kid who peered out of *Sports Illustrated*'s "Faces in the Crowd" section in the January 26, 1970, issue. As a senior at Helix High in La Mesa, California, he had been named MVP of a prep cage tournament after scoring fifty points and pulling thirty-four rebounds. Irrespective of his hair length, seven years later Walton would become a fixture of flamboyant aggression in hundreds of pictures run in national magazines and newspapers throughout the season. His mouth gaping, lips pulled over teeth, Walton resembled a mongoose poised for a strike as he braced against the muscle of opponents under the basket. His arms were coiled at near shoulder height, fingers flexed wide—seemingly bent backward—as spider webs ready to snatch. He became the epitome of expression on the court, a symbol of animated aggression.

He was on his way, finally. And in the crowning hours of the championship season—when a nation's basketball fans caught themselves celebrating Walton's prowess—he would provide a setting that influenced me to choose a new way of life.

4
Getting Acquainted

Camp and exhibition games paraded by in days filled with a steady serving of optimism. Burleson was looking good. You win in the hole. There was hope in Sonicville.

"I'm just a lot more ready mentally and physically," Burleson said of himself after one practice. "Last year I tried to do things and I was just out of it at times. It got me down and I was fighting myself mentally."

A couple days after that statement, in an exhibition against Phoenix, Burleson missed a short jumper, grabbed the rebound, jammed it back up, missed, got it again, shot again and finally lost the ball to Dennis Awtrey. "He didn't quit on it," commented Russell. "I'm not sure he would have kept after it like that a year ago." Hope, hope, everywhere there is hope in preseason.

Burleson and Ricky Sobers had a virtual war going during the previous spring's playoffs. In one of the exhibitions, Burleson popped Sobers in the neck with an elbow. The officials didn't see it, but Sobers, enraged, stomped over and put a mule kick on the courtside shooting clock. That earned him a technical and rendered the twenty-four-second clock useless. Sobers was not about to nominate Burleson for a good conduct medal.

The scrimmages in camp were rougher than ever as players fought for survival. Watts commented, "I look around and see those rookies all worried about what they have to do to make it. I remember it, oh man, it's awful. It's the worst pressure there is. There's some good talent out here. I hope they get it cut down pretty soon. I been stopping at the top of the lane and shooting my little jay—it's so rough in there all you get if you try to drive is a broken leg."

Fred Brown remained on the sidelines. He wasn't making any friends among those who were out there taking their bumps. It was a resentment that would carry through the year.

Hopkins was impressed with a 6'5" guard out of Washington State, Norton Barnhill. A quiet, graceful player. "He's been the most impressive guard in camp for all-around play. Offensively he's been head and shoulders ahead of the rest. He's playing like a five-year veteran." I sat down with Barnhill to do a column. It developed he had grown up with a lot of time on the streets of Winston-Salem, North Carolina. He'd studied under Earl Monroe's collegiate game there. He'd played summer ball with Bob McAdoo. His mother worked in a tobacco factory. He wanted to get her out of there. "I used to hang out—you know, the wine and the gang going on all night. I used to get tossed out of school for fighting and the typical childhood hassles. I came to the point where I had to decide between the street or the game."

It was the sort of story that a journalist has to be careful to avoid trying to create a dime-store novel. At the expense of either the truth or a man's dignity, there is a tendency to try to fill in the script with a "Hood to Hoop Hero" sequel. Still, there was the drama of a cool, street-wise figure pursuing his dream.

Sometimes you get the feeling "cool" is more important than the rest, though. Such as when he lost control of the ball just before the end of an exhibition game against the New York Nets. The ball rolled across midcourt and John Williamson scooped it up for what would have been a layup if the buzzer hadn't sounded. Barnhill had just stood there with hands on hips, blank expression, seemingly oblivious to Hopkins' shriek: "What are you doing? Go after it!" I wonder how many guys never made it in the NBA because they didn't want to blow their cool?

Dr. J couldn't come to terms with the Nets. An exhibition with the Sonics was canceled by the Aladdin Hotel in Las Vegas. No star, no show. So much for good times in Crystal City.

There was a story brewing that Sidney Wicks, who couldn't come to terms with New Orleans and was still on the block by Portland, was Seattle-bound. I got his phone number and called him in Los Angeles.

"HellOOOOOOOOOO," he sang.

"Er, Sidney, this isn't who you think it is, but while I've got you on the line . . . what are the chances you'll come to Seattle?"

He laughed at it not being who he thought it was. "All I can really say is that I want to play ball, I want to get paid the money that I am worth and I want to win. I don't care about anything else."

Evasively curious.

The Sonics were working out in closed session. I decided to risk the wrath of Russell and ask him if any deals were working. It was also reported Portland would unload Malone and that Curtis Rowe was going to be dealt by Detroit and that Paul Silas was to be dealt by Boston rather than paid his raise demands. I wandered in. Russell glowered. He didn't want to discuss anything, he didn't want me there. I figured I had to get some sort of an answer.

"Bill, all these stories are popping around and I *have* to have some sort of an answer. I know you don't want me here and I wouldn't have come if it wasn't important. Let me just ask you one question. Is there any chance you'll be interested in going after any of these forwards?"

He paused for a moment. In my mind I cursed him and my job and . . . he said, "I would say it is very, very improbable we will add any more players. We have more players than we can use already."

Well, it was better than nothing. I headed off to call in a story built around the comments of Russell and Wicks. When practice was over I came back to talk to Russell. We've had a very good rapport rolling since late summer. One day I was heading out to cover the racetrack and he sent along two dollars. It was his first bet on a horse race. I wrote a piece on how I selected the horse to bet on. It lost, but I got a good story out of it. I didn't want to lose the good rapport. I found him shifted into a good mood and we talked for over an hour—about how he thought Walton was the player who most resembled his own game, how he doubted Brown would ever become hard-nosed enough to be a winner, how he wished his oldest son, Buddah, would get back into college, how he doubted pro basketball would ever allow the circumstances of togetherness and camaraderie that had meant so much to him on the Celtics. He talked about how much he liked Seattle and how he was having a forty-thousand-dollar addition to his house which included a "bathtub for eight." He talked about how he didn't think he could ever get married again and how he hoped Gray would control his temper better this year and how Phoenix wouldn't go anywhere this season even though they'd finished second last year and how much he loved his father, although they had gone for weeks without talking to each other during various squabbles along the way. He talked about how a father and son could only be so close because there was a generation gap and a disciplinarian factor that would always be there and how that was a lot like the relationship between a coach and the players. We talked about jobs. He didn't think it was right that "seven people work full-time around the world to support the materialism of one wealthy American." But, as long as the system is the way it is, he's going to enjoy the good life. He thinks sportswriters take their jobs too seriously. He thinks everybody takes their jobs too seriously. "There isn't a job that can't be done in four hours a day if a person is organized."

It was the casual sort of conversation that leaves one feeling he has been with a friend.

Two days later LaRue Martin was waived, four years after being drafted as the league's No. 1 plum. The Portland scout had caught the 6'11" center in his greatest collegiate game while at Loyola of Chicago—a contest in which he outplayed Walton. He hadn't done a thing for the Blazers and they had sent him to Seattle with the condition they would pay all but forty thousand of his salary the first year and all but eighty thousand the next. Seattle could hardly afford not to take a look. There wasn't much to see.

Things were amazingly warm with Russell. I caught him coming out of his office and we were talking again. I wandered onto a matter that had never been discussed by Russell—his refusal to join the NBA Hall of Fame. He was the first black player chosen for induction. There was speculation that he thought other blacks should have been chosen earlier. There was speculation he had heard that it took a campaign by Auerbach to gain the selection. Russell always remained silent.

"Whatever your reasons were for not being inducted into the Hall of Fame, wouldn't you have made better use of the stand to explain them to the public—to make them more socially conscious of whatever philosophies they were based upon?" I had asked.

Russell, standing with his hands casually draped from the top of the doorjamb, replied, "Let me tell you a story, you may have heard it: There was a man and a boy traveling down a road with a donkey. The boy was on the donkey's back. They came upon a traveler who said, 'Isn't that awful, that healthy young boy making his father walk while he rides?' So they switch places. The next traveler comes by and says, 'Isn't that awful, that big strong man riding while the little boy has to walk?' So they both get on and the next traveler to pass says, 'Isn't that awful, those two loading down that poor little donkey?' So they both get off and the next traveler says, 'Look how stupid they are, they're walking when they could be riding the donkey.' "

His crackle bounced around the room. Then he turned serious again. "You see, the thing I long ago learned was that you can't explain things to people who don't want to believe you. If I gave you five reasons to print in the paper why I didn't go in the Hall of Fame, people would come back demanding five explanations for each reason. It's better to just leave it alone in the first place."

A few days later I walked into the gym to discover Russell lying flat on the floor. He was on his stomach, elbows propping up his head, which was covered on each side by a big hand. A TV cameraman swooped down on Russell. It looked like he was loafing, but actually his back was giving him trouble. All those shoves and slams under the hoop, all those trips up and down the court, all those plane and bus trips crammed into small seats, all those nights in beds too short and too soft. His lying there seemed melancholy. It was the worn-out warrior at the end of the road that all those on the court were fighting each other for the right to travel. His face wore an expression of dejection, but he actually was enthused—or was it bemused?

"We've got some good young players here. We should be able to use five guards—keeping fresh people in there all the time. I like what I see in the rookies, Bob Wilkerson and Dennis Johnson. Frank Oleynick is coming along. Some others show promise. We can press and run and no one will have to get worn out."

Upon hearing that statement, Watts commented, "That's great. I can play ten years if I don't have to carry the whole load. I hope he means it." Those words would last barely a step beyond the starting gate, however.

Meanwhile, rumors were afoot that Brown might be traded. The only member of the Sonics who was aboard before Russell came, Brown had riled his coach with his injury-inspired sit-out. So I wasn't surprised when I came into the office one afternoon to find a note from a fellow reporter: "Fred Brown, Jr., was to register at the same school where my kid is going. His mother told the registrar yesterday they can't keep Freddy there. 'Something very big is happening to change our whole life around.' Check it out."

I called Brown. His wife, Linda, answered. She said she didn't understand where the school got that idea. "Must be a different Fred Brown. There's nothing to it." Russell said Brown wasn't going anywhere. I called a few general managers around the loop to see what they might have heard, or were doing. Nothing. He stayed a Sonic.

No sooner had the circuit ride through opponent's locker rooms begun again than I was reminded of how even the simple function of interviewing people becomes a chameleon act. You see, shaking hands around the NBA is like making love to someone for the first time—you never know how far they want to go or what they want to do getting there.

You walk into the Warriors' locker room, note pad in one hand and a pen in the other. You don't *have* to shake hands, of course. But with visitors there is the self-introduction and unless the guy has both hands in use pulling off his jock or combing his hair, it's an almost uncontrollable response to stick out a hand. So as you climb over travel bags and step around gold uniforms tossed on the floor to reach Phil Smith in the corner, you find yourself wondering how to handle it. "Phil, how ya doin'?" you say, switching your pen to the left hand. He switches the tape cutter to his other hand. You hold out your hand sorta cupped and thumb out, going for the "soul shake." He sticks out his hand and you grip and slide and slip an uninspired greeting. He might just as well have had some doubts about your roots and have caught your palm with a conventional "whitey" shake. You wouldn't have been ready and the two of you would have been left to fumble through a handsy exchange that is a mixture of Kiwanis breakfast and Alpha Tau Omega secret session. You wipe off his perspiration on your $40 (well, $22.95) slacks, pick up the pen and start interviewing.

Finished, you turn to the tall body at the adjacent locker. Rick Barry, besides being the best free-throw shooter in the league, is white. So the handshake is as straight as a Presbyterian sermon. You wipe off your hands on your slacks and begin taking notes. On and on it goes around the locker room, your pants getting damper by the handshake and all the while you're feeling like an actor who has forgotten his lines.

Soulful evolution in the sixties brought the three-step shake. The thumbs-hooked wrestlers' grip slides across the "Pleased to meetcha, Joe" conventional shake and slips off to a gripping of half-cupped fingers. Sometimes this is toasted by a warm covering of the opposite hands—creating a fleshy ball extended halfway between the principals.

If you're graying a bit at the temple or simply lack any qualms about being labeled straight, shaking hands is pretty well defined. But, if you're halfway hip, two-thirds cool or just plain white in an environment as cluttered with behaviorial mores as the NBA's, it's a constant hassle. The shake is a mirror of a relationship, or more a distinction of social classification. In the time it takes to stick your hand out you're trying to anticipate how your partner-in-shake judges you. You don't want to sell yourself short, but then you don't want to push yourself on someone who doesn't regard you as being "among 'em."

I had gotten a couple of calls at the office questioning the Sonics' inability to make any deals for the big names who were reportedly floating around.

"Bill, a lot of people have been wondering why clubs like Los Angeles, Milwaukee and Philadelphia have been mentioned in the paper as trying to make a deal to get Paul Silas from Boston, and some of these other name forwards. Why don't the Sonics seem to be interested in picking up a forward with Silas' obvious abilities?"

Russell snapped back, "What's everybody think I'm doing with my time? Do they think I just show up at games and don't think about the club any other time? Do they think I'm not trying to improve this team every way I can?" He was bristling. I thought, "Damn, man, just like that you blow a good thing."

What seemed like an hour, but was probably only five seconds, saw Russell's glare fade into a grin.

"Besides that, Red said no."

Molding a team, analyzing young talent, that is most of the aim of the exhibition season—other than to make a few extra dollars for the owners. Preseason days are also times of looking for signs—as in who seems to be in the coach's plans and who isn't. An incident as the Sonics' plane arrived in Oakland from Los Angeles for the final exhibition game could have gone either way for Dennis Johnson, a second-round guard drafted out of Pepperdine. At 6'4" he was big for a guard. His freckled face and reddish Afro gave him a rather puckish image—kind of a black Huck Finn.

The aisle was packed as everyone stood to deplane. I was in the front of coach class with Johnson and a couple of others who hadn't been able to squeeze into first class. Suddenly Johnson called out for Russell, who was in front of the line, black fisherman's cap bumping against the ceiling.

"Hey, coach," Johnson shouted. "Hey, coach."

Players nudged the message up to Russell. The rookie wanted him. Everyone looked at each other, perplexed. Russell turned around, trying to muster a menacing stare to indicate he didn't like to be yelled at in a crowd.

"Hey, coach," Johnson chortled, having Russell's attention. "I know I haven't been up there where you could keep an eye on me, but I'm okay."

Russell gasped his most unstudied laugh and returned, "Thanks, I was really worried."

The door opened and Russell led the troops out. Players shook their heads. Bruce Seals turned and reached across two passengers to slap Johnson on the head.

"That boy's one crazy nigger," Watts giggled as he slapped hands with Dean Tolson.

Johnson couldn't help smiling. He had tried the water and found the temperature warm and inviting.

That night Portland destroyed the Sonics so convincingly, there seemed a little room for concern. Malone came out of his preseason shadow to show some of the things that had made him an ABA star. I went up to him in the locker room and started asking questions. He put a toothbrush in his mouth and started to walk away, mumbling something that I couldn't understand. A Portland writer motioned to me with a shake of the head. "He doesn't talk to the press."

At the hotel I ran into Walton and Wally Walker, a rookie out of Virginia. We walked a mile to Francisco's to eat. As we kicked along in the darkness, Walton related how myths kept being painted around him. Things that had no foundation kept appearing in print.

"I don't understand why writers are so careless that they don't even care about the truth. There was a guy who just wrote a story how I was finally healthy and playing good because I'd started eating meat again. He never even talked to me. He just made it up."

Russell's comments about not wanting to explain why he didn't go into the Hall of Fame came back to me. How reckless the media can be with honesty. The desire, or the demand, to come up with big stories about big people so often is pursued with no concern for the protagonist. And it takes only a few reckless journalists among the whole fraternity to discourage any access for cooperation from these so-called superstars of society.

As we flew to Los Angeles for the final exhibition game I talked with Tolson, a 6'8", willowy leaper who had played a rookie year with the Sonics, was banished to the Eastern League the following season and was now trying to keep his spiderlike on-court wildness under control enough to reclaim a berth in the NBA. "I don't want to do nothing but play here," he said. "I came here marked as a wild player. I've learned some things about myself and about the game. It's not just the materialistic benefits. Playing in the NBA is the only thing I want."

Russell had constantly taunted the former University of Arkansas cager. He told him he was going back to the Eastern League or Mexico or Europe. Tolson, who had spent the entire summer in the weight room and earned an invitation to camp by impressing Russell with his determination, was awash in agony throughout this preseason.

As we rode the subway through the Sea-Tac airport upon the return from Los Angeles, Russell was on Tolson. "Do you have your passport ready, Dean?" Tolson fidgeted under a pale yellow Panama hat. His eyes couldn't face Russell. "You'll like Europe, Dean. Fascinating people."

"No, I won't," he stammered.

Russell had him on the run. "*Parlez-vous francais,* Deano?"

Tolson snapped back. "No comprendo."

Russell almost went to the floor with laughter. Tolson wished he could share in the fun, at someone else's expense.

Two days later the final cuts were made. Two-year veteran Talvin Skinner went. Collis Temple went. Tolson went on the injured list. Norton Barnhill stayed—but only for a week, until Tolson's hamstring injury healed to allow him to go back touching the clouds.

I sat down with Russell to get his assessment of where the club stood as it headed out across more than half a year's schedule on a campaign that would bring more surprises than even he could have expected as he hung up a caution light.

"The biggest single improvement on the team this year is Burleson. He's about halfway to what we think he can be. Last year, well, he was about a quarter of the way there. And that was on an average. At the start, on a scale of one to ten, he was about minus zero.

"You just have to wait to see what happens to team attitude over the season. When somebody is fighting for a starting role and is delegated as a backup, how does he adjust? When a player is used coming off the bench when he thinks he's a starter, how does he adjust? When a player isn't getting the playing time he thinks he deserves, well, you just have to see what happens to these individuals. I guess I'm a little apprehensive about how some players are going to react."

An hour later I was going across the Evergreen Point floating bridge in a Mercedes 450 SLC. Watts was driving—with no more restraint than his insane down-the-lane style of play—to his home in suburban Kirkland. He was upset.

"I just want you to know that this ain't gonna work," he said. "Russ says Fred and me ain't gonna play but ten to fifteen minutes a game and that we gonna run a five-guard offense. We won forty-three games two years in a row with me and Fred out there and I know this for a fact and anybody who knows anything about basketball knows that Fred Brown and Slick Watts had a lot to do with that. He's taking away my motivation, man. He's just trying to keep me down. I don't want to say nothing in print yet, but you wait and see, there's gonna be a real disaster on this team if Russ tries to go with them kids. Them kids ain't ready. It took me a couple years to get ahead of this game and now he wants to put us on the bench. He's just head-trippin', man, and you just remember what I told you here today. We ain't goin' nowhere the way he's treatin' us."

5
Even if You Win, You Lose

Spencer Haywood reminds me of a "new rich" who has attained the wealth and the material grandeur, but cannot achieve what he wants most—acceptance into high society.

His circumstance is not unlike that of Sam Schulman's, who as owner of the Sonics, teamed with Haywood to write sports history in court recorder's code. Schulman is high society, though. He is Beverly Hills society, where everybody is new rich—sometimes as recently as last week's hit parade. But he, too, hasn't accomplished the clear-eyed celebration he coveted when he picked up his NBA franchise in 1967.

Haywood desperately wanted to be accepted as the greatest player in the game. He desperately wanted to be a champion. Schulman was equally obsessed with being a champion. They each wanted more than anything else to be called "a winner." To be a winner: to have grace under pressure, style, dignity, strength to achieve where others tried and failed. That is what made Russell such a glorified subject: he *always* won. Some few individuals seem to establish their own standards and compete within themselves. For a Haywood or a Schulman, like most of us, the jury is one's colleagues and the public who sit in judgment with adulation and respect to offer.

They both lost out, even if they win those championships now. They will have been tainted by events that will never let go of their character images. They were too much the renegades, the mavericks. They both lunged, hand in hand for a while, too desperately.

Principles screamed at them too loudly. Principles and greed. The former are a man's drummer—who can say what is right, where he should make a stand? The latter is certainly acceptable in sports—it's the foundation, actually. Greed for achievement, for recognition, for as much of the full array of rewards as are attainable. Haywood had been denied too much—everything, in fact—as a racially beaten, economic and socially impoverished youth. And there is no counterbalance to be attained, try as ruthlessly as he has. Schulman battled his way up the classical American success ladder. After receiving an MBA from Harvard School of Business, the New York-born Schulman took eight thousand dollars left him when his father died and planted it in a bankrupt book manufacturing firm, George McKibbin & Sons. From there he directed Executive Car Leasing, the National General Corporation, Great American Insurance Companies, Bantam Books, Grosset & Dunlap, Mission Pak, Peninsula Savings & Loan and Bergen Trust Company. Like most men who go into the ownership of sports franchises, he went in search of the applause that was the only thing lacking in all his other enterprises.

The events that will never let go of either's reputation developed through the winter of 1970–71. Haywood had already established himself as a controversial individual with the potential to become the best forward in the game. He was the star of the United States gold medal effort in the 1968 Olympics and then signed with the ABA after two seasons of college ball. He was soon unhappy with his contract there and after it had been renegotiated once, jumped ship to sign a contract with Schulman. The latter thus became the first owner to sign a collegiate underclassman to an NBA contract and his fellow board of governors wanted to boot him out of the league for the act. But the courts ruled in favor of Schulman and Haywood in decision after decision and the result was that Haywood became a Sonic and the four-year college rule was declared illegal. That opened the door for many others to abandon their colleges short of class graduation. George McGinnis was the first to make such a move as he immediately departed Indiana University for the Pacers.

Schulman had won, but it was a bitter triumph minus the celebration he would have liked. "The discrimination and all the rest was terrible to live with. In retrospect, no player is worth challenging the whole organization. The league was bitter, the player turned out to be ungrateful. It's sad, even when you win, you lose."

Such sentiments were expressed years later. At the time, Schulman remained on the prowl. A year after securing Haywood, he had gone back to the ABA well to sign Jim McDaniels, in his rookie year with the Carolina Cougars, and Pittsburgh badboy John Brisker. He got burned on both of them, finally having to settle on McDaniels' contract ($1.8 million for six seasons) because Big Jim couldn't cut it in the NBA and on Brisker's ($900,000, five seasons) because he incurred the wrath of Russell.

Haywood failed to deliver the Sonics to the promised land and after two seasons under Russell, he was dispatched to the Knicks. He said he was elated to be escaping and took a shot at just about everybody in the community, excepting First Avenue drunks and underprivileged children:

"Watts doesn't have the pride a black man has to have. He lets people slap his hands and his head and does the Globetrotter thing. . . . Russell could not have me around anymore. I'm a man and he's a man, but he wants boys around him. There's no superstar allowed in Seattle—only Russell. . . . Basketball is the only pro-sport in Seattle and I put the city on the map. But nobody remembers that. . . ." When you came right down to it, Watts ran Haywood out of town because Woody needed to be king. He had the money and the life-style which was the mountaintop compared to his youth, but he had to be king, too. And there was no way he could compete with Watts's ability to entertain people. Where Russell's ego fit into all this remained for conjecture.

A year after Haywood's departure, on the eve of the new season, Schulman and I sat over a tape recorder in a suite at the Washington Plaza Hotel, looking out on the Seattle waterfront at the ferry boats scurrying to and fro. It seems the powerful are always operating from high stations—like the chess player leaning over the board. Schulman's offices in Los Angeles are on the twenty-third floor—shared by the editorial staff of *Playgirl* magazine—of the Century Park Plaza Building. Floor-to-ceiling windows provide a 180° view. Telephones ringing, he wheels and deals with the best of them. Schulman now presides over First Northwest Industries, which operates, besides the Sonics, Racquet Clubs of America and Universal Gyms. The rest make money, the Sonics make headlines.

I asked him if he had read Frank DeFord's novel *The Owner*. He hadn't. I read him a passage where Duncan Radnor, the owner, is talking to his mistress:

". . . The other owners are just fans anyway. They worship the players. With me, I worship more what they can do, what they can create. When I'm in that arena and something real, something beautiful happens, and the fans are going bananas, and the players are slapping their hands and cheering, I sit there and I swear to Christ, I say: 'You own this sonuvabitch, Duncan Radnor, you own a thing like this.' It's a certain power. . . ."

I asked Schulman if he ever felt that way. He smiled and nodded. "Sometimes, I guess I do."

"It must be fun."

"It is," he countered, a rather wistful look on his face. "But it gets so complicated at times. Seems like whenever you try to make things better, you get burned. But I do feel I've put Seattle on the sports world map. It's a great feeling. I guess it's partly ego, but it's also a great feeling of accomplishment for a town which has supported me tremendously through thick and thin. Some of the things we've done wrong here, why, if we'd done them in New York or Los Angeles they'd have thrown us in the dungeon."

I asked him why the Sonics hadn't reinvested that $2 million in Haywood moneys on new talent?

"I'm prepared to bargain for a player if Bill Russell determines one is sufficiently attractive to us. But I'm not going to make the mistakes of the past. If I had more seats I could afford to go after a Julius Erving, but you just take a pencil and paper and see that if we are playing to ninety-six percent capacity there's no way I can spend a lot of money and recover it. Besides, there's no guarantee it will work out. Look at Haywood."

I thought to myself, What have we here? Has Our Man Sam suddenly compromised his lust to be "a winner" in favor of a fondness for balanced books? Will a destiny of mediocrity be established because this man can't justify spending any more in search of a champion? That was a set of questions that would confusingly peek out of several major events on through the season.

Now he seemed a little anxious about the state of the team. Apparently Watts had been filling his ear. He asked me, "How do you think the team is going to do? Are there some internal problems?"

"I think they have lost some of that real togetherness that they had before the playoffs last year. But I really think Bill is putting more of himself into the job than he has before. I think he's genuinely enthused. But there's friction. There seems to be a clique formed around Leonard and Fred and Bantom. A lot of the guys are pretty down on Tommy. It'll be interesting to see how they go."

"Well, I'm a little worried, but I don't know, it's so hard for me to really know what's going on."

I moved on through the interview, not realizing how profound certain of his answers would seem within a few months.

"Out of all the players who have played for the Sonics, is there one who would rate as your favorite?"

"I have no compunction in telling you this, and if other players don't like it, I'm sorry. In the city of Seattle, players get more from the fans than they give. In the ten years of the Sonics I don't know of one player on a par with Slick Watts as far as desire on the court and ability to make people happy. That's a fact. I wish I had twelve Slick Watts on my team."

"You made your biggest commitment in the granting of power and finances to land Bill Russell. Are you satisfied with the job he is doing?"

"Bill and I are good friends and I have to respect him for having that innate something that enables him to take an average player and make something out of him. We now have one of the lowest payrolls and we had one of the highest a few years ago. Yet we are winning more now. You can love a guy, but that doesn't mean you have to agree with everything he does. I wish Bill was a little more exposed to the community. I guess some people would say I shouldn't make statements like this, but I never want to reach the point where I'm not going to express myself."

"If Russell had a poor year this season and next, is there a possibility his contract would not be renewed?"

"Well, that's something that is a ways down the road and I really don't want to get into it now. I can tell you that when I hired him I did something I am adamantly against, one person being both coach and general manager. But those were his terms and I felt it was important to our franchise to get him. As a coach you want to win and as a general manager you want to govern the budget in the best interests of the club. There's a conflict in getting the best deal and keeping players happy. I think Bill has made some contracts that could have been done more economically, but he has done a lot of good for the franchise, don't get me wrong. Whether he has a good year or a poor year, this year or next, I have to do some serious questioning of renewing his contract—frankly, primarily of the cost. His salary is beyond what those roles customarily pay. You have to evaluate by comparison. I think Al Attles is a pretty good coach, I think Tom Heinsohn is good, Gene Shue is apparently pretty good, and I doubt they are being paid what Bill is receiving.

"It just boils down to good sound business judgments. This is a delicate issue and I think it is premature to discuss it now. Yet it's going to come up."

Schulman asked that I show the interview to his main man in the Sonic organization, Vice-President Zollie Volchok, before I used it. We had wandered off the path on occasion, mixing in personal reflections. I assured him I knew what he had meant to be off the record. A few days later Volchok and I were having a casual conversation at the Sonics' office and he asked me about the interview. He was particularly concerned about the statements being made about Russell. Sam had called him and asked him to be sure to check it out, to be sure that I understood that what he had said about Russell was off the record. I explained how I obviously had to acknowledge that I had asked about Russell's future, even if the matter was two years down the line based on his contract. I went back and looked over the transcripts of the tape. Where Schulman had said, "I can tell *you* that when I hired Bill . . ."—that must have been his cutoff point. Well, it was a long way off and why turn off Schulman over something as seemingly insignificant as this? So I agreed to go with:

44

"I think it is premature to discuss what will happen two years from now, but naturally, it is going to come up. He makes a large salary and his value to the franchise will have to be judged accordingly when the time comes."

6
Close to the Maddening Crowd

I stewed all afternoon as to whether I should talk to Russell. I kept trying to set it out in priorities. Was it worth risking his wrath? This was a man who had shown once he gets down on somebody, he was through communicating with them. Did I have the right as a reporter to possibly jeopardize my working rapport? I knew I wanted to make the journey more pleasant for all concerned and even though the regular season was just three games old, there were some disturbing trends in attitude developing on the team.

After opening the eighty-two-game schedule with a victory at home over the star-robbed (Erving had gone to Philadelphia) New York Nets, the Sonics had been humiliated by thirty at Indianapolis and kicked again the next night in Detroit. It seemed so terribly early to be declaring a crisis, yet storm warnings were flapping over the Sonic camp. I felt I was in a position to act as a mediator. (Or was it meddler?)

Maybe it was just a helluva lot of ego tripping on my part, though. As a journalist, especially one involved with a beat covering politics or sports, there is the opportunity to influence public response to the decisions of the principals and therefore there is a chance to influence those making them. If I encourage Russell to trade Fred Brown and he does, I can have almost the same satisfaction of control as if it was I instead of Russell at the helm.

It wasn't a trade that I was advocating this day, although Russell's threat of making a trade had partly motivated the commentary I had written for that morning's paper. Russell had benched Gray and Brown during the Detroit game, although the former returned to action and redeemed himself, somewhat. Russell had said: "I didn't like the way Mike Green played and I didn't like the way Fred played. . . . What's wrong with Fred? I don't know. That's something I can't relate to. He's just not coming to play."

Would you consider trades?

"Yeah."

The plane ride back west had been noteworthy in the petty discontentment and cliquishness among the players. This was in contrast to a wacky, all-for-one atmosphere that had prevailed among the Sonics the previous season—even during losing streaks. There had been a hassle over the division of playoff shares at the end of the previous season and those scars seemed to be showing, along with jealousy over playing time, the prominent role of rookies Johnson and Bob Wilkerson and a lot of words being uttered behind Russell's back. In the commentary I had made a point of these things and even suggested that Russell might relax and soften his rapport with the players. It was nothing profound, but it did represent a challenge for the crew to get its act together. It at least made the public aware of some of what was happenin' to the Sonics off the court.

My stomach felt as though it had been simmering in its own juices all afternoon. I called Russell earlier in the day and told him I wanted to talk to him that evening. I wanted to catch him before the game—but he arrived too close to 7:15 to make it possible, as he went directly into the locker room and closed the doors. I waited for the team to come out onto the court for warm-ups, then started down the corridor toward the locker room. I felt no less tense than the previous year when I had gone out to midcourt before a Coliseum sellout crowd and presented Watts with the Pro Basketball Writers Citizenship Award. I gave a ninety-second speech in sixty seconds and didn't breathe once.

So much for public speaking. This was private, and I still had thunder in my chest. Russell and Hopkins were starting down the corridor. I walked up to them, Russell stopped, Hoppy paused and then decided to go on out. Russell looked down on me curiously. I started to talk but felt my voice croak.

"I hope you understand what I'm trying to say and realize I'm not, well, I'm not trying to play the big shot. Er, ahhh, damn, I can't figure out why I'm so fucking nervous."

"Maybe it's because I'm so tall," he offered, trying sincerely to get me enough at ease to spit it out.

"Well, you read that commentary this morning, I'm sure, and I just thought that since I have heard some things I would lay them on you and you can take them as you want. The players are afraid of you. They are pissed about a lot of things and yet they think if you get down on them they'll get shipped out or benched like Brisker, or whatever."

Russell looked at me without any response.

"A lot of guys have said they didn't understand their role. Maybe, I don't know, maybe since you started all your career you don't realize how a guy reacts coming to a game and not knowing whether he's going to play ten minutes, forty or none. They also feel like they should be able to run more. They think the new offense is too precise. They don't have any flow. Another thing, while I'm spilling it all out here, the guys say that Hoppy talks too long before a game. They say they can't understand him. That he goes on too long and they can't keep up with him. I don't know how valid all this is, but I just wanted to get it out. Maybe some of it has merit."

He laughed about Hoppy and turned casually to go out to the court. "Thanks. I appreciate it." We small-talked the walk out. I wondered how he had taken it. What was really registering behind the mask?

Seattle fumbled around with Detroit and was down 57–49 at the half. I was still on edge as I called in my halftime report for the first edition.

The Sonics caught fire, pulled even and eventually went on to defeat Detroit behind Brown's twenty-nine points. I found out later Russell had told the team during the intermission: "Relax, get loose. Have some fun. This game isn't supposed to be so serious. Play your game, don't fight the plays, just run these guys."

I wanted to tell some of the players how I had gone to bat for them—in the commentary, by suggesting Russell might relax, and talking with Russell. They, of course, weren't aware of the latter. And there was no way I could tell them.

After meeting with Russell in the interview room, I walked across the hall and into the Sonic dressing room. Willie Norwood, a usually amiable veteran, walked toward me from the side. "Get the fuck out of here. We don't want no reporters pokin' around here—tellin' shit on us. We don't want you around here, boy."

I thought, Oh my. I'm trying to get this ship on course and they want to throw me overboard. Ah, we martyrs have it rough.

I said, "Well, that's gratitude for you."

The burly 6'8" Norwood broke into a big cackle, slapping me on the back.

Gray wasn't so frivolous. I walked over to his booth. He was pulling his jersey over his head, exposing a barrel chest and thick arms. His face can bear a menacing expression, lips pursed and eyelids lowered like shields of armor. What had been a relaxed, if not wordy, communication between us the year before seemed to be fast disappearing. "Would you say the guys were looking more for each other out there than in the first three games?" I asked. "Do you think things were a little more together in the second half?"

"You're putting words in my mouth. You got your quotes mixed. Ask the question," he said, his voice thick and flat like a sheet of lead.

"Okay, what has changed to get the running game going?" He was pulling off his socks, didn't look up. "Is there more free-lancing?"

He stood up and shrugged his body as if to push back what now was a group of writers. He bent back over and cut the tape off his ankles. "Well, you can probably get an answer from Bill Russell. He's right over there. He's got all the answers."

Another reporter tried. "Now, you said . . ."

"I'm not talking to you guys. I like you but get out of my face, please. I ain't got time to talk about tonight. I'm thinking about this Sunday's game. I'm just out there playing. You're getting paid to watch the game. What do you want to know what I saw? You saw it."

"The fans want to know what *you* think."

He stepped through the group, heading for the shower. "Well, with all due respect to all four of you writers here, please don't ask me no questions. I'm only a ballplayer." And he rumbled across the locker room and was gone.

The cluster of writers were around Brown. "Were you back into a game that everybody was more into?" a writer asked.

"How do you mean?"

"Running."

"Oh, yeah. We were a little tight in the first half. We missed I don't know how many layups. But we loosened up in the second half." He paused and looked away from me. "Contrary to whatever you hear or read there's no tension on this club. Everybody enjoys one another here." He glanced around to see who was writing that down. He looked at me. I snorted and walked away.

Minutes later Gray was back. I sauntered over. I didn't want to leave things on such a brittle note. "You've got the prerogative to re-main silent." I smiled. "I just want you to feel free to come forward if you ever have anything you want to relate to the public. You know, if something really important needs to be presented, please keep me in mind." He offered a thin smile. I turned to leave, leaned back and asked, as casual as possible, "Did you think that commentary maybe loosened Russell up? Did he say anything at halftime?" He shrugged. "Hey, I'm not taking notes, I'm just asking."

"No comment, thank you."

Ah, what price duty? I would have to ask myself that night after night through the following weeks as a Gray-Brown faction inspired a mess-with-the-press campaign. The dressing room, which is supposed to be open to the media up to forty-five minutes before a game, became a bastion of player contempt as Gray would usually run the media out at any time. "Out, out. We don't need any reporters in here to help us get dressed. There is nothing to discuss here. See you at the game," he would singsong as he ushered us to the door. Most of the others would just smirk and certainly give no encouragement that they disagreed. And Russell—if one happened to be interviewing someone in a corner while a Brown or Gray or a Bantom or whoever fussed and fumed—would always make a big point of telling you to leave, even if the time limit was on your side.

The postgame game became just as disturbing with the players dashing off to the steam room to outlast the media. This didn't work on the road because they didn't have a steam room, but long showers sometimes were sufficient. If you waded into the "off-limits" shower area to ask a question that you felt was pertinent and needed a response, someone would usually holler out, "There's nothing to discuss here. No press allowed."

It was terribly early in the season, and it was tough to decide how to make a stand. Without a lot of discussion among the writers, except to share "get the hell out of here" stories, the plan seemed to be to suffer and endure in hopes that things might smooth out. The previous year hadn't been marked by this sort of thing, so it must be just a little flexing of the ego which would eventually pass. Gray had always been taciturn, but adequately cooperative. Things would improve with patience, surely.

Everyone in the media had to realize that they could end up with a situation as inconvenient as that which radio broadcaster Wayne Cody had encountered with Russell.

In some ways, Cody's boycott by Russell was a boycott within a boycott, for Cody wouldn't quit asking about the shelved John Brisker. It seemed inevitable Cody and Russell would have their eventual problems, what with the size of their egos. Cody, who is as distinctively round as Russell is tall, waddled into Seattle at the same time Russell took over the Sonics in 1973. Cody announced in his own "You probably think I'm kidding" manner, "I have a five-year plan, and at the end of that time I will be standing on the floor of the Coliseum before a Sonic game talking with Bill Russell, and everybody in the stands will ask, 'Who's that with Cody?' "

All this puffery didn't deter the two of them from teaming up for the Saturday morning *Bill Russell Show* on KTW radio. "We did the show the first time, second time, third time, no problems," recalls Cody. "I'd go on the air saying, 'Hi, everybody, I'm Wayne Cody. Welcome to the *Bill Russell Show*. Now, to answer your phone calls, here's Bill.' After about the third week, I had a note from my station manager that Bob Walsh, the Sonics' assistant general manager, had basically told him I should lay back. Bill apparently thought I was saying too much. I would sometimes interject a further question if I didn't feel the caller was getting the answer he wanted or sometimes ask him to elaborate on something. I was a champion for Brisker and kept sticking in little questions or comments about what was happening to John and why. Bill didn't like that, apparently. So I simply changed over to 'Hi, folks, here's Bill.' Then I sat there and read the paper for two hours while he was on the air."

Russell was getting six hundred a week for the show, three hundred cash and three hundred in trade-out promotional time for his

Kenyatta Corporation, which sold books, record albums and the like. He was also getting two hundred a week from the Seattle *Times* for his weekly "Take-A-Shot" column in which he would sit down with Heberlein and fire off some answers to fans' write-in questions. Part of that gravy train was derailed when KTW went off the air at the end of Russell's first season.

Cody went over to KIRO and began the *Wayne Cody Sports Talk Show*. He had a gift for gab, as they say in the business, and he wouldn't let an occasional confused fact get in the way of entertaining dialogue. Keep it moving, keep things stirred up. Cody called Russell 181 times over two years, by his counting, asking the Sonic chief to be on his show. Cody set up the phone interviews with sports stars from throughout the country and, of course, on the local scene. But he couldn't rouse Russell. It became a joke. "After a hundred or so calls, I sent Bill a Candygram saying I didn't really know what was going on between us, but I would like to clear the air," Cody explained. "He sent back a reply: 'Candy is dandy, but I'm still not going on your show.' "

Along the way, KIRO television contracted to carry a number of Sonic games. Russell let it be known that KIRO wasn't going to use Cody as part of the telecast team. A letter to the "Take-A-Shot" column asked if Cody, who had told his listeners he wanted that duty, had been passed over because of a personal feud between the two. " 'We didn't choose him because of information we have which would not make him the right person for the job,' or something like that, is the way Bill answered the query," explained Cody. "I called Bill many times trying to find out what that was. It made me sound like I had a criminal background. Apparently he had been told I was a large bettor on sports events, which is a total lie. I never bet a dime on anything except the horses, and that's totally legal. I liked Bill and I respected him. He's probably the greatest basketball player of all time. I don't think the feelings toward me were mutual. I don't have to like everybody I work with nor do they have to like me—but everyone should be professional enough to work together. But he just shut the door on me."

Russell could shut the door, all right. And he had the discipline, or the determination, or whatever, to keep his mouth shut—leaving the guessing to others as to why it all happened. No case better illustrates that than that of Brisker's. He was a powerful athlete, muscled with a rather menacing aura, enhanced by his reputation for violence on and off the court while compiling some dazzling statistics in the ABA with Pittsburgh. How founded those rumors were didn't deter the image he carried into Seattle. He was a starting guard for a season before Russell showed. Halfway through Russell's first season, the coach sent Brisker to the Eastern League—a dramatic humiliation. This came shortly after Brisker had scored forty-seven points against Kansas City. It shocked the Sonics and their fans and John. The official word was that he needed work on his defense—but the Eastern League is as much an atmosphere for defense as a brothel is for Bible reading. He was in the East on weekends and in Seattle during the midweek for nearly a month. Then Russell hauled him back into Seattle and planted him on the bench. Fans chanted, "We want Brisker," but got nothing but a glower from Russell.

One player later related, "None of us really knew what was going on. I know John didn't. Someone told me once that Brisker had been bad-mouthing Russell's coaching to other players around the league, and Ray Scott, who was coaching at Detroit then, heard it and told Russell. I don't know if that is true. Might have been something else, but I don't think it was John's game, though, and I wasn't there, but another player told me that John said to Russell the next year, 'I'm willing to do anything, just tell me what it is you want,' and Russell told him, 'Just keep the fuck out of my face.' That's cold, man. But that's the way Russell could be and a lot of players were afraid of Russell after that. They didn't want to end up like John."

Where Brisker wound up was on the bench all but 276 minutes the next season and when he was ready to report for the start of the 1975–76 season, he found the door shut. It seems he had undergone surgery to remove a bone spur during the summer and the Sonics ruled that was a violation of his contract. They charged him with breach of contract and eventually were forced to settle through arbitration by paying Brisker off on roughly half the balance due on his contract. He never played professionally again.

Such accounts aren't without their influence on a journalist who is dependent upon a communication with a man and his team. Whether I am striving to simply report facts as they happen or to entertain the reader or to interpret personalities and events, the contemporary style of covering a beat necessitates dialogue with the principals. We are dealing with the realm of quotes now—quotes, contact representing pregame and postgame commentary and quotes for personality profiles and quotes from everyone so the reader will know how everybody feels about everything.

The emphasis is on what is said in the huddles and locker rooms. Most of all, take the reader where he can't go on his own. Give him the coach's strategy and the player's interpretation of same. And don't forget to get the gripes of the guys who didn't get to play. Trying to honestly relate these expressions is not without some profound conflicts, as will be illustrated shortly, but the question can be posed: What more does anyone need to know about Dr. J other than what he does on the basketball court? Why does anyone need to know what he thought of the game? Fans want to be taken on a tour of the athlete's head. They want to know what he eats and why and what he thinks about when he's falling asleep. They want to know why he changed religions and wives and how much he makes and what he does with all that money. The writer is constantly forced to go deeper into the athlete to come up with new headlines.

And so the writers come trooping into the locker rooms sometimes feeling not unlike a bunch of chipmunks scurrying around for an acorn. Sure, too many of the questions are innocuous, but the game of basketball doesn't warrant that kind of scrutiny eighty-two times a year. Understand, too, the only thing worse than having to answer a stupid question is having to ask one. As a reporter you want the reputation among your colleagues for being a guy who can dig out the best material, handle the tough issues.

What makes it difficult for many writers is the feeling they are always crowding the athlete—clamoring for material they would resent being asked to express themselves. Forward Bruce Seals came to the Sonics from the ABA's Utah Stars. He had left Xavier of New Orleans as a sophomore and his immaturity had caused him problems in dealing with the challenges of the pros at Utah. He wasn't playing much and eventually got to drinking beer with a flourish. A year later, during an interview as he joined the Sonics, he alluded to this, but didn't want to make a big deal out of it, because he was trying for a new start and didn't want fans to look at every slump he delivered as being back on the bottle. The temptation was to turn it into a sensational and therefore unfair account, titled "A Boozer Tries to Shape Up." But he wanted to keep it as a passing comment. I decided to cooperate with him rather than to exploit him.

Respecting the fact there is a limit to what the athlete is comfortable giving up to the public, there is a problem in that many athletes forget the role the media plays in their career. A reporter helps him become a salable commodity. The pandering to athletes and the indulgent salaries have given many athletes the feeling that the money they are getting and the adulation and all the rest is their natural due—that they are justifiably superior people. But the athlete is dependent on the fan's support and since the fan cannot get to know the player directly, he must rely on the media as a surrogate. If the fan, through the media, develops a fondness for the athlete, he will be more apt to respond to the products he is endorsing or buy his book or send his kid to the player's summer camp, or just spend the bucks to come and watch him play.

And in the process of pushing for more, the writer runs the risk of sacrificing his own values and pride to cajole and wring out ever more provocative material. Yet it was my feeling going into those early season days of turmoil with the Sonics that there was a tightwire running through all this, and the challenge for me was to find a meaningful, fair and entertaining journalistic trip across. It was a challenge to see if I could constantly fulfill the readers' interests and still be decent with the athletes—especially when the decency was not being reciprocated.

7
Hyphenated Hypocrisy

Willie Norwood, who could be mistaken for a teddy bear if they grew to 6'8" and played pro basketball, hugged the ball in fingers thickened by adhesive tape and searched the court anxiously, trying to unload an inbounds pass. Players on the Sonics' bench behind him yelled confusing advice. Only seven seconds remained on the clock. Seattle had a 115–114 lead over Chicago. A frantic look dominated Norwood's bearded face as the Sonic guards tried, without success, to shake loose. Norwood pumped the ball in a fake pass—only the ball spilled off his fingers and out onto the court.

Mickey Johnson, who was already worth twenty-nine of Chicago's points, gobbled up Norwood's gift at midcourt, took flight toward his basket, was cut off by the desperate pursuit of Norwood (have you ever seen a scared bear flee downhill?), fired off the rim from fifteen feet and heard the final horn sound. Of his near game-blowing error, Norwood explained:

"I was just going to fake it and get some reaction. The next thing I knew, the mother-fuckin' ball was gone."

Enter the reporter's dilemma. I know Richard Nixon left as his greatest presidential legacy the "expletive deleted." I know "bleep" is very popular with the PTA and that "bleep-bleepin' " can be employed in some circles, and even "m——-f—— ball" will go with editors who know they should be working at *Esquire*, anyway. I know it's customary with many writers to simply substitute some cotton-candy phrase such as "doggone ball" or "darn ball." But this is corruption, or a plasticization, if you will, of the truth—and I find that distasteful, probably as much as some persons are disturbed by the word "mother-fucker."

A season is inundated with events and encounters to the extent that a reporter can feel he isn't doing his job, because he doesn't report everything. And yet, there is too much that develops when a reporter travels with a team. It is unrealistic to think that a group of men can be covered under a microscope twenty-four hours a day. The pressure develops as the reporter tries to determine where to draw the line—weighing fairness for the athlete against fanfare in the paper, weighing today's headlines against tomorrow's rapport with the arena he is assigned to cover.

If, as we have discussed, the reporter wants intimate communication with the individuals he is covering, then the conflict over what to relate of that intimacy is confused when society's taste buds are taken into account.

Unfortunately, a reporter can often feel as though he is the perpetrator of the sugarized infatuation which is part of sports world worship. He doesn't print that Willie Norwood said "mother-fuckin' ball," so a parent chews out a son who gets caught swearing. "You stop that kind of language. You don't hear Willie Norwood talking like that, do you?"

The communication conflict is greater in pro basketball than any other pro sport because the NBA is culturally colored (I'd never stoop to such a pun) and while what is said and done out of the public's eye seems casual within its own realm, to present it undiluted or to try to interpret it for the average white fan is just too much to expect of daily sports coverage.

As Russell once reflected: "I went to an all-black high school. When I got to the University of San Francisco, there were about eight blacks on campus. It was a real cultural shock—a different language. They thought mother was a word all by itself."

Pro basketball is unique among sports in several major aspects, not the least of which is the predominance of blacks. The NBA has 67 percent black players. This is more than all other major pro sports combined, with football's 40 percent, baseball's 12 percent (we're not talking about Latins) and hockey's (anybody seen Willie O'Ree?) zero percent.

This contrasts with a much whiter picture only a decade earlier when there was an unwritten quota system—no team had more than four blacks. It was Red Auerbach and Russell who broke that with the 1965–66 championship team as the Celtics started an all-black five. "As despicable as the quota system was," Russell said, "I must say that it won a title for the Celtics. In the 1963–64 season Cincinnati had a better team than we did. The Royals could have beaten us, but in my opinion they virtually gave Bob Boozer away to get down to their black quota, and that gave us a championship in the bargain."

Former NBA writer Merv Harris reflects that "in the early sixties what you saw were some pretty remarkable people fighting through the system and making it into pro basketball. Tom Hawkins, for example, was a sociology major from Notre Dame. Now with expansion, more players and a higher percentage of black players, you are getting more of a cross section of the American Negro society. There are some

54

guys who don't have very good educations and there are some guys who are inarticulate—not necessarily in white society, but probably in black society as well. With more players representing less education and more recourse to vulgarity in common speech, there is a different attitude expressed among the blacks in the league than you found in the mid-sixties."

The racial prejudices are not as overt as they were twenty years ago when Russell became the NBA's first black star. He was drafted No. 1 by St. Louis but was hesitant to play pro ball in a border town still filled with open prejudice against the black man. The way they called him "nigger" and "worthless nigger garbage" and "black gorilla" the first time he played as a Celtic in St. Louis so enraged Russell that he dedicated every subsequent appearance in that city as personal punishment for Hawk fans. In fact, barely six games into his pro career, Russell was ready to quit, convinced that he was the worst shooter in the league and dispirited by the racially incited taunts of fans. Only the encouragement of his since-divorced wife, Rose, kept him in pursuit of what eventually became a legendary saga.

Lenny Wilkens, who later confessed to being "none too pleased" about being drafted by St. Louis in 1960, remembers the atmosphere when segregation laws opened previously off-limits restaurants to blacks. "Some still refused you service and others just made you feel very uncomfortable. I remember a place called Mrs. Hullings. They had pictures of all the Hawks, including me, hanging on the walls. I went in there, got a lot of hostile stares, but I stayed. You could always go to a movie though. They couldn't see you in the dark.

"Russ did some important things. I was in the service when he refused to play in an exhibition game against the Hawks in Lexington, Kentucky. Sam Jones and Tom Sanders couldn't get served in the hotel coffee shop, so Russell just got all the blacks together and they flew out without playing the game. That was unheard-of then. But if Russ had come in Jackie Robinson's era, he wouldn't have lasted.

"Even in the mid-sixties there were a lot of blacks who just went along—tried to stay out of the way, to be inconspicuous. We had the best record in the NBA in 1968, but as we got more blacks on the team there was less support from the community. So they moved the team to Atlanta. One thing I learned from Russ, though, was that you can deal from strength."

A national magazine article printed in 1964 proclaimed of Russell: "Beware of the Mad Negro." These were years chronicled by a sports writing generation that, for the most part, had a limited understanding of "the Negro," let alone an empathy for the fires that burned inside a proud black man. The derisive sports department humor of the fifties and sixties was captured in: "The reason Negroes can run so fast and jump so high is that the ones who couldn't got eaten by the lions." The Negro athlete was seen as a finely developed animal.

Russell was celebrated for his basketball magnificence throughout the country—at least by those who didn't get too much exposure to his outspoken diatribe on race and the religion made of sports. But he was never fully accepted as a hero in Boston, the city to which he brought sports world fame with eleven NBA titles in thirteen years. "After the last championship all I heard was that there were too many black guys on the team," Russell said at one time and added a few years later: "The main problem in Boston was that I went there as a man and they weren't ready to accept a black person as a man—the press and everybody."

When Russell hit Seattle to take over the coaching and general manager duties with the Sonics in 1973, he said: "As I read it, this is a city that accepts a guy for what he is. I am what I am. If you can accept me for what I am and I accept you for what you are, then we can make it." Seattle has its bigotry and racism, but it seems to run a little thinner than most of America's major cities. Although one of the smaller population bases in the league, Seattle produced the No. 2 ranking attendance (second only to New York) in the three years since Russell took over the club. The Sonics often have five blacks on the court at the same time—a lot of times when they aren't even behind. (Remember Russell's old NBA ditty? Three at home, four on the road and five when you're behind.) Watts is a bald-headed mumble-mouthed cross between a Globetrotting clown and a New Orleans pimp, who came to be acclaimed as the state's No. 1 personality. As a *Sport Magazine* piece just into the 1976 season proclaimed: "Slick Watts Towers over Bill Russell." Part of the reason that headline came down so hard on Russell was due to the fact the Sonic coach refused to meet with writer Ralph Barbieri even when he came to Russell's office. It is true Russell's protective nature and pious personality have cost him much of the popularity he owned when he came to Seattle—but the criticism hardly ever includes the epithet "nigger."

Still there is the ugliness. En route to the Boston Garden one evening a cabbie told me, "You couldn't *pay* me to watch those niggers play ball. Thank God they've kept 'em down in baseball." Boston still may not be ready to accept a black as a man.

Sit in first class sometime on a commercial flight with a party of eighteen. Make ten of twelve players black. Make the coach and his assistant black. Give the scene six whites in the form of a trainer, a broadcaster, two reporters and two players. Your impression of where people's heads are at comes when flight after flight over a full season a stewardess, a pilot, a public relations official or just a curious fan seeks "the coach" or "the owner" and goes to the trainer or the broadcaster because they are middle-aged whites among a group of blacks and shaggy-heads.

You have to be clever in your timing, but if you are, you too can walk back through the coach section about the time some of those blacks are running around the aisles laughing and singing and drinking and shouting over a card game and talking about mother-fucker this and muf-fah that and they're hustling some white chick like she was the last piece of sweet potato pie on earth. Walk around then and you too have a chance of finding someone leaning over to a partner and saying, "Ain't them niggers riding high now?"

" 'Sport reflects American life,' " Russell once said, parroting a common spiel among sports followers. "Yes, it does. The fans bring their prejudices right along with them.

"How much has it all changed? Well, when I first got involved in the big-time sports world twenty years ago, most energy was being expended in finding good polite colored boys who would play the game, take abuse with a smile and shuffle and thus be . . . a credit to their race. Now all the energy is spent in searching for white hopes (of any character) who can play, and thus be . . . a credit to their race," Russell reflected during the early seventies.

Basketball thought it had a "white hope" in Walton, but it turned out he didn't want the part. The white players feel the strain of racial alignment. Sometimes there is humor in it. Rick Barry advocates a dunk contest for white guys who can't jump with the blacks, and before he retired as one of the game's best forwards, Billy Cunningham felt embarrassed by a newspaper story calling him the best white player in the NBA.

"They shouldn't say a thing like that, should they?" sensitive Cunningham said to teammate Chet Walker.

"No, they shouldn't," Walker replied. "Because it's Jerry West."

Most of the time it isn't a chuckling matter. The cultural or ethnic circumstances never go away in the NBA, and just when you forget that, invariably something stirs the consciousness. Racially based animosities are part of the NBA life extended by blacks as well as whites. Sometimes it's within the race, as Spencer Haywood's chiding of Watts for being "a clown." Haywood, the cold and stern pride, versus Watts, the effervescent and rollicking pride. Attitude collisions within a culture. So much of the friction and awkwardness in the NBA, including the fans, is mainly a result of cultures scrubbing on one another like icebergs floating through too narrow a channel at the same time.

Once I figured out that a "bad mother-fucker" was an all-right dude, I at least had a shot at communicating in the world I was supposed to be relating to my readership.

8

Around Beer Town

Outward bound again, Milwaukee via Denver this time. Election Day U.S.A. tomorrow. Russell was musing over his absentee ballot. There was nary a word of conversation among the players regarding the presidential race between Jimmy Carter and Gerald Ford. There were a couple of quiet backgammon games in progress. Wilkerson was sleeping. Green was sleeping. Even the human mosquito, Watts, was slumped in his seat, eyes closed, earphones snapped onto his head. His arm, sporting a massive turquoise and silver bracelet, rode his knee as it bounced to the music, the bracelet shooting reflections of the sun at the walls. The autumn rays filled the cabin with a soft yellow glow. It was a lazy sun porch mood. You felt like you should be shooing away a fly. It was a chance for contemplation.

I stared out the window as thirty thousand feet below a world went about its business. What an abstraction, this flying of thousands upon thousands of miles each season. I thought of the journeys I had taken crisscrossing the country. There is something in traveling on land that at least gives you an awareness of distance and space. Regardless of how little you interact with people, you still get a feeling for the country. Even in the cover of night, when all you see are big interstate signs counting down the miles to some destination (which will be followed by another) in chunks of fifty and one hundred, there is an understanding of place. Little towns come up and fade not unlike the lights of ships passing in the night. The radio wavers in and out of contact with dozens of faraway stations. The truckers are out there like hundreds of wild horses trampling across the plains. Maybe there is the sweet scent of spring grass and cattle. Maybe there is rain or wind or even a nasty snowstorm to fight through. With a beer between your legs and that long thin dawn coming in your tired eyes, you comprehend what 474 miles means driving from Oklahoma City to Memphis.

You don't get any of that in the NBA. Instead, you get frameless hours to stare below, trying to get some feeling from the lovely hazy autumn day taking place down there on earth—where the foliage goes through its October orgy. You are left only with time to flirt with other dimensions.

Over the prairie skies, I'm riding above the clouds like a traveler over the ice sheets of that frozen age long past. I'm locked in a time-absorbing machine. I have reflections on what I last touched and anticipation on what I will next touch on earth, but in between there is nothing but the passage of time. What is said, what occurs, could be anywhere in the universe. I might as well be a spirit. And to think that just one hundred years ago the adventuresome and the trapped toiled on clutches of prairie for survival. Beaten down by the odds and the elements, the farmer lifted his immigrant's eyes to this sky asking for help—for mercy. Fifty years ago the adventuresome and the desperate plunged up and down narrow concrete ribbons seeking a way out, a new chance. When that traveler stopped at a sun-bleached gas station or a gray-graveled café, he looked up to the sky for answers. Now I'm in the sky, given a drink and a magazine and a cushion for my ass and another for my head. I'm in the prairie sky, but I don't feel any closer to their answers. I have only the lust for survival that rode with the motorist and met the farmer quietly in his fields.

As the plane whined eastward it was indeed a time to relax, to indulge in the state of being among the privileged of the world's workers. I flipped through some some mail I had grabbed at the office before departure. There was a Telex message from *Sports Illustrated*. "We are doing an early season pro basketball story on the performances and effects of the former ABA teams and former ABA players on NBA teams, on the rest of the NBA. We would like comments, opinions, quotes (on or off the record), anecdotes, funny incidents, surprising performances, etc., on or about the players, coaches or fans of your team. . . ."

After listing a number of specifics the magazine would like responses to, the message concluded: "Need by Nov. 4." That was three days away, not even two weeks into the season. How can you draw any conclusions in two weeks? Such is the pressure of having to deliver a national product every Friday—if nothing is going on, you have to make something go on. Well, I appreciated the bread *SI* spends on such stringer reports and it was nice to see quotes and observations I dredged up featured in a national piece, and who knows, maybe I would stumble across something that would make a good column in the process.

I looked around to see if anyone was bored enough to be interviewed. No one was stirring. Burleson was across the aisle from me, sprawled across two first-class seats and sound asleep. He looked as though he had been blasted into his present position by a roundhouse barroom punch. His shaggy hair spilled across his face, his head was twisted sideways against the capsule wall. An airline blanket covered him from neck to knees, one arm dangled like a hose filled with hot water. The legs, one wandering far under the seat in front and the other projecting a massive Adidas sneaker nearly to my elbow, shouted a message: This man is seven feet plus two inches tall. He doesn't fit normally into any of society's trappings.

There were some who questioned how well he fit on a basketball court as he began his third season in the NBA, although he had performed admirably the night before, picking up eighteen points and ten rebounds in twenty-three minutes as Seattle waltzed past hapless Atlanta for its nineteenth straight regular season home court win wrapped over the end of last season and the start of this one.

I recalled the day we first met. He had come to Seattle in the summer of 1974, the club's No. 1 draft choice. He was a towering, ultra-polite, "Yes, sir" and "No, sir" and "Thank you, ma'am" boy out of the hill country of eastern North Carolina. He arrived in Seattle flanked by his quiet and cautious mother and his three-year-old sister, who stood eyeball to his knee. He wore his hair in Dutch Boy locks then. He was fresh off the North Carolina State NCAA championship team and came to the pro ranks to study under the master, Bill Russell. When Russell got through with him, why Burleson would be the greatest center in the game, or at least one of them. NBA titles comin' up.

Now his hair was longer, his body heavier, his manner more worldly. But the performances hadn't brought championships. In fact, after developing convincingly as a rookie to lead Seattle into its first postseason playoffs after seven previous years of trying, Burleson had come back off knee surgery to play his sophomore season like a slug. Partly because he and David Thompson had led N.C. State to the stunning upset of Walton and the UCLA dynasty in the NCAA semis, and because everyone figured Russell was going to make Burleson into a superstar, the nation still kept a close eye on Big T.

As we drew closer to Denver, Russell had awakened and became restless enough to move into the aisle. Burleson joined us. I mentioned the ABA query. Russell frowned and said, as if he had just been waiting for the chance to jump on *Sports Illustrated*, "I think it is really dumb to be trying to make big things out of nothing all the time. I don't have time for that kind of story because there's nothing to them. Boston's not going to change. Denver's not going to change. The league is just twenty-two good teams now instead of eighteen. What's the big deal?"

"Yeah, well, I tend to agree, but not every story can be profound. I usually come up with something interesting," I said, wanting to drop it. "You vote for Ford?"

He laughed warmly, changing his mood on a dime. He explained to Burleson: "I got a letter from Ford a while back asking me if I would campaign for him. I was tempted to write back and tell him, 'Sure, as long as I can make appearances as a team with Earl Butz.'" Butz was Ford's Secretary of Agriculture at the time he made an offhanded comment to a traveling companion that "the attitude of the coloreds is no interest in the political process as long as they have tight pussy, loose shoes and a warm place to shit."

"What made me mad," said Russell, "was that Ford had to wait to see what public sentiment was going to be when the story got out before firing the guy."

The "fasten seatbelt" order interrupted our discussion at that point, and I was left to ponder what Russell would do to someone like Butz if the two of them had ended up sharing a podium. That would be entertaining, but the whole idea of endorsements and advertising promotions by athletes deals with manipulation I find sobering.

The power of influence people will let their heroes have with their minds is exemplified in the amount of money organizations and businesses spend to recruit athletes and other entertainers for endorsements and promotions. It makes sense, to at least some semblance of logic, to have an athlete tell the people which shoe is best for the sport he plays. He might be wearing the shoe strictly because it outbid another company for his services, but at least it's convincing because it is a tool of his trade.

The athlete can make some embarrassing statements along the way, though. Like what Burleson stated, in an article I was doing on the rapid growth in the number of companies making shoes for basketball. I knew he had been offered some pretty nice bucks to wear Pro-Keds, but turned it down, explaining to me, "I really don't feel very comfortable in them." But he signed a pro-services contract coming out of college which paid him a flat fee and entitled the service the right to make deals with various firms for his endorsements. Not a month after he made that statement, the pro-services people made a deal with Pro-Keds and you know what Burleson wore and endorsed shortly thereafter.

What is especially disturbing is the "image through association" advertising that companies produce by using a personality or a theme that really has nothing to do with the institution or its services.

What does Russell have to do with the services of the telephone company? Nothing. But he's known nationally as a witty, dynamic guy. So he trades insults with some guy named Ron Watts—no one knows who he is, but if he's a friend of Russell's, well he's probably a pretty witty, dynamic guy, too. Russell walks down a street and stands next to a small boy. White picket fence, cozy middle-class neighborhood in the background. "Ever seen a giant before?" The laugh. He throws a basketball over his shoulder and into a hoop hanging on an executive's office wall. Cackle. But for what? For the image that the phone company is pretty witty and dynamic. They're still going to want a hundred-dollar deposit when you take out service in a new town, though. They're still going to charge you thirty dollars to move your phone from the bedroom into the kitchen.

It's sad that "Massmind" is treated this way. It's worse that it responds just the way it is supposed to.

Probably no athlete ever surprised his colleagues more with an endorsement than did Chamberlain when he backed Nixon for the 1972 election. In his autobiography, *Wilt*, Chamberlain explained how he thought he could help the blacks and gain some influence on programs he was interested in by siding with Nixon.

"Some blacks thought I backed Richard because I was getting paid for it; some thought it was because I 'had it made,' and didn't care much about other, poorer blacks. Neither was true. I didn't get a penny for helping Richard, and I hoped to use my contact with him to help other blacks. . . ." Chamberlain found out later he had very little influence. "Does that mean he exploited me? Sure. All endorsements and testimonials are exploitation, though. When I do a commercial for Volkswagen, they're exploiting me to sell their cars, and I'm exploiting them to make money for myself. It's the same way in politics. Richard and the Republicans exploited me to get black votes, and I exploited them to provide black input—and to learn something about the political process. And I learned quite a bit indeed; . . . I've had about as much opportunity to influence him as I have had to influence the Pope."

As we climbed out of Denver, bound for Milwaukee, I wondered just how many of the players had voted, how many even cared who won the election. No one had mentioned it other than Russell's pitch on Butz. You assume because most of them are black, and they are all relatively young, and they lead this free-spirited life-style, they would naturally be liberal, Democratic. But then they are in the 50 percent tax bracket. They aren't likely to be too concerned about welfare. Most have business investments, maybe real estate holdings, stocks, bonds. They aren't stumping for socialism. These people want the same tax protection programs sought by any bank executive.

Still, culturally, they must have some contrasting emotions. I contemplated interviewing each player as to his presidential preference. Then I decided that constitutes an invasion of privacy. If there are curtains on the voting booth, why should these citizens be asked to convey their sentiments publicly? Some of them would refuse, as would be their right, and others might cooperate reluctantly. If I wrote a story that implied they weren't interested, that would make them look bad. They'll say, "Why did you bring it up?" Hell with it.

Squeak, bounce, reverse engines, we were there. Where'd the day go? It was nearly dark. We walked down the ramp and across the open apron. There was a momentary flash: Where are we? It felt like Buffalo. Why is it the worst weather airports have open-air boarding? We went inside and waited for the baggage. Filing through the terminal, the players drew stares and comments and a couple of autograph requests from the good folks of Milwaukee. I renewed my ABA query. *SI* was particularly interested in Mike Green, since he had spent the previous three seasons in the ABA, the last one with the brink-of-collapse Virginia Squires.

"Yeah, I'll tell you what the difference is, man," he answered, his eyes darting between myself and adjacent players, checking out his audience. "First thing is, I like it over here 'cause you know your check's gonna be there on time." He snickered and Seals, two years with Utah, said, "I hear that." They slapped hands loosely. Comrades. "And I'll tell you something else," Green continued in a sheeet-man-you-just-don't-know tone of voice. "There's too much jamming the middle in this league. Guys spend half their lives learning to play the game and then they can't use nothing because it's all jammed up. Ain't no fun. They don't know how to have fun here, man." He spotted a bag coming down the conveyor and called to Furtado, who was pulling Sonic luggage off into a fast-growing pile. Wilkerson and Johnson were lending an occasional hand. The rest of the players sat on the baggage area perimeter. "Hey, Frank, grab that bag there, will ya, man?" ordered Green.

Furtado looked over his shoulder, delivering a messageless smile. "Don't worry, Mike, we'll get 'em all. You guys just relax. It's all being taken care of." He was saying, I'm not your servant. I just do a job that happens to look that way.

It was past eight by the time the bus moved out for the hotel. The NFL Monday TV Night Game of the Week had already started. Some were anxious to get there to watch it. They needled the driver to hurry. Others were just anxious to get out into the night. They needled the driver to hurry, too. One of the players was taking action on the game. "Hey, B.J., what's the spread?" he called to me.

"Houston and six."

"Houston favored?"

"No, it's Houston plus six."

"Who you want?"

"I'll take Houston, but you gotta give me six and a half."

"You on. How much?"

"Let's see. You owe me anything? Naw, well, let's make it five."

"Deal. Who else out there wants to give me some chump change?"

We checked into the Marc Plaza, downtown Milwaukee, a nice, older hotel two blocks from the arena. The rooms were preassigned, two to a room, the pairings determined by Russell's secretary, Anita Dias. Brown and Watts had private rooms. Brown because it was in his contract and Watts because he drove everybody crazy. They picked up their keys which had been set out on the counter with their names on the envelopes. They hollered out room numbers, and having had only eight hours to talk it over, tried to decide who was up for what. They disappeared into the elevators. Russell had a suite. The players were on a different floor, the media on another, per Russell's orders.

I threw a few things in the closet. Flipped on the tube. A knock on the door brought in Oleynick. A minute later Watts wandered in. We watched the game. Baltimore was killing Houston. Someone was about to get my "chump change." We had a straight shot courtesy of the airline's little bottles. We reviewed Howard Cosell.

"Howard's all for himself," said Watts. "He don't care what he says as long as people notice him."

"He's fucked, man," added Oleynick.

"He's rich, though," countered Watts.

"He fucks it up for other journalists, though," I added. "His ego gets out there so far people get to thinking all journalists are arrogant assholes."

"He is," concluded Oleynick. "He fucks up the game so bad you can't even understand what's happenin'. Let's go downstairs and get a beer."

We headed downstairs to a tame lounge. Watts gulped down a tequila sunrise and ducked out, needing more action than our conversation, which centered on Oleynick's relationship with Russell. Oleynick grew up in Bridgeport, Connecticut, the inner-city kid. He talks tough, probably to offset his baby-faced appearance. He became an All-American, one of the nation's leading scorers, tops in free throws, as a junior at Seattle University. He went hardship and Russell drafted him No. 1, calling him a real solid pro prospect with Oscar Robertson-style possibilities for greatness. Oleynick is one of the two whites on the Sonics this year, but his being is ghettoized—his game is him, his game is everything. And his game isn't going where he thinks it should. His rookie year was marred by a serious knee injury early in the spring. The players got down on him because he took off for home. "I'm no cheerleader, man. I'm hired to play ball. Can't play, so I'm gone."

He's solidly built at 6'2", 190 or more pounds of muscle. He signed a nice contract, $100,000 a year plus a bonus, which became a new Mercedes. He traded that in on a new one the next year. He had his agent, Jerry Kapstein, handling all his finances, paying his bills and sending him spending money which he went through to the tune of C notes per week. He was living high and we were gulping the good life, Heineken dark, as he talked about himself. "Man, I never had any bread in my pockets. What'd I need it for? I didn't even know how my checkbook worked when I signed my contract. All I know about is ball. That's where I'm at. When I was in high school we just played all the time, go down to New York, get into some games, man. When I was at SU I would get up and go over to the gym and play. I wasn't into school much. I liked a couple classes, talked about some shit that was kind of interesting. But school is for some folks and not for others. I got my thing. I used to spend all day in the gym, shootin' by myself when no one was around. During the summer that's all we do, man. Just play ball and swim and hang out at night. You know Pat Jordan of *Sports Illustrated* is workin' on a book on me and Walter Luckett—you know the dude from Ohio U. See, it's kind of like a contrast of stories between the two of us. He's black, but he came from the suburbs. He was the star all the time we were in high school in the same city. He averaged forty points a game for his high school career, really. Everybody wanted him. And then he was a big college star at Ohio U. The Pistons drafted him last year—only he didn't make it. Now, me, I'm white, but I was in the streets, see. And I was always in Luckett's shadow. But I'm the one who made it in the pros."

The degree to which he had made it was bothering Oleynick, though. Russell had traded away guard Herm Gilliam to Portland at the start of this season, telling Oleynick he would be filling those shoes in the backcourt. But even this early in the season he was getting erratic treatment from Russell. Starting some games, but playing as little as five or six minutes, coming off the bench other games and playing as much as a half. It was conjecture who was guilty of the breakdown, but Oleynick didn't have any doubts.

"Russ is fucking with me, man. I don't understand him. I'm making good bread and the life is fine, but it don't mean shit to me if I got to go through all this. I'm just gonna wait awhile and see what happens. When it comes time I'll make a stand. I don't care what happens. I'll go anywhere. I just want to play ball. Now, don't you use none of this till I tell you. You my man and I'll tell you when it comes time to write something if things don't improve. Okay?"

"Deal," I said, toasting my good fortune to develop what will probably be a helluva story. Be patient, be fair, it'll all come your way, I said to myself as we ordered another round.

The next day came on with sunshine and only slightly chilly breezes. I went into the coffee shop around 11 A.M. Russell and Tolson were just finishing. I was surprised to see Russell out like that. Rare indeed was the occasion when he didn't stay in, using room service. I sat down, ordered and dug into the morning paper.

Heberlein sauntered in. He told me how some chick had pounded on his door in the middle of the night looking for a certain ballplayer who happened to be in the same room a floor above. We lamented how easy it was for the damn jocks to score, and I talked him into taking a walk, even though he said he should wait for Russell to do the "Take-A-Shot" column. I reminded him the team had shooting practice for another hour.

We walked down to Lake Michigan and kicked along through the breezy day, up a hill and along a bluff with some grand old houses looking out over the water. We talked about what a crazy life it was to be jetted from environment to environment to cover a bunch of guys playing a game. How it was a dream job for thousands of individuals who go into sports journalism. It had been with us. He told me how he had been into newspapering since he was in high school, working as a copy boy and anticipating the day he would move up—up into this sort of position. I told him how that must really be something to know what you want like that when you're so young and just keep at it, not doing anything off the track. I told him how I had been in high school journalism, but thought I'd make my way as an artist or a basketball coach or maybe a merchant seaman—Lord, the world's full of options when you're eighteen years old. I told him how I had wanted to become a wheeler-dealer contractor, but couldn't entice any of my buddies who were good at math into teaming up with me. I made sure he understood that more than anything else I had loved to travel and that was how I had ended up in New York hanging out with a friend at Columbia University and that I had gotten recharged about journalism then while reading Red Smith and Jimmy Cannon and that sort every day. A couple years later I drifted back toward coaching. When I was in the Coast Guard, I would stand up on ship's watch and practice speeches that I would give for half-time inspiration. I used to get so worked up, one time I actually started bellowing and the captain strolled out onto the bridge, arched his eyebrows and asked, "Something wrong, sailor?" But by the time I got to the University of Nevada, I was managing a hotel in Reno and didn't mind that too much, and then a professor of journalism turned me on to David Halberstram's *Making of a Quagmire* and I was back to my first love, being a journalist—full of causes. I was writing protest poetry and trying to be the Phil Ochs of the *Nevada State Journal*'s "Readers Write" column. And then it was into the trenches on the typical small-town daily, this one being the Bellingham *Herald*, working for the hard-assed but lovable city editor and covering the parades and the school board meetings and taking fire pictures which went either all white or all black in the developer and thinking that I was going to be a national star the day we got a tip that fugitive James Earl Ray was supposed to be on a Greyhound due any minute at the Canadian border thirty miles away, but all I got was a ticket for making an illegal U-turn leaving the parking lot and the message that it was a false alarm before I could clear the city limits. But soon thereafter, I got the so-called Big Break. The local college basketball team was going on a six-week People-to-People tour of the Far East and Australia and I muscled my way along to do some articles and went to the Seattle papers to see if they would like some, too. The *P-I* was looking for a reporter and since they were offering $135 a week compared to the $80 I was making in Bellingham, trying to support a wife and child, I jumped at it when I came back from the trip. And after two years I decided the wait would be too long to get to cover something like the Sonics, so I went out and became publicity director for Longacres Race

Track and pursued free-lance writing and four years later, the *P-I* said they had a better idea, and I came back to cover the Sonics.

Between Heberlein and myself there were two very diverse backgrounds to the career we now shared. I wondered which best qualified one to sit in judgment of other individual's careers. We sauntered back along the sidewalks sprinkled with people en route to or from the polling place and we were interviewed twice by some marketing research group doing a study on political sentiments. We took a swim in the hotel pool and reposed in the sauna for a while and talked some more about how this was a damn nice way to make a living. It was like covering a nation, instead of just a team, yet there was much more pressure on a guy than even most of the guys in the office realized, maybe even the editors, since they hadn't ever covered beats where they traveled in such intimate circumstances, where the lives of the participants and the press were so intertwined. We talked again, as we did at the start of the season, about how we had both been pretty burned out at the end of last season and how he had actually really felt like he was cracking up last summer and wound up taking tranquilizers to get back on course and how I had gotten so I never felt I was sleeping because all these faces kept riding through my dreams. But here we were clawing at scoops, pouring out the copy, putting in the hours. It all seemed pretty attractive on this sunny Milwaukee day.

A quick bite to eat, a glance at the first election returns coming in from Maine and a quick visit with people setting up the Carter Election Headquarters on the fifth floor, then time to tune all that out and go to work. The Milwaukee Arena is weirdly lit with banks of fluorescent lights which cast a whitish glare into the small arena—its seating not quite eleven thousand. The place seems bigger, more important, because it still wears the ghost of Kareem Abdul-Jabbar and those glory days when the Bucks actually ruled the NBA. A few of the Sonics are dribbling around, loosening up when we get to the arena. Press row runs along the sideline, backed by the main walkway. People constantly kick the legs of your chair, bump you in the head with purses and Cokes, cough down your neck, so we stay in the press room as long as possible. The hallways and the press room are painted what is called forest green, but actually is kind of a neon-fungus color. There are a dozen card tables in the press room, none of which stand up very well to the vibration of a typewriter. They do have beer on tap and cold cuts and a relish tray and they have a little plastic reader board which says "Welcome Blaine Johnson, Greg Heberline, Bob Blackburn." Heberlein laughed at the latest in an unending parade of misspellings of his name around the league. We pick at some salami and read over the pregame notes.

As the teams warmed up I watched Milwaukee's coach Larry Costello sitting on the bench, legs crossed, hand held to the back of his oily hair. His sports jacket seemed too loud, his tie too narrow, his face dominated by a nose that looked like it had been laid one way and then the other too many times to remember which was front. His hair just long enough to comb over—dark, definitely the wet-head look—something out of a 1965 Vitalis commercial. He looked like a farmer who had reluctantly put on his Sunday duds for a Grange social. He was heading into his ninth season as coach of the Bucks—the only coach they had ever had. They won it all in 1971, three years after the franchise was founded, because Lew Alcindor came to town. Costello had been a sparky, rugged guard for the 76ers up until he became the Milwaukee coach. He was from a different era. I remembered a passage from Roger Kahn's piece on Alcindor's rookie year in *Sport Magazine*. Costello was sitting in the locker room after a loss. The players were shuffling out on their own:

"I returned to Costello, who was becoming more upset. The performance was disturbing him slowly but surely, like a bad clam. 'I don't understand some of these guys,' he said. 'Here they play a terrible game like this, and now they're taking off, going their separate ways. It wasn't that way when I was playing.' Costello gulped a soft drink from the bottle. He has a flat, pleasant, tough, Irish face. 'If we played one like this, we'd want to sit around for a long time and talk, talk among ourselves.' At that moment, not twenty feet away, Alcindor slipped out of the dressing room alone.

" 'So many outside interests,' Costello said. 'So many things on the side.'

" 'What about all that money?' a reporter asked.

" 'Look, the more money a guy can get, the more power to him. And everybody on the team feels the same way. I'm just saying when it goes bad, sit around and talk. Stick around. Hang together like a team.' "

He got a championship out of that team the next year, and yet you couldn't forget those words. It was a different world nearly a decade later, all that ABA-NBA war money spread around, all those long-term no-cuts. Why wouldn't the guys gut it out like it was before? Costello was in trouble, his team had lost all their exhibitions and the first five games of the regular season. He needed the guys to stick around, to suck it up. His team was young, they had gotten some chances on tomorrow when Abdul-Jabbar forced his departure for Los Angeles. But it was going to take time. Doggone it, he was putting in the hours on the sketch pad, if the guys would just bear down.

Seattle let the old warrior off the hook this night, though. Plenty of good Election Night metaphors for this one, too. The Bucks ran off a 17–2 streak midway through the opening quarter and it didn't take a Barbara Walters with an ABC Early Projection to tell you the Sonics were destined to suffer their seventh straight road loss wrapped over two seasons. The Sonic starters accounted for only twenty-eight points, and although Seals was credited with seventeen, two of those belonged to Johnson on a heavy-traffic tip-in. Pressure building on the Seattle road show. Getting to be a good theme for the media.

Game story wrapped up and dispatched via Can-Fax, I headed back to the hotel to catch up on the election. Polls were just closing in the Far West. Looked like a close race. Headed out for a steak down the street at Clock's. Getting ready to close the kitchen but slipped by. Headed back up to Carter's room. Everybody's drinking, waiting, trying to outguess the prognosticators who loomed down from two TV sets. No real action, more people pouring in. Tried a few conversations, everyone's too nervous. Headed back up to the room. Pushing 3 A.M., looked like Carter's victory. Can't stay awake any longer. Flight out at 10 A.M., bus leaves hotel at 8:30. Try it again tomorrow night in Kansas City.

9

Kansas City and the Midnight Oil

Out of Milwaukee at 10 A.M., down in Chicago at 10:30, out of there again at 11:45. Down at Kansas City International at 1:00. Sit and wait for luggage. Players were loose. Norwood, a heavy gray wool cap seemingly a part of his head when he isn't on the court, tossed a quarter into the trough of a good-luck bronze replica of a wild boar statue from Florence, Italy. Others kicked in their tokens. Green, wearing a multicolored heavy-knit sweater that hung to his knees, reached into his purse and flipped in a dollar. "Bad as my luck is, I better spend some mon-neee if I'm gonna get any help." The bags were collected and put on the bus. It's a long ride into the city. Several players spread around the bus and tried to catch some sleep, but a raunchy conversation between two of the players made it impossible.

"Hey, your boy here's talkin' 'bout you."

"What's he sayin'?" One called over his shoulder from the middle of the bus.

"He say you a mother-fuckin' dog."

"I'll come back and kick his mother-fuckin' ass."

"Fuck you! Eat your face," chimed in a third voice.

"Watch you tongue, boy."

"I know what to do with my tongue, nigger. Do you?"

"I hear you don't know *when* to do with it, boy."

"Whassat?"

"I say I hear you so fuckin' dumb you don't go down on the lady like she want."

"You know thas a lie, you depraved nigger."

And so on.

Others picked up the submerged train of thought and it was still going strong when the bus pulled up to the Crown Center complex a few minutes past 2 P.M. Six hours later the Sonics took the court against K.C. Nineteen minutes later they were down 34–19 and well en route to Another Road Disaster. What a tiresome theme, I thought as I searched for a lead while waiting outside the Sonics' dressing room. And waited. We could hear Russell's voice rise and fall, but couldn't make out the words. He was obviously stinging the troops. Yet when he opened the door after some fifteen minutes, he flipped on an easy posture, as if to say, "Everything is under control. Don't push the panic button on me."

This was the eighth straight road loss. There was a ring-around-the-rosebush feeling to Russell's comments. One game threatening trades and punishment. The next saying things would work out fine if everybody stuck together. I wanted something more direct tonight. I was flanked by Heberlein and two K.C. reporters. Often outside reporters seem a little in awe or unsure of Russell, and wait for us to set the tone.

Heberlein opened: "What was the lengthy conversation about in the locker room?"

"Well, we talked about our defense. It was pretty weak tonight, especially up front."

"Isn't defense pretty much a reflection of attitude?" I asked.

"Well, that's hard to say because attitude is a funny word."

"Why is that?"

"Well, you usually think of attitude as good or bad attitude. Attitude can mean different things."

"Well, in this case, isn't it a less than aggressive attitude which is getting you in trouble early?" I persisted.

"Our front line has been dominated every time we hit the road. Leonard had an exceptional game tonight, but except for that, our front line has just been dominated in all our road games."

Heberlein jumped in: "Okay, then what's the difference between the front line at home and the front line on the road?"

"Ahhh, if we only knew."

"Is it a matter of not coming to play?" I tried.

"It looks that way. They don't even seem like the same people."

Heberlein: "Is the defensive problem stemming from the middle?"

"Well, you can't just say one guy because we do a lot of switching and things and we're not getting any defense from either the centers or the forwards."

"You're oh and four this season on the road—clobbered in every one of them. Is there anything left you haven't tried?" I asked.

"Yeah, there's a lot of different things. Bigger sticks and clubs." He laughed.

Heberlein: "After the first quarter you seemed to be making very rapid substitutions. Is that just a matter of looking for something that might work—a certain combination?"

"Yeah. Looked all night without finding it, I guess."

K.C. writer: "Are you going to sue just to play at home?"

Russell gave a polite little laugh.

K.C. again: "Isn't this the eighth in a row your team has lost on the road?"

"Is that all? Seems like more than that."

I feel put off in a way, like nothing is really being acknowledged here. I didn't know what I expected him to say, but I didn't want to quit.

"Pardon me if this is a stupid question, but are you more worried than you were a week ago?"

"No, I was sufficiently worried then." He smiled.

K.C. writer: "Well, what are the coaching tricks or styles to get a team going again?"

"Oh, there are a lot of subtle technical things we can do, but it's difficult because we play so much differently at home than we do on the road. So different that it's unbelievable."

"Have you ever seen anything like this with any other team you've been associated with? The Celtics? In college?" I asked.

"No, but I've seen it in teams we've played against."

K.C. writer: "Is this a new challenge for you?"

"I'm too old for challenges."

"Well, somewhere along the way there has to be something that is consistently happening. Are these people sleeping and not waking up or do they need a crowd behind them that much? What the hell can it be?" I tried again.

"Well, I'm going to find out. There's no doubt in my mind that I'm going to find out. This is a good team and I'm going to find out what the problem is and straighten it out."

"You must have pursued threats."

"I don't like to use threats. We've got eighty-two games. You can't just use threats and threats and threats. It comes down to different kinds of motivation."

"And there are some you haven't tried yet?"

71

"Oh, there's a whole world full of them out there."

K.C. writer: "Is it a situation where it can become progressively downgrading mentally?"

"I'm not going to let that happen."

"How can you prevent that?" I asked.

"I just won't let that happen. Period."

One of the K.C. writers switched tracks with a question about Russell's impressions of the Kings' new ABA guards, Ron Boone and Brian Taylor. Russell said something about being too concerned watching his own team to notice much and I headed into the Sonics' locker room. I didn't feel like I'd gotten anything satisfactory from Russell. I looked around the room. Seals picked at the tape on his ankles, in a corner, seemingly on the verge of tears. Others sat staring at the floor while the rest pulled off wet uniforms, tossed them at their feet and trudged to the showers. I was struck with a feeling of futility.

"I don't suppose there are any new questions to be asked, so if any of you have anything to offer, I'll just flip on the old tape recorder here and let you speak your piece," I hollered out, holding my pocket-sized tape recorder over my head and smiling.

Oleynick returned the smile faintly, as if to say, "Aren't you some smart ass?" Others ignored me. Gray and Burleson were in the shower. Suddenly Brown, who had been sitting with an ankle in a bucket of ice, arms folded across his chest, scowling, spoke up.

"If we don't hurry up and get it together, the word is going to get around the league. The fans are going to know it, the refs are going to know it, and the other players are going to know it. Then we'll have an even bigger hole to climb out of. Everyone will just *plan* on us losing on the road."

Fair stuff, Fred. Best of the night. I looked around again. Nothing going on, I wanted to catch the K.C. dressing room before they all disappeared, so I headed down there. Boone was one of the few left. I went over, introduced myself. I was glad he kept buttoning his shirt, not bothering to shake hands.

"What did you think was wrong with Seattle tonight? I'd like to get the opposition's view."

"Well, I don't think they executed very well. They seem to have good talent, but I mean . . ." he faded off.

"Was the execution breaking down in any particular place? Was it out front or in the hole?"

"Well, I'd rather not talk about that . . . you know. . . ." Of course I knew.

"Okay, tell me this, off the record, just for my own observations, did you think they played with much intelligence?" It was a stab, but he might go for it. One chance in twenty.

"Well, it's pretty hard for me to know," he answered, smiling thinly.

"I was concentrating mainly on our game. You know, it's . . . well, you know." What he was saying was, Hey man, don't make me have to give you meaningless answers when you know I can't give you what you want.

It's another rip-the-fellas review, built around the aroma of the stockyards adjacent to the arena with a few shots at Russell's dance around the questions, a couple of pointed technical blasts, Brown's quote, and a see you Friday in the Coliseum where Sonics shoot for their twentieth straight at home. Tell me this isn't a weird team.

Took a ride to a cabstand with a K.C. writer. Hit the hotel close to midnight. Restaurant was through serving. Burleson and Blackburn were finishing their dinners. We chatted aimlessly, Burleson obviously depressed by the game. We kicked around a few ideas as to what might be wrong, none of them really making any sense. As we were leaving a woman called out to Burleson, "Too bad you lost. See if you can do better next time." It was rather derisive in tone. Burleson walked past her, muttering under his breath, "If the hoop had been as big as your mouth, we couldn't have missed."

I wanted a beer, but the bars were closed. I asked if we can get room service. Just closed. I dashed into the service area, pleaded with a pleasant matron who promised to dig up some beer and a sandwich of some sort. Burleson and I headed up to my room. We settled in for a rap.

"You know there are a hundred things going on in the world more important than the Sonics, even to the people of Seattle, but what's happening to this club is sort of a fascination," I was saying about 1 A.M. "I mean this home and away shit is weird stuff."

"Yeah, you've got a job to do to tell all the people what you think is going on. . . ."

"Yeah, and I can't figure the fucker out."

"Well, this is my livelihood. If we are rotten and don't draw attendance just like if people don't read your paper, then there are problems. If they don't give a hoot, I'm in trouble."

"It's show business, but I don't think you can just show it off at home. If you're stinkin' it up on the road, it gets to be like a spoiled product, even at home when you're winning."

"Yeah, I suppose you're right," Burleson mused, sucking absently on a beer, slumped in a chair. Lord, he's big.

He was just talking the loose, fill-the-time kind of talk people settle into when they just want to unwind. "If you're playing ball you go out and have some beers and the next day—I mean you don't get shit-faced drunk, but you have a couple—and the next day, you've built up some water weight, but you sweat it off. The first part of practice you get out there and you say, 'Shit, I don't want to be up this morning and I feel stiff and lousy.' Then all of a sudden you break into a good sweat and you start fast-breaking and after a while you hate to quit because you know what you are doing is good for you."

I suddenly remembered I hadn't put in a wake-up call. "What time's the bus leave?"

"Seven-fifteen. Damn, it's nearly two. Better finish this and get going." I put in a wake-up call for 6:45. We babbled on. I didn't realize how vague my concentration had become during the next half hour until he was saying, ". . . now I live on about a thousand cash a month. I feel like I'm living so high on that it's unreal."

I blinked. Here was a guy making $350,000 a year living on twelve grand?

"Okay, all I pay is my car insurance and house payment. Okay, two hundred forty-four times twelve is about three thousand. That leaves me a lot for food and gas and heat and clothing. All right, during the season I get a per diem of twenty-five dollars per day, so I'm not having to buy my own food on the road. And my wife, Rhonda, doesn't eat much. It's not like I'm living on a twelve-thousand-dollar salary, though. We're talking about cash. Usually I have about three thousand left for the summer. Now the Sonics bought my van as a bonus. They buy me a van every other year for four years. The one I have now is completely shot. I went across the country twice in it. I completely destroy a machine, just drive like hell all the time. I don't drive super fast, but I accelerate fast. I guess that's the redneck in me."

"You came out one of the real winners in the war between the leagues. I wonder what would have happened if you had jumped to the Carolina Cougars after your sophomore year at N.C. State like they wanted you to?"

"Even though I felt basketball was the thing I could do, I felt I needed a college education. I felt I needed the experience and the education to deal with something as complicated as professional basketball. In my sophomore year I was on the Olympic team—nineteen years old. I was the youngest guy on the team. If I'd gone to the pros then, I'd probably be out by now. A Carolina Cougars contract would be no good. They went defunct. I feel like patience was a virtue there. I feel like I should be thankful I saw things with patience then. I guess that's partly due to my conservative upbringing. Then, I knew if I finished school, I'd have my education to fall back on." He paused for a moment, finished a beer with a gulp and reached for a new one out of the ice bucket.

"We're sitting here tonight talking about basketball. I know more about basketball than the average person. At the age of twenty-four I should know more about basketball than an armchair quarterback twice my age, because he has not had the experience and involvement that I have. Weird, isn't it, how somebody young knows more than somebody older, even if it's in a certain field?"

"There's bound to be fields of knowledge that one person will have over another, but what is sad is that a lot of people never know much about anything. It's not just lack of intellect or education. It's more like they don't want to work at anything," I offered. "It's like they'd rather let other people sweat and commit themselves and then sit back and take shots. You know, Schulman is obviously a bright guy. I don't know if you saw that article in the paper today on him. Well, I did an interview on him for the *P-I*. He's got a lot on the ball, yet he gets desperate to have a winner and he makes a lot of mistakes like going after Woody and McDaniels and Brisker and maybe giving away more than he should have to get Russell. But he's out there trying to do something with his life and while he's aggressive and strong-willed, I don't think he's trying to screw people over. Yet so many people sit back and say, 'Ah, Schulman's just another of those pushy Jews trying to rule the roost.' They think he's an asshole because he's grabbing so hard for a championship. When they aren't out there asking anything of themselves. I don't know if that makes sense."

"I hear what you're saying. It's like us out here on the road, the team, I mean. If we were trying and losing, then there would still be people criticizing us, because we weren't winning—and they need for us to win for them to be better or something." He swallowed a pull on the beer. "Only trouble is, it's us who isn't looking respectable. We're not looking so much for that first road win. We're looking for that first road game where we are respectable. You know what I'm saying? These last four games have been a hoax. This isn't basketball. This is a total waste of the fans' money. The only reason those fans will come to see the Sonics the next time we come to town will be to see Bill Russell or maybe Slick or Freddie or me. But that's minor. Hey, they'd rather see their team lose by one point in a thriller than stomp on us that way. Right now we're just embarrassing." Burleson was getting worked up. He sat up, leaning forward, long elbows on tall knees. He set his beer down and slapped his hands together. Sat back, put his hands behind his head.

"We should have enough team pride to go out there and play to gain respectability. We're a team, we're a helluva team. And when we are at home the fans can see it. They say, 'Hey, those guys are good.' But on the road it's just a total embarrassment to go out there, to put on a professional basketball uniform and lose within the first twelve minutes of a game. There's no sport in history that lasts that short. Except maybe a first-round knockout. I can't think of another sport where people pay to see a game that lasts less than six to twelve minutes."

I was delighted that we were attacking the issue from inside. Maybe we'll come up with something for our loss of sleep. "Well, maybe. It's just that some guys have enough pride to perform well, whereas on the road they don't feel like they have to live up to anything."

Burleson pondered that for a moment, then slammed his hands down on the arms of his chair. He was pissed. "Well, I hope not. If that's it . . . *if that's it* . . . this is totally off the record . . . *if that's it*, then trade me. If that's it, trade me. That's a bunch of spineless dogs. Play at home to please the fans and then lay down on the road. Man, if that's it, that's a bunch of spineless dogs. If the team's that way, trade me. I mean I don't want to hurt feelings or anything . . . well, my game of basketball is one of the things that I do best—a lot of people may not think it's all that great, but I try. Dammit, I try all the time." He was riled. He started to stand. Then he sat back down. "You know, it's just like tonight I was so frustrated that I got an offensive foul—but I felt so good because I took the shot I wanted to take. It was not the shot that their defense dictated. It was sort of like breaking a barrier, you know, getting over a hump. God, they were making us pass the ball here and take certain shots we didn't want and their defense was dictating our offense. They had us. It was like they were saying, 'Hey, you can have a shot over here. No, not there. Over here, fellas.' And when I took that shot and got that offensive foul, it pissed Sam Lacey off. He got mad. He looked like he wanted to fight, which I would have been glad to oblige. Because I was doing something they didn't have in their game plan for us." Burleson stood up and paced toward the window.

"At the start of the second half, I was hustling, but still half a step behind. I got the ball on Two play and I went into the middle and went up to take a right-hand hook and Sam was there and I just pushed him away with my arm. It was something I had to do. The whole team has to do that—to just shove somebody over. We've got to set some goals, we got to try to hold somebody under twenty-five points in the first quarter. You'd be amazed how much that would help our offense."

"Well, is it the coaching, the direction or the lack of it? Do you think everybody is frustrated because strategically the team is all fucked up? Or is it just attitude?" I wanted to zero in.

"I don't know. It's like Russ is dealing with a series of complicated minds that have to be put together like putting a puzzle together. And with us, those vital pieces are not there. I get frustrated and I start pointing the finger at Slick or Fred or Leonard or Bruce or Tommy— but then that's me, and I know it's not just me or any other one guy. Basketball is a team game and when an individual is getting burnt, Russ says, 'Hey, Mike, get Tommy out of there.' Yet five minutes later he's made five substitutions and it's still not there. You make a change. Nope. You make another. Nope. Then you've got five more new guys out there and we're still getting our asses kicked."

"What if the game plan is fucked up? What if Russ and Hop have things so out of whack that it doesn't matter how hard you work?"

"This is completely off the record?"

"Hey, yeah. We're talking as friends. I'm just trying to learn something. I'll save it for a book sometime."

"Okay, so you say, 'Coach Russell, you're leading the team completely wrong.' And he looks at you and he says, 'We haven't lost a home game. We play defense, we play offense at home. Is the wood we're running on so different?' This is hypothetical, of course. But he says, 'I know my game plan can work. We've proven it can work. We beat by thirty at home and lose by thirty on the road.'"

"Yeah, but you beat 'em by three at home and lose by thirty on the road, that's the difference," I reminded him.

"I don't disagree with or question Coach Russell or Coach Hopkins. You may wonder, you may think sometimes—but if we can do it at home, why can't we do it away? Is it the pride at home and no pride on the road? Gutless wonders, is that what we are? Why did Leonard play good tonight? Because K.C. is his hometown? Oh, that is a helluva theory you've got. Dean played well tonight, but he's been playing well all along. He's not smart enough to think. He just plays, he just goes hard all the time. Oh, that's heavy. When you get into pride it's so hard to judge. But, like you say, there's a pattern there. Damn, Leonard was the only one who played well and he was the only one who was at home. Isn't that a bitch?"

It was a bitch. And it was quarter to four. Christ, wake-up in three hours.

Morning hit like a wet towel. There was no jive, no oral sex lesson. People slept against windows, a hand for a pillow, mouths agape.

Everyone was eating ice-cream cones as we waited to board. Blackburn was trying to run down his morning paper. Players must eat them. Mike Bantom, a quiet, almost bookish forward from Philadelphia, and I sat on a railing, awaiting the signal to board the homeward plane.

"Who we got tomorrow night? Phoenix?" Bantom asked.

"Yeah, the Suns Who Also Haven't Risen," I mused. He winced. "They're having their troubles," I continued. "Hard to believe how fast they've lost that momentum from almost winning it all last year. Think they're one and seven now. First twelve on the road is killin' them."

Bantom played at Phoenix before coming to Seattle. "Yeah, they thought they were really going to have the town turned on this season, but the road is killin' them. Killin' us too, but at least we get to go home enough to even things up. Bring your thesaurus Sunday, though. The Doctor's coming to town."

That did seem suddenly exciting, the thought of the glamour guys from Philadelphia rolling in. I wondered when I might be able to catch Erving for an interview. Saturday afternoon, no doubt. My only day off this week. Sheeeee-it.

Once boarded, Watts, Tolson, Johnson, Heberlein and myself were

77

spread around in coach class, the front end being too crowded. Tolson flopped across two seats as soon as the "fasten seatbelt" sign was off. He grabbed a blanket, took off his shoes and covered himself up. Watts was after him even before his head hit the pillow.

He put his fingers to his nose to give his voice a metallic sound: "For the courtesy of the passengers, will Dean Tolson please put his boots back on."

Tolson was lying with his head against the capsule wall, his feet sticking into the aisle. He responded with a muffled "Fuck you, Slick."

Watts repeated his command: "This is your captain speaking. Will passenger Dean Tolson please put his boots back on for the courtesy of his fellow passengers."

People in the area were beginning to laugh. Tolson ignored Watts. Suddenly Watts was in the aisle, his grand, wide-lapelled, dark-green, three-piece suit giving him style, if his behavior was not comical.

"I'm sorry, miss," he said to an attractive young woman sitting across the aisle from Tolson. "Is this rude fella's smelly feet bothering you?"

"No, not at all." She laughed, deciding to be on Tolson's side.

Tolson mumbled from under his blanket, "See, now sit down." But Watts had an audience.

"We are sorry for the unconsideration of this here dumb ball-player," Watts told the seated assembly. Then he turned to Tolson, bending over him. "Hey, boy, what if everybody took their shoes off? This place wouldn't be fit for no kind of man or beast. Oh my, so awful."

"You hide your bald head and I'll put my shoes back on."

"Now don't get nasty, boy." Watts grabbed the demonstration oxygen mask and turned back to the passengers. "Ladies and gentlemens, in case of an emergency, like some dumb ballplayer not wearin' no shoes, we want to show you how to get some clean air." He was laughing, giggling, gettin' ready to get real crazy. Lookin' for ideas. Someone passed him an aerosol can of deodorant. He sprayed it on Tolson's feet. Tolson kicked at him.

"Now, boy, you colored and you makin' it look bad for all of us. Please show some class." The beverage cart forced Watts back to his seat. The stewardess asked him to quiet down so passengers could relax. Watts looked over at me, laying a hand out there for me to slap. "We've got the people of Seattle already wonderin' about us, B.J. Man, we got more crazies than the circus."

"I hear that, Slick."

10

Selling the Doctor

He even seemed to sweat with class. Julius Erving hadn't been forced to push himself during the 76ers' workout in the Seattle Coliseum. The club had trotted through some half-court drills, working on a few plays designed to set up shots for the brightest gem in Philadelphia's bag of jewels. Coach Gene Shue picked away at the players in somewhat hesitant tones—partly perturbed, partly nervous, as though he didn't want to offend anyone. Now Erving stretched out on a table at courtside to be consumed by another barrage of writers and broadcasters and cameramen.

His body wore a dewy glow, accentuating muscles that were defined and potent, yet smooth, supple. The hole designed into the front of each knee support exposed skin about the size of silver dollars—like cinnamon cookies sitting on top of his knees. When he spoke his voice was strong and manly-deep, yet refined—a partner to his muscle tone or, for that matter, his gracefulness as a player.

The arena was now dimly lit, most of the court lights having been doused as the 76ers concluded their workout and headed for the hotel—leaving Erving behind to sell "The Doctor." This wasn't a strobe light and TV camera press conference with a podium and a lot of pomp. This was more intimate and Erving was comfortable with himself. If you didn't notice the note pads and the tape recorders and the cameraman ducking in and out among the reporters going *whiz-click*, *whiz-click* with his 35 mm, if you just looked at Erving sitting on the table with his legs stretched out and his hands propped behind, it almost felt as though it was just a gathering of jocks relaxing after a Saturday frolic.

The white towel draped around his neck softened his face, giving him a handsome profile. As I stood by his side among the seven or eight other media representatives surrounding Erving's table, I was captivated by the total control he conveyed. Here was a man at the very uppermost precipice of public infatuation and celebration. He seemed so calm and composed, so naturally belonging at the top, that there was no doubt he would withstand all the fickle winds that lick at a person of his stature.

The questioning was close to conversational. That was partly due to the low-key reporters on hand. There weren't any egomaniacs wanting to "bring the hotshot down." And it was partly due to the mood Erving set with his voice and his mannerisms. It was interesting to note as the interview began how prominent this man was in name, and yet how

79

little was known about his attitudes. For that matter, there were probably many less renowned NBAers who would be more readily recognizable walking through your average major city airport. It was known that he did magnificent things on a basketball court, but not many major markets had seen him to know exactly how magnificent that could be. He had been everything in the ABA the previous four years, but the ABA didn't play on national TV. The ABA played in Memphis and Louisville and Norfolk and San Antonio instead of Los Angeles and Chicago. Even though he played for New York, it was on Long Island, not in Madison Square Garden.

Erving had been tremendously important in the ABA's bid for merger and he, more than any other player, was the cause for the league to adopt a new schedule that would put every team against every other team four times—abandoning heavier emphasis on intradivision play so that all arenas would get equal billing of Erving. Everyone wanted to see The Doctor. When Philadelphia bought him from the New York Nets on the eve of the first post-merger season, figures were cranked around to make him "The Six Million Dollar Man"—after a popular TV show. If the show had been called *The Five Million Dollar Man* somehow the press would have come up with different figures than the $3 million Philly paid the Nets for Erving to go with the $3.1 million salary over five years. Big figures, nonetheless, and it all helped to hype the gate for a nation that best evaluates greatness when it is spelled out in dollars.

As he sat there in the Coliseum, fielding reporter's questions, lifting a hand from behind to gesture, wiping his thick nose with the edge of the towel, looking into the eyes of the various men around him, I wondered how he could help but feel like a five-legged calf being shipped across the land by Barnum & Bailey to be gawked over. The 76ers had drawn sellouts along the trail to the Pacific Northwest, as they would throughout the season, and at every stop there had been sessions with the press. Many of the questions had to become repetitious. So it wasn't only his patience but his depth of expression that was impressive. He admitted he didn't particularly like being there with notebooks and microphones poked in his face, but it was a task that went along with being Julius Erving. Some superstars don't see that they need to share themselves with anyone other than by what they do on the court. Others will subject themselves to the media, but their reluctance to do so is so obvious that even interesting material is delivered in an attitude that they are being ruthlessly abused in the process. Erving doesn't have the unpredictable brashness of a Rick Barry nor the flighty charm of a Slick Watts. He just seems to present himself more openly and more comfortably than all the rest.

After fifteen minutes of this session, reporters alternated leaning on one foot or the other. One pulled a chair up and sat on it backward.

I slid my butt onto an edge of the table. Erving reached down and halfheartedly stretched toward his toes to keep loose.

"I don't get a big kick out of sitting around answering questions," Erving said as he delivered a polite grimace to indicate he would appreciate Sonic broadcaster Bob Blackburn withdrawing his microphone a couple inches back out of his eye. "I try to answer questions because I feel I have somewhat of a responsibility to the 76ers. I don't think a major press conference in every city is something that will continue forever and ever, but I choose to do it now to sort of set the record straight about myself, about my team and what we're all about. It's a way of setting the record straight with new people."

Someone asked if he felt he was being promoted to death.

"No, because the demands on my time are limited. Like we'll sit here answering questions for half an hour, then I'll go do something that I initiate. Promoting an individual and a team collectively is part of the business. Filling seats is part of the business. That's something you acknowledge when you become a professional. Every team has the right to do it and I think there are some teams who do not do it enough. As long as it is constructive promotion, I'm all for it."

He casually reached forward and wiped away a drop of a reporter's spittle which had landed on his thigh. He acted without belligerence. His answers were preceded by just enough of a pause to indicate thoughtfulness, but not so much that it seemed he was having to struggle. He was asked if he had been subjected to the same sort of media assault his first time around the ABA.

"No. I caught the ABA by surprise. When I left Massachusetts after my junior year, no one was very concerned about my signing with Virginia. The Nets were the only ones who voted against it. As a result they got to draft Jim Chones. I was a third-team All-American and the first time around the league most people were more aware of Artis Gilmore, who had just signed, along with George McGinnis, Johnny Neumann. It wasn't until like midway through the season that people realized that Virginia had a find."

Heading into any interview, a reporter tries to fill himself with as much background as possible. He should know the significance of different events and incidents that have occurred. If he is familiar with what has been written and reported, he can then try to push deeper into the personality—trying for new material, greater amplification and fuller commentary than has been previously developed. In anticipation of eventually encountering Erving, I had read Marty Bell's book titled *The Legend of Dr. J.* I moved in with questions built out of my knowledge of his youth on Long Island. I asked about the role basketball played in his teen-age years.

"I tried to expose myself to as many experiences as I possibly could. Variety was one of the key terms in my approach to life. I tried to expose myself to things so that I could pick and choose which things really turned me on. To pursue something earnestly, you have to really like it. You have to be a leader, not a follower of the crowd. You can't just let others influence all your thoughts and actions. I think I learned that and put it into practice at a pretty early age. Basketball was important, but I tried to see life beyond the playground."

I made several references to things that had been expressed in the book, feeling he would be appreciative that a reporter was coming from a point of informed reference. It was obvious from what he had been relating during the interview and what events had been described in the book that Erving possessed a philosophical outlook virtually unchallengeable for a public figure. I asked what had been instrumental in the development of what read as a very attractive philosophy.

"I think my high school coach had a great influence. He was a good man and he took a personal interest in his players. There were a couple of events in my life that really opened my eyes to how life is and how powerless individuals are in controlling things. My father died when I was young, my brother died when I was in college. I got a lot of strength out of that. I realized you shouldn't take anything for granted. They can call your number anytime and your turn might come tomorrow. I just try to live with a clean track record so I can look back at any time and not have any regrets about what I have done. I'm very conscious of making that my life's pattern."

Served more philosophy than they had expected or planned to use, the reporters shifted the questioning in pursuit of controversy. Erving had come into the headlines on the heels of the merger with demands for a renegotiation of his contract. He had four years left on a seven-year contract which called for $1.9 million with the Nets. Owner Roy Boe had said if there was ever a merger, the contract would be renegotiated, Erving contended. What with his obvious drawing power, a lot of big NBA arenas were now going to be filled by this man and a lot of owners were going to make some nice revenue. Additionally, there was now the television exposure he had not had in the ABA. More revenue for others. He wanted a piece of the rock. But he had left college early and then tried to jump from the ABA's Squires to Atlanta of the NBA. He'd been sent back to the ABA, going to the Nets, by the courts. Now he was jumping for more bucks offered by the 76ers. He was asked if maybe a lot of people weren't going to look at him as a greedy guy?

"There is bound to be jealousy and criticism from people who see it only as a dollar-and-cents issue. But if they look way down inside it at all the details, they'll know that it involves more than just money. Only someone who has experienced a similar situation themselves can really know. I could talk myself until I am blue in the face to defend my position, but I don't really feel that I have to do that. You just can't let the opinions of the vast majority dictate your life. You have to have a close group of friends and those are the people who really know you and you look to for guidance and influence."

"There is a lot of talent on this team. Do you anticipate any problems sharing the spotlight with the likes of George McGinnis and Lloyd Free and Doug Collins and Caldwell Jones? That's a strong cast of characters."

"People have asked about the possibility of there being dissension on the team or an inability to complement one another. Of course, we're all optimistic that we can play together and will play together. I've always approached the game that you are more of an asset to your team if you are a complete player, able to do a little of everything offensively and defensively. I think George also had that type of coaching philosophy."

Anyone who knew anything about Erving was aware of all the artistry he was supposed to possess. There were magazine and newspaper pictures of him floating above his colleagues, windmilling reverse dunks, snaring one-handed rebounds and slamming opponents' shots back in their distressed faces. There were reports of the "ohhhhhs" and "awwwwws" he inspired from ABA crowds. But what was his game, technically?

"On defense I would rather try to gamble on a steal or try to block a shot or overplay the passing lanes as opposed to just hounding a guy all over the court—beating on him, so to speak. If you call it a difference between physical and finesse, I'm more of a finesse defensive player. On offense I'd prefer to face a guy about five-two. Give me a Monty Towe. Actually, I prefer to play guys taller, because I feel I'm able to go around them. They're usually hesitant to come out on me because I'm usually able to go around them. So I can either get my shot outside or drive to the basket easier than when I'm playing a short and strong player who is maybe a little quicker than the taller one. The shorter one can probably deny me the ball better. As for playing with a lot of other very talented players, instead of having the show sort of revolve around me, I think it will help. Right now it's a wait-and-see situation as to how everyone reacts, but at least they can't double-team me and allow anyone else to go free. In the past a lot of teams could overplay me on the fast break. But if we keep the floor spread and move the ball, I think we'll all benefit."

The questioning lost its steady momentum. Where the next question had piled in on the final words of his answer, there now were pauses, a little shuffling. No one wanted to let this prominent piece of copy get away, but the interview was getting to the picky state—like a diner nibbling at the final crumbs on a pie plate. Erving sensed the slack. He swung his legs over the side of the table and ran a mild ripple of shrugs through his shoulders and back to loosen up muscles that had cooled under the coating of dried perspiration.

"Does that get it?" he asked, standing unhurriedly. He was in control even after the race was run. He had given an obviously entertaining and informative interview and now he smoothly closed the notebooks for reporters—letting them convince themselves they had gotten all the cooperation they wanted. Blackburn wanted to tape a special pregame bit and offered to drive Erving to his hotel while they did it. Erving agreed. As he headed toward the parking lot, I walked at his side, asking him how he had come to adopt his attitude of collaboration with the media.

"Most of the people who do not want to cooperate with the press either have bad experiences or lack the confidence to relate to the questions that they are asked. I believe in dealing with the truth. I will be reserved about certain things—some things are private and personal. If asked about that sort of thing I will either lightly dismiss them or evade them. Issues relative to the game are worthy of discussion."

As he reached the car, I mentioned the book again. I thought it was pretty well done, I told him. Erving looked at me as he folded into the back seat of the car, his facial expression and tone of voice more relaxed than the feelings his words reflected.

"I didn't want to do a book at that time. I didn't feel I was ready yet. I didn't have anything to do with it. But Marty Bell went to work on it and *Sport Magazine* backed him and they went ahead and did it anyway. I've never read it."

The door closed and the car moved away toward the hotel—toward a few private hours for Julius Erving. I watched the car leave the lot and turned toward mine. I found myself muttering, "He didn't read the book. He didn't even read the fucking book. How does that make you feel, Marty Bell?"

Seed for a Saga

The next evening as Dr. J was gearing up in the 76ers' dressing room, I walked across the parking lot and through the Coliseum pass gate. People were jabbering away with unusual zeal. The crowd, a sellout almost from the day it was announced Erving would play for the 76ers, was early in arriving. The fans wanted to see the Philly dunk line—to get a full serving of The Doctor and the rest of Philadelphia's highly publicized scootin'-shootin' payroll. There was genuine excitement in the air, expectation of a treat. Seattle had run its home court streak to twenty by nipping Phoenix two nights earlier. The atmosphere served as a reminder of the role a superstar plays in sports—like the trapeze artist or the lion tamer in circus tent days of yesteryear.

Beyond the winning and losing and the match-ups of various combatants and the team attitude and execution and all the rest that gets kicked around the sports pages, fans come to see players do things with a basketball that are out of this world. Most everyone has at least bounced a basketball off a driveway backboard so that he or she comprehends the physical factors of the height of the rim and what it takes to put the ball into the hoop. Erving, of course, represented the best in magic acts.

As I walked along the corridor beneath the stands, Collis Temple appeared at the other end of the hallway and headed my way. He looked handsome in a new suit, not quite as rough-and-ready as he had in a basketball uniform. Collis Temple. Hey, what was he doing here? Nearly two weeks before I thought it such a melancholy scene when he had stood in line to board a plane for his native Louisiana as the Sonics boarded a plane out of Sea-Tac bound for their road season opener in Indiana. We had developed a good rapport in camp and I hated to see him fade away. I had wanted to go over and say good-bye, but there hadn't been time.

"What are you doing back up here?" I asked, genuinely surprised.

"Russ brought me back," he said, leading me over to a pocket in the corridor. "Now, if I tell you something, will you promise me you won't use it or tell anyone else until it's okay?"

I tried to think of anything that he might have access to that I already knew, couldn't come up with any ideas and said, "Sure."

"Look, if this gets out, it could be the end of any chance I have to play in the NBA." He looked into my face. I nodded. "Russ brought me back up because they're going to get Bob McAdoo for Tommy and Mike Green. So when the deal is made I'll be activated."

"No shit," I responded. "I hope it works out for you. Wouldn't that be something? What's the timetable?"

"Soon, man, but you gotta sit on it until it comes down. We're cool on this, right?"

"Yeah, no problem," I promised. I still can't figure out just why, but at the time I didn't believe it was going to happen. I know Temple was standing there in all his 6'9", 225 pounds, telling me. But more than one player who has been cut from an NBA team had come back around, trying to work one last angle to catch on. Maybe it was all a cover-up story to protect his own pride for not having been able to stay away.

Interesting. We had developed a sound enough communicaton

that it was possible he would trust me with the story. If it were true, well, maybe that's why it didn't seem plausible—McAdoo was one of the few players in the NBA who owned enough talent to pack a team on his back. The league's leading scorer the past three seasons, the 6'10" long range bombing center would be a dramatic catch for the Sonics. But then why would Buffalo let him go? But I didn't feel compelled to start digging on it. I figured I would casually check it out when the time came. Besides, I had given my word to Temple. I really couldn't pursue it in any other manner without betraying his trust.

I sauntered out to courtside and took my seat at the press table. During the hour preceding a game, there is a nervous-sluggish time that can become almost uncomfortable. On the road this pregame period can be worked off with a tour around the arena. But, at home, there isn't the same sense of stimulation. The press room gossip gets as old as any other form of gossip. I sifted through some mail from the office.

There was a fat letter written in a way to make a guy pay attention. It is difficult for a journalist to know what one's audience is thinking but this essay didn't lack for impact. It had been written after the Kansas City loss:

"Well, the magic died. It died about 15 minutes ago as I listened to the Kansas City game. The magic has been dying for quite a while now—perhaps it started with the playoff money. I don't know.

"It was fun last year, you know? On our long, wet winter nights, nothing could excite me, nothing could warm my heart like the Sonics. I would grab the sports page every morning after the game and look for your column, eager to grin over the latest Slick Watts' malapropism. It was fun. That game—remember?—when we came from behind and Slick leapt into Tommy's arms at the buzzer? Or remember Willie Norwood faking injury and stealing the ball? Or Tab Skinner's infectious grin? Or the night we were so far ahead that Tommy decided to play guard, and was dribbling around in backcourt, much to the coach's dismay, as the whole bench dissolved into laughter? Or the night Slick gave a high feed to Tommy and the ball dropped through the hoop?

"I loved to read your columns then, because they were a reflection of the fun and camaraderie. Were they as easy to write as they were to read?

"But I listened tonight and nearly cried. Where was the coaching? Is it coaching to substitute 4 cold players and leave in a panting, tired Mike Green?

"What's wrong? Is there dissension? There must be. I remember last year when a New York sportswriter said Seattle was the most insane team in the league.

"The honeymoon is over, Bill Russell. I've never read it in the papers, but I feel it everywhere. We were thrilled when he came to coach, excited when he decided to live here, and overjoyed when he said he actually liked it here. But that was several wet winters ago, and what have we seen? I cringe when I read the papers and see 'Trade Talks.' Someone doesn't perform? 'Trade Talks.' We lose a big one? 'Trade Talk.'

"Russell's 'Take a Shot' column in the Times may still be as funny as I thought it was two years ago, but I am hard-pressed to laugh.

"The old run-and-gun too-crazy-to-be-scared offense will win some. But it will never win big. When they do it well, they are the best in the league. But when they do it badly, they look like shit, and leave approximately the same aftertaste in the mouth.

"I am angry with myself for caring. Have I been sucked into the world of professional sports? What do *I* care if they win or lose? They're making their money, raking in the bucks. As long as they fill the Coliseum (how long will that last?), what do they care? I am an intelligent woman, a college graduate, with other interests. Why do I agonize over the stats? What's going on here? Do I see the players all as phallic symbols? What's the deal? Why am I scribbling on old stationery to someone I wouldn't know if I tripped him in the street?

"I blame you, Blaine Johnson. Damn you and your infectious glee. Damn your ability to make me like a dozen or so people I don't know and maybe wouldn't even like if I sat down for a beer with them.

"So what do I want from you? A pound of flesh? Jesus—I don't know. Naively, perhaps, I expect a letter, soothing me and telling me that nothing is rotten in the bowels of the Coliseum. Do I feel better now? I don't know. Will the magic return after the next game? I don't know. Will I switch my allegiance to the Seahawks? I don't know. (For a college graduate, I am not exactly brimming with knowledge, am I?)

"The season is young. Normally this would thrill me. Not this year. The thought leaves me cold and tired.

"The bloom is off the rose.

"Damn you, Blaine Johnson. Even Slick Watts can't make me smile.

"Respectfully, Lisa Remted.

"P.S. Please do not contact the FBI. This was *not* a threat on your life."

Then there is a note attached, written after Friday's four-point win over Phoenix.

"HOLY MOTHER OF GOD! I sat with my nose inches from the stereo. My eyes were wide. My breath, short. WHY MUST THEY WIN LIKE THAT? How can I possibly say I don't care when I spent the last ten minutes of the game rolling my eyes heavenward and asking God (or whomever) to shine on the Sonics just this once? O yes, I'm a tough one. To hell with the Sonics, right? What do I care? I obviously care enough to risk cardiac arrest. So how can I be so cruel as to send this to you after reading your column (twice)—a column which sent shivers down my spine? Easy. I'm a cruel person.

"Besides, I already bought a stamp."

Well, at least somebody out there is paying attention. Have to give this lady a call. I sat back in my chair, hands locked behind my head, and watched the 76ers going through their warm-ups. Caldwell Jones bounces a ball high off the floor, takes it as it starts to drop a foot above the rim and shoves it through. The crowd ohhhs and awwws. It seems amazing how much people are into all this, the Sonics, all sports. It is something that completely envelops the lives of us covering it and playing it and managing it. But I wonder how many people out there feel like this Remted—not making a big deal out of my writing, but using that writing as a means to get at the world these guys live in. What a trip.

The crowd's anticipation for a show from Erving is immediately dampened when the Doctor picks up three fouls in less than five minutes and sits the half. He comes back in the second half to do some of his tricks, but Seattle hangs on for its twenty-first straight home win. Road time again tomorrow morning. San Antonio and Houston this week. No pause to refresh.

12

Magna Cum Elbow

Men who cheat while teaching someone the rules of a game get shot—or it seems that ought to be the code, anyway. Probably is down here in Texas. Watts and I were in the middle aisle of a DC-10 for the forty-five-minute run to Houston from San Antonio. He flipped out his backgammon board and decided it was time to teach me this captivating game. He was free-lancing and calling options so often I thought there surely must be some mistake in his method, but that wasn't confirmed until Gray leaned over the back of my seat and said in his quiet voice, "He isn't teaching you backgammon, he's teaching you crime. Don't pay any attention to him."

The Sonics had executed another of their patent-pending road debacles the night before, getting clobbered by the Spurs. That really wasn't even news anymore in Sonicville, but there were some other events that had come down in the past seventy-two hours which now seemed, on this Wednesday morning, to be destined for bold headlines.

It had all started with my conversation with Temple on Sunday evening. What would have been a sleeping dog was kicked to life innocently during dinner conversation with Furtado Monday evening in San Antonio. The next afternoon, Tuesday, at 4:10, a phone call had jangled me out of a nap. Russell was on the line. His voice was strangely focused. So often it seemed only partly interested in what it was saying. Now it had purpose, concern.

"I think you know something that I can't have getting out. The news is a fact, but it won't be if it gets out."

"Hmmmmmmmmm. What's the timetable?" I murmured, knocked off balance by the circumstance Russell had called, bumped again by the confirmation of the McAdoo deal. I assumed that's what he was talking about.

"There's been about three thousand dollars in phone calls between Hong Kong and Buffalo," Russell explained. Schulman was on vacation in the Orient. "The whole thing will probably happen in about a week, but it just can't get out now or Snyder will call the whole thing off."

I told him I would cooperate, but I wanted him to be damn sure the story broke my way. I wouldn't have had a clue of this without Temple having told me in confidence and I wouldn't have given it much further thought if Russell hadn't called. When I had mentioned it casually the night before over dinner with Furtado, he had passed it off so casually I had given it no further thought. Furtado had obviously told Russell I had wind of the deal and was worried that I might go with it—not knowing how lightly I had evaluated it.

It was disappointing to me that Furtado had drawn the line on what I regarded as a warm relationship to serve his loyalties to his employer rather than trust me with the full story. I was reminded again of how the role of a reporter often precludes the opportunity to be totally open in relationships with those he is covering. Some words to that effect that Furtado had spoken last night loomed in my mind. I had gone to his room after the loss to the Spurs. He was splashing around in the shower while we talked.

"Russ called you, huh?" Furtado called over the running water.

"Yeah."

"Well, I just couldn't say anything last night. I guess it's a pretty touchy situation with the Buffalo owner. Russ really wants to make the deal. He really thinks it'll make this team a winner. Boy, was he pissed at Collis. He called him and chewed him out. I feel like doing the same thing. Boy, these guys are dumb. Why in the hell would you tell a reporter something and expect him to keep it quiet?"

"You can trust some guys, Frank."

"You couldn't if you were doing your job." He laughed.

Thanks, Frank. But maybe he was right. What really hurt was the dawning, after nearly ten years in the business from the various perspectives I had held in journalism, that I was a poor risk to be trusted—because of my job.

Blackburn and Heberlein wandered in, ready to go for a midnight dinner. There was no more discussion of the McAdoo topic. It was quickly becoming an obsession with me, though.

I had been awakened the next morning at 6:40 by a health freak jogging on my ceiling. It was more than an hour before our scheduled wake-up for the flight to Houston. I pondered the trade details and tried to handicap the likely course of events.

Russell had said the deal was a week away to keep me cooled off. It seemed to me the timetable was to get Tommy and Mike through that night's game at Houston and back home and off the plane before it all came down. So that put it at midday the next day for release, which— even if Russell tried—would never be contained until the evening so that I could break it on Friday morning. I would have to be careful not to put him in a squeeze, but if it was only a matter of his dealing with his players rather than some conflict with the Braves, I'd have to take aim to write the story that night and break it the next morning. I'd call the morning paper in Buffalo. At least the morning paper there would have the same concern as I as far as time, but with a three-hour edge on Seattle, if something got stirred up and out on the wires before 5 P.M. in the East, it would still give the *Times* a shot in their last editions.

I got out my league schedule. Buffalo was at home against Denver the next night, idle tonight. I wondered what *they* would do if this broke the next morning? The whole problem was keeping things under wraps if indeed Snyder would scoff the deal if it got out before he wanted it to, and keeping communications open with Russell.

Now, as we waited for the luggage at the Houston airport, I sat down on a lounge bench next to Brown to see what Temple might have told any of his soon-to-be teammates. It was the usual sparring match—he slipping and sliding on the edge of issues, sounding me out, giving nothing that wasn't calculated to get back more. Smooth, cunning.

"You heard any words floating around, like about certain people moving on?" I asked.

"Always talk. There's always talk." He looked across the room. "What do you hear?"

"Don't know for sure. Maybe something big."

"There isn't much to work with—maybe T. Slick and myself are the only other ones I can see being valuable to anybody in a big deal. We aren't much right now. We're five and oh at home, but who've we beat? Philly was without Collins and the Doctor was on the bench the whole first half; Phoenix didn't have Adams or Perry; Nets were playing their third straight road game in three nights; Atlanta is helpless; Detroit hasn't won in its last fifteen games on the coast. We haven't done anything really and you *know* we haven't done anything on the road. Lost all five."

"Maybe the man figures he's got to make a change then," I suggested.

"Could be. We need something," he said as he rose and sauntered off to the bus. "We sure need something," he repeated as I decided to follow. He noticed Green in a barbershop getting his big ol' red-tan boots shined. Brown went into the shop. I headed out to the bus.

The November sun felt surprisingly warm on the bus as the wait for baggage extended to a quarter of an hour. Russell had picked up his rented car and disappeared. Hopkins sat fuming. Furtado directed a skycap with a load of luggage to the bus, left for the rest of the load. The wait on the bus was becoming uncomfortable. The sunshine was making the bus stuffy. Someone lit a cigarette. The air became worse. Furtado was back. Where were Green and Brown? He went to find them. Someone opened a window. The bus driver, a fiftyish man with a cold expression, looked over his shoulder. His salt and pepper brush cut came across as too much redneck to suit the players.

"You want to be cooler, keep the window closed," the driver said loudly, standing, looking back at the passengers.

"Fuck you, Texas Ranger," someone murmured, just loud enough so that the driver might have heard it.

"It's cooler with it closed."

There were some more murmurs and some hands whipping open more windows. There was something in the way of bad vibes going around that seemed to have come from beyond that which was apparent, as if the players and the driver were old enemies. Maybe they were, symbolically. The driver sat down, his back to the players.

"Hey, let's go."

"What the fuck we waitin' for?"

"Where's Freddy and Mike?"

"In the barbershop."

"Leave the mother-fuckers. Let's go."

"Fuck 'em. Let 'em take a cab."

"Long ride out there, man.'"

"Fuck it. Let's go. Where's Frank?"

Everyone was talking shit, but who would say anything once those two got here? Furtado came back and sat down. He told the driver to wait a minute. Hoppy looked like a volcano getting ready to erupt.

What was happening was that Fred and Mike were screwing around, stalling, so that they'd have to take cabs. Even the fat price of the long ride from Houston airport to the Summit was worth not having to go to shooting practice. The rest of the guys didn't really want to leave, because if they got hung up long enough they'd all miss practice.

91

Fred and Mike finally came out, sauntering toward the bus. Climbed aboard. Dean Tolson was the only guy to challenge Mike.

"You got those ten-gallon boots shined, boy? They don't look so shined to me."

"They shined just right." Green giggled. He was feeling loose, full of jive. "He shined 'em just right, Dean. Hey, Fred, they shined 'em just right, didn't they?" Brown was sitting across the aisle from me. Green was in the back. Brown waved a hand without looking around. Green was laughing with Norwood, telling him some story. ". . . so they said he stole two cases of RC Cola and a *Jet Magazine*. Now, you tell me he wasn't some crazy nigger. Nothin' but RC Cola and a copy of *Jet*. Man, can you believe that?" There was hand-slapping and more stories. The bus was moving across Houston, taking nearly as long as the flight from San Antonio.

Houston has no natural charm. Flat, blah. But there is money there and there are Big Money buildings. And more coming. Big Money monuments to insurance companies, oil companies, airlines. Houston is growing, growing, like oil poured on a flapjack pan. There are no boundaries. It can go and go and go until it becomes bigger than Los Angeles. Why not? It has the central location for shipping east or west. Cheap labor. In the gut of America. Seems like an uninspiring, muggy place to live. But it's open space compared to the East. The sun shines a lot. Better place to be poor than the East. It'll be the monster by the year 2000. It'll be the big daddy, maybe. Someone from Texas once said about Houston, "All this place needs is a little water and a better class of people."

"Man," the other replied. "That's all hell needs." But Houston will be big. Real Big.

I felt sluggish by the time we checked into Stouffer's Greenway Plaza Hotel, a beautiful new high-rise structure—part of an office complex, all concrete and glass, spread over many newly constructed acres. The Summit, where the Rockets play, is just a block's underground walk away from the hotel. I put on my running gear. Decided to check out what the Buffalo media might know about McAdoo deal first. Called a writer for the *Courier-Express*. Got him at home, day off. I don't want to give anything away, but have to check it out. Wish I knew someone personally in the media there.

I related how I had heard McAdoo might be on the block and maybe Seattle was interested. Was there really a chance the Braves would let him go? He said McAdoo was in the last year of a five-year contract. Mac claimed he was free to go anywhere the next year. The club said they still had him on an option year the next season. There was confusion as to who was calling the shots between Paul Snyder and John Y. Brown, the latter in the process of buying control. Apparently, the Braves were willing to let him go if they could make a deal. The writer would check around to see if there was anything imminent. He would call back.

I headed out for a run through a residential area adjacent to the hotel. The air was musty, smoggy. The area was trying hard not to become completely run-down. How long could the few houses tucked in among some small apartments hold out against the commercial mushroom crowding it? Just as long as it takes for someone to plan another office building. Houston on the grow.

While I'm running, the McAdoo matter loomed in importance. It was like something you feel is immediately vital, yet every time you try to analyze it with facts, it floats away. Russell says it's not "today" immediate. Buffalo doesn't seem to think it's even "tomorrow" immediate. Yet Russell called me. That was a bold move on his part— asking for something. And do I have the right to be casual about this? I'm paid to dig up big stories. I'm paid to be on top of things. I can't tolerate the chance of getting a beat on this story, professionally, egotistically. I've got to keep on top, not wait for someone else to spoon it out to me.

Back at the hotel there was a message from Buffalo. "Nothing cooking as far as I can determine on this end. Will let you know if hear anything new." Good, no danger of anything breaking back there right away. Of course, what if someone had called Heberlein? Same answer.

I called Bob Walsh—Russell's alter effort in the Sonics' managerial ranks. Officially known as assistant general manager, Walsh was the chore horse in the everyday GM's duties, making advertising and television-radio deals, handling the execution of player personnel deals, after Russell had made them. He had made his mark producing a provocative talk show in Boston and had been moving up with ABC in Los Angeles. Landing Russell to host his popular talk show on KABC radio was a big feather and it opened a close relationship between the two. When Russell got the Sonic job, he asked Walsh up to Seattle with him. His wife was an attractive, well-known TV news personality in Seattle. Bob and I had established a good rapport since the first days I had covered the beat. We had gotten into all sorts of mischief on Thanksgiving night the year before at his native Plymouth Rock. We had that kind of good-buddy rapport two guys sometimes develop raising hell in a far-off place, sharing problems—like sailors who have staggered about in a foreign port together.

Heberlein always thought Walsh was giving me the edge on stories, because we were close. He didn't, but he kept me from steering too far off course if I was guessing on something. I wanted to bring him in on this. I wanted to make sure I had his efforts working on my behalf to make sure the story broke my way. It was insurance of controlling the announcement. Walsh said to trust the situation. It was in the works, but probably wouldn't come down that day. That day! Hey, wait a minute. No, no, don't worry. It'll all fall in place. He'd take care of me. Damn.

I wondered how much Russell appreciated this. I wondered how much he was even aware of what he was asking, of the position I was in. I thought of calling my editor, but figured why load the strain on him. I wanted to tell someone, to let someone know I was on the inside. Yet there is an expanding risk of leak the farther you get from the source. Those closest to the issue are primarily concerned with protecting their interests, which outweigh the urge to flaunt what they know. The farther you get from that, the freer a person is from suffering if the news is out and the greater the ego desire to be in the know. Russell has a lot to lose by telling anyone else, so it's not in his interest to go around bragging about the big deal he's going to pull off. Now, Temple (why the hell did Russell tell Collis? Courtesy?) didn't seem to have a bubble ready to burst inside him when he told me—he seemed to be motivated mainly out of friendship that we had established during training camp. He was just being a nice guy. (I make friends fast, but you can see how tough it is to keep them.) Still, Temple probably wanted to tell someone, share the good news. Why not a player? I didn't have any feeling of a big secret when I mentioned it to Furtado. That feeling didn't come until after Russell confirmed it. But now . . . well, I was wearing it like a mountain in my chest. It wasn't just the news responsibility. I wanted to be the guy who broke the story nationally. Because, after all, you can't be a good newsman if you aren't curious about things. And you can't be a good reporter if you aren't basically like the proverbial washwoman—when you hear something, you just can't wait to tell it. Can't wait.

I was lying on my bed thinking about all this. A thunder shower had passed and a glorious purple-plum and gold sunset was spread across the horizon beneath a lid of black clouds. Big Ol' Texas Sky. Seems like there is more purple in southwestern sunsets than anywhere else. Might be, but this one was probably 90 percent automobile fumes.

I decided I had to talk to Russell before this evening got away. I wanted to remind him I was here, waiting. I wanted to make a stand. I was not going to toss and turn over this thing another night. I called him in his room. It was 6:30 P.M. I told him I wanted to talk to him. I was coming up to his suite. He answered the door with just his slacks on, his face puffed with sleep. As we stood and talked, I felt in control, not flustered like the hallway discussion.

"We've got a problem, Russ. The more I think about this whole thing, the more I figure it is going to come down on the wrong side of the clock. We wouldn't have any problem if I didn't know about this— but I do, and that's the reality we have to work from."

I imagined him imagining himself strangling Temple.

"You know how Snyder is," he replied quietly. "He's so emotional that anything could blow it."

"Well, what if I just come out tomorrow morning saying that the Sonics are on the verge of a major deal today. That Burleson and Green are expected to be traded for a major center?"

"Obviously I can't stop you. I've told you this is a very fragile deal. If you write anything about it you will probably be writing about a deal that almost was."

I believed him, as much as I didn't like the fact that nothing had changed.

"I will do everything I can to make sure you get the story," he continued. "I hope it happens tomorrow night so you can have it for Friday morning. But I don't know how it will happen. We aren't calling all the shots, obviously."

I had gone there prepared to make a stand. To hell with the risk of angering him. But what was there to stand on? I remembered how Snyder had fired his coach after just one game in 1971. The guy had to be pretty emotional. I wondered, as I took the elevator back down, if anyone had ever been sued for causing another's ulcers?

Around 7 P.M. Heberlein and I walked through the huge parking garage from the hotel to the Summit. What a beautiful arena. Built in the modern, shallow-bowl style, the place features 15,600 seats in delicious pastels of orange, lemon, purple and gold. Too bad they can't draw a crowd. This is football country, they say—some also say that folks won't support a black sport in Texas. Whatever, the Rockets wound up winning the Central Division that year, going 34–7 at home, and averaged only 8,486 in the Summit. That was about double what they had done the year before, though.

We headed into the press room for some salad and a sandwich. It was a nice lounge, people sitting around on couches watching the evening news.

"... and this startling announcement today in Boston. Dave Cowens, center for the Boston Celtics, has said he is quitting basketball immediately. No reason was given. The Houston Oilers today announce . . ."

Dave Cowens is quitting? Everyone looks at each other babbling and shaking their heads. The fierce Dave Cowens, the guy who would dive through fire, crawl on broken glass for a loose ball, is quitting basketball? God, he must have cancer. You heard anything about this? No. I heard he's a fag. Bullshit. Probably some chick just left him. Boy, I'll bet ol' Auerbach is ready to shoot himself. God, you know, I just bet Cowens has got cancer. Isn't it a shame? Jesus, what a great competitor. He'd never quit unless he was dying. Isn't it a shame?

The minute the ball went up to start the evening's work for the

Sonics and Rockets, Mike Newlin tried to take Brown out of his game. He banged Brown with a forearm, and everywhere the Sonic sharpshooter tried to go, Newlin was in front of him, chesting, hanging, shoving—trying to take away Brown's heart. He knew Brown, he knew as a shooter, from twenty feet, twenty-five feet and beyond, there is no match in pro basketball. Brown employs a delicate right-handed jumper that is as soft as baby hair. He can double-pump fake and go up with two or three players on him. He can toss up shots full of English off the glass while floating in the wings. He can sit out front and pop his fadeaway jumpers until you think you'll have to use a shotgun to stop him. But Newlin knew it didn't take a shotgun, just a hatchet. Brown is not hard-nosed. But, then, they didn't expect Chopin to split firewood between recitals, did they?

Brown was in his sixth NBA season at this time, coming off a campaign in which he finished fifth in scoring. He was on the brink of becoming one of the best guards, certainly the best outside shooter, in the league. He had the physical tools. But he'd been on the brink for at least three years. He didn't seem to have the ambition, the obsession it takes to go from good to great. I found out later Russell had sought to deal Brown to Houston at the start of this season for Newlin. Houston coach Tom Nissalke, who coached Brown in those terrible times of 1972 at Seattle, said he liked him. They thought it over and decided they wanted about half a million and a top draft choice as well. Russell must have said, "I think we have a poor connection, Tom. I'll call you back some year."

What the Sonics would be gaining in a trade like that would be a more aggressive player, commendable shooter, supposedly a real cerebral giant and, of course, a white for a black. Russell wouldn't be concerned with the latter, but a good white ballplayer is better gate than a good black player, so the marketing thinking goes. Newlin teams a strut-the-beach body with a Dave Cowens competitiveness (isn't it funny that when Cowens quit no one figured it was a squeeze for more money. "He loves to play too much for that") and a keen mind. A keen mind becomes so labeled by the media if he is white. (They call Abdul-Jabbar religious, not intellectual.) Newlin graduated magna cum laude in English from the University of Utah, and throws around a lot of clever statements.

He says things like, "Pressure doesn't matter to me in a game because whether you win or lose there is going to be a final score." And, "I firmly believe that a basketball player tends to have a great quality in performance if he has had, in the past, a tougher time in life. A physical flaw . . . a personal setback . . . an unhappy personal experience. As kids we form feelings of inferiority or superiority. Kids aren't sophisticated enough about their feelings, but psychologically, how those feelings affect him later determines his ego." Also, "Sometimes players think too much about what's happening, who's getting the ball and who's not. . . . Intellect must be used spontaneously. . . . Intellect is also knowing when not to use it. That equals wisdom, and that's when a team wins. . . . Once again, it's simple. Either you box out or you don't. Either you make a five-footer or you don't."

I don't know if those sort of observations make Newlin an intellectual, but it is unique and that is endearing with the media. He can also be pretty nerve-wracking for opposing players. And Leonard Gray doesn't like to have his nerves wracked, let alone his body run into. But that kept happening all during the first quarter as Newlin banged away on Brown and the rest of the Sonics as the most aggressive of Nissalke's aggressive troops. Hopkins picked up a technical early in the second quarter. Russell collected another shortly thereafter. Finally, midway through the period, Newlin trotted down the lane, set a couple of picks and caught Gray in the chest. The man they call Mister exploded. He rocked Newlin with a right. Newlin went down on his back. Newlin got up. Gray staggered him with a right and put him down with another. Someone yelled out, "Stay down, you dumb son of a bitch." But he was starting to get up again when hands reached around bodies and fists stopped flying. Gray was ejected and the measly crowd of 6,200 booed as hard as it could.

Fights are instant headlines in sports. They are the unusual—the spilling of emotions, the exposure of personalities out of the performed role—that captivates the fans. What started it? Who landed a punch? Anybody hurt? A fight usually breaks out away from the ball so only a few people see the first punch, or sometimes even any of the action, before other players jump in and pull the players apart. What happened? Who started it? A major fight dominates any game story. The fan wants to know what happened and it won't be told in the box score.

I wanted to catch Gray, at least try to get something out of him, before he disappeared into the night. I waited until the team had come back out onto the court for the second half. I waited until Russell and Hopkins had sauntered out and then strolled into the room. Furtado was picking up a couple of towels. Gray was walking across the room toward the door.

"I saw you warning the refs before it started. What did you say?"

"Nothing. They didn't do a thing. I told them. I warned them that if they didn't control the game we didn't have no choice but to defend ourselves. I told both officials twice, in a nice way, that I was getting clobbered out there. Newlin just kept bumping me with his forearm. I set a pick and he hit me. I set another one and he hit me again. Finally, I just let him have it. What was I supposed to do?"

I shrugged. Gray was at the door, looking out into the corridor. A guard stood with a cannon on his hip. "Is it safe for me to walk back to the hotel?" Gray asked. "I don't want to fight the whole state of Texas getting there."

"No, we have an officer who will escort you. Just wait a minute until he gets here." I went back to the game.

Moses Malone was sucking rebounds like a vacuum cleaner for the Rockets. And Malone had been on the move—three teams in the season's first two weeks. Ramsay had figured there just wasn't any way to justify keeping that kind of salary around playing behind Walton and Lucas and had dealt him to Buffalo. As the story goes, Snyder dealt Malone to Houston for a $100,000 profit while Brown was vacationing in the Bahamas. Brown was infuriated, especially when Malone bloomed as the season progressed. That tells you something about the communication among the owners in the Braves camp and the likely confusion ol' Sonic Sam was probably having trying to get McAdoo. But it also supported a mystery that Malone only plays like a superstar for Nissalke, who had him at Utah.

And after Seattle had come close but still lost by two, what did Newlin have to say about all this? "It was sloppy more than rough. I've had nightmares that were more organized." He was combing his beard, looking at me in the mirror. "It's ignorant to fight—it's the most uncreative thing in the world. Besides, the total story is that we won and they lost."

Newlin had hit the game-winner from the top of the key with 0:47 remaining after Brown had tied it with a soft high-arching lob off the glass as he drove the lane. Watts had twenty-five points and thirteen assists. He was pretty pleased with himself even though the team had lost its tenth straight on the road. "I been talkin' to myself all week 'bout how I gotta slow things down and make things happen for Slick. I've just been feeding others and winding up with bad shots when the clock runs down. I averaged thirteen points a game last year and when I take that little jump stop and get my jay working I can score. I hope it doesn't upset anybody, but I plan to do more of this. And another thing," he said, grabbing my arm to make sure I didn't leave. "Russ has been sayin' he has to use his big guards against other big guards. Well, I led the league in assists and steals last year against big guards and little guards. Keep your eye on me."

The next morning, as we sat in the airport, players were pestier than ever about wanting to read the papers bought by Heberlein, myself and Blackburn. I could never figure out why guys making $100,000 a year couldn't spend a dime for a paper. They were all interested in the Cowens story that morning. Big Mystery, the paper said. "Auerbach said Cowens had undergone a complete physical before leaving the team, but added, 'Anything concerning his physical condition is between Dave and the doctor.'" Players guessed as wildly as the TV watchers had the night before. "Auerbach said he was talkin' fluently and reasonably," Watts read to his mates. "Said he never had nothin' like this happen in thirty years of professional basketball. Nothin' of this nature at all." He handed the paper over his shoulder to Gray. I winked at Blackburn, sitting in a chair across from me. It's even-money he would never see his paper again.

"That's some deep shit about Cowens, ain't it?" Watts said to me. "That Cowens's gonna' drive ol' Auerbach crazy. Already almost did, workin' on cars all the time. He's a crazy son of a bitch. Good ballplayer, though."

We went up out of Houston and down into Dallas. Seemed impossible it was less than seventy-two hours before when we came down to San Antonio. Half an hour later, we took off, circled and headed north by northwest. I looked down at Dallas. I found myself thinking, Gee, it isn't powder blue. Images of a city through sport: Dallas is the perfect study. Big D, Big D. We don't stay here, we don't play here. We just stop and wait here. So like millions of Americans out there who never come here, we don't touch here. What is a city that you have never touched? If it's Dallas, it's powder blue football uniforms. The success of the Dallas Cowboys. A clean machine. Thin-lipped Tom Landry, religious, disciplined, a winner. Dallas. President Kennedy died here. Dallas. A clean champion of a city with a black eye. A black eye on a field of powder blue.

I wanted to talk to Russell on the plane about the McAdoo thing. No opportunity. I told him I'd call him in the evening. Now it was evening. I was calling:

"How ya doin'?"

"Awwwlright," he answered in his customary way, depicting a little impatience, like you're interrupting something, like maybe a nap.

"What's developed on Mac?"

"Nothing new."

"Damn, how long? How long we gotta wait?"

"I don't know," he replied rather peevishly.

"So I have to stew it out. Still don't think there's anything to be printed, huh?"

"You can print it as long as you're willing to accept responsibility that you will probably wreck the deal."

"You know this is a big story or I wouldn't be going on this way, but damn, I can't just hang like this day after day. It's going to come out somewhere."

He paused, then asked, partly with a tone of curiosity, partly with intimidation. "How old are you?"

"Thirty-two."

"Well, you'll never live to be forty if you keep worrying like this," he stated with a touch of humor.

"That's probably true, the only problem is that some jobs require more worry than others. I can't just lay back and let the pieces fall where they may and I can't instigate anything as far as making the deal happen—so I have to just keep after it and be ready."

He didn't bother to respond. We concluded the conversation. I should have said, "I'm getting harassed for being so tense from the guy who used to be so tense for games he threw up in the locker room. Man, think about that."

Wish I had thought of it in time.

Speaking Out

Fog, tinted gold by a ball of sun demanding a role in the morning's mood, embraced me. I was running around a picture-pretty inner-city park which provided a pleasant way to clear out the head. Fog gently lifted as I circled the lake, changing the angle of the sun's rays with every stride. Ducks quacked, leaves crunched, dew glistened, sweat ran. My, the morning tasted good. Almost too beautiful to be real.

Kansas City and Indiana had paid respective visits over the weekend and served themselves dutifully as the twenty-second and twenty-third victims of the Monsters of the Home Court—five- and three-point decisions, as they were. It was so nice not to be climbing on a plane, first Monday in a month not to be outward bound. A day off, some time to work at rebuilding my Victorian house on top of Queen Anne Hill. A day to pick up the hammer, been nearly a month since I'd had a chance. Of course, I had to be sure I didn't bang too loudly. I had a call in for Bill Fitch, trying to put together a feature on his hot Cavaliers, who would visit in two days. Almost was afraid to be away even for this run. Had to check around again on McAdoo deal. That issue kept building and fading like a distant radio station. It seemed so immediate one hour, then almost like an idle thought an hour later. I wished I could just be cool about it. Russell seemed pretty cool. I would bet Sam wasn't being cool trying to deal with Snyder. Ah, suck in the morning air, move legs move.

That evening the team headed for Oakland to meet the Warriors the next night. The *P-I* figured it could save a few bucks having me cover this one on the tube. I headed to the office to put together the Fitch feature. I talked to a Buffalo writer who said Snyder wanted to deal McAdoo to the Knicks, but Brown wanted to make it with Schulman. Frankly, the writer felt, McAdoo wasn't going anywhere. I wished

Schulman would get back from Hong Kong so I could see what was going on.

Anything out of the ordinary catches the reporter short in the monitor coverage. Barry ran a consecutive free-throw string to sixty for an NBA record. I stole a couple of TV postgame quotes to cover that, and there it was, an eleventh straight road loss in the books. Cleveland in tomorrow night.

The Cavs came in as the hottest team in the league, 11–2. They put up a great fight, but Seattle was up 65–45 in the third quarter when Fitch threw in a whole new lineup. Forty-seven seconds later it was 70–45. A fan called out, "Bring in five more, Fitch. Play all twelve if you want. You guys still ain't shit." Nervous titters rippled through the crowd. I was sure it was the same guy who called out in the first quarter, when Russell was talking to Burleson on the sideline: "Don't waste your time talking to him, Russell. He can't help himself any more than a baby can help wetting his diapers." Harsh.

But it was another win at home, a club record defensive effort as Seattle held the Cavs to seventy-eight points. And guess who was coming to dinner Friday night? Bob McAdoo and his friends.

It was still too much of a secret, the possibility of the trade, to have appropriate fun with, but I couldn't help but imagine the swap would be made just before game time. What a classic scene: "Ladies and gentlemen, boys and girls, before introducing tonight's starting lineups, we would like to take this opportunity to make a special announcement. Will Bob McAdoo and Tommy Burleson please go to midcourt. All right. Now will each please remove his jersey, exchange it with the other and put on the new one. There it is folks: the trade of the decade. Welcome to Seattle, Bobby Mac!"

It would have been worth my not getting to break the story to have that happen. I guessed the reason they hadn't was because they didn't want to have to mop up the floor under fourteen thousand Sonic fans. The worst of it was that by the time the evening was over, you knew there wasn't a chance in hell the deal would ever come off. Oh sure, Seattle destroyed Buffalo, 130–101. But while McAdoo was collecting twenty points, Burleson was going 0–5 from the field, zero rebounds and being benched after eleven minutes. Way to sell yourself, Tommy.

Everyone was ready for some escape. The next night, a Saturday night off,puts the group into party time at Watts' house. People upstairs, downstairs, sitting on the stairs. People eating and talking upstairs, mingling. Burleson stooped over talking to a short girl. His wife standing beside him, quiet. Relaxed conversations among players, wives, girl friends. People upstairs sitting on white couches and chairs, standing on a white carpet. Big paintings of modern art on the white walls. Big pictures of Watts on the walls above the stairs going downstairs. Tolson and Watts jiving in the poolroom. Dark in the rec room. Big fire going. People sitting on low couches, pillow furniture. Big stereo speakers. Pong being played on the TV set. The music strong, filling in around close conversations, filtering upstairs where it's easier to talk. Plenty of beer around, some bourbon, the grass must be outside. Jump, jump music. Pick it up, get stronger, take over. Slick moves and talks, moves and sings, his jump suit open to his navel, heavy silver and turquoise jewelry against his cocoa skin. The pong game goes away. The stereo goes louder. Fuse blows. Music stops. People stop. Replace fuse, get loose. Watts sings in a hoarse falsetto, "Love to love ya ba-beee, love to love ya ba-beee." He's bumping with Janice from the Sonic's office. Sing and bump, sing and bump, move, move. Turn the music up. Others step, step, clap hands, step forward, back—they're together, five, six people. Do the hustle. Eight dark bodies moving in unison in the darkened room, the fire giving most of the light. Everyone steps forward, half-step back, erect, faces quiet. Step forward, half-step back, turn 90°—all together—turn, clap, step forward, lift right knee, back down, step, step, turn 180°, clap, step, step. . . . It's seductive. It's so mellow, so *together*.

The upstairs crowd fades, the downstairs mood grows, settles in thick and warm. Plugged into the music and the people and the warmth, it's too good to leave—like a warm fire in a November field. Stay tucked into each other, ride on friendly voices, music. Makes you feel like dancin', dan-sinnnnn. Bump, bump, bump, feel good, feel good. "Oh daddy don't it make you feel like dan-sinnnn? Dan-sinn. Dansinnnnn." Clap, clap, nice and easy, clap-clap, come on and shake yo' bottom, dan-sinnnn, dan-sinnnn. It's all a nice easy bounce, on daddy's knee. Slick Watts hostin'. Feel good. Feel Good. Don't change anything, don't change a thing. Feel good. Step, step, bump and bump and get down, get *down* ba-beeee, get down. Dan-sinnn. Dan-sinnn. Clap, clap, nice and easy, clap, clap. Don't let it get away. Do Not Let It Get A-W-A-Y.

But it always does.

The next evening brought a visit by the NBA lowlanders, the 3–15 Milwaukee Bucks with Larry Costello, dying in the saddle.

The Bucks' coach looked even more slumped, beaten, than he had two weeks earlier in Milwaukee. He'd been publicly criticized by Bucks' management. The scent of dismissal was in the air. After Seattle whipped the Bucks for their twenty-sixth straight home win, Costello sounded like a man who had been framed in a murder charge. He tried to analyze the game, he tried to comment on his team and how they just needed some more time. Finally it poured out of him: "I don't care what they do to me. We don't have any talent, we don't have any muscle. We're just a bunch of kids. No coach in the league could do any better with the situation we have here. Nobody could expect any more." He threw up his hands. There was nothing else left to say. The next day he announced his "voluntary resignation." Don Nelson became only the second coach in Bucks' history.

A whole four days before the next game. Four days, the longest stretch of game-time inactivity over six months' span of the season.

Relaxation is a very dangerous word in the beat reporter's world. And no sooner did I allow myself to do it than the proverbial slap on the blind side was administered. A reporter is always looking over his shoulder in fear of getting scooped. You notice some small observation or a quote that someone else had in their story that you missed and it rankles like a sliver under a fingernail. No one had broken anything major on me. Nobody had come up with any dramatic features I hadn't gotten around to, or thought of. Even to a close reader, I doubt the elements of competition between journalists are discernible. But among one's colleagues, getting scooped hurts. You want to be known as the guy who does it all—the jock world nomenclature is very prevalent. "He's strong, doesn't get beat. Hard worker, diligent, perceptive." Can't go to his left, though.

So you can understand the slam it was to pick up my own paper on one of those "idle" days and see the lead story was a UPI piece on Bob Wilkerson, telling how he was upset with Russell and his teammates. Ouch.

Wilkerson had been the silent one. His image seemed pretty well captured in the kayo punch he took during the previous spring's NCAA championship game when a Michigan elbow took him out of the game and out of this world for nearly twenty-four hours. He hadn't said much at all since training camp opened. His postgame quotes were barely audible and far from provocative. He was the serious and silent type. He didn't play around with his mates—which didn't enhance his stature since he was already courting jealousies over playing time. But he made it clear he didn't want anybody hassling him and he was tough enough to deter anybody from trying to change him. He had played for Bobby Knight—the military man, the bootblack disciplinarian—at Indiana. He was used to paying the price for victory and already in a month of the Sonics he had lost more than in four years of college. He couldn't stomach it, the lack of effort. His circumstance seemed very lonely.

"If there are guys not willing to do the job out there, then Coach Russell should let me play. When we go on the road and the guys would rather mess around and not take care of themselves than do their best, then I should be out there."

Not the sort of thing to endear himself with the troops. But then he hardly ever said two words, anyway, except to his roomie, Johnson. Wilkerson always sat in the front of the bus, quiet as a stone. I figured I would take a long time getting through, if ever. Now, John Engstrom, sports editor for United Press International, had stumbled upon the story. Engstrom had gone to a Sonics' public relations practice at a local high school and had just been shopping for a feature. He started talking to Wilkerson, was surprised by the course of words and put his tape recorder to good work.

Owen, my editor, asked, in a matter-of-fact way, why I hadn't come up with the story. I told him I had found Wilkerson noncommunicative. He accepted it. But there it was again, that athletic world competitiveness—somebody had bettered me on one story. A mark in the loss column. Johnson complained to me the next night, as the team was preparing to play Chicago, that Wilkerson had been misquoted. I told him I had talked to Engstrom and heard the tape. How could it be? Johnson just said it was distorted. Wilkerson, standing next to him, didn't say it was or it wasn't. Here was another example of a player saying words that sounded okay, but looked pretty out of proportion when they were in headlines.

The Sonics squeaked past stumbling-fumbling Chicago for their twenty-seventh straight home court win. Someone remarked that it didn't seem to make much difference, Wilkerson speaking out. He played his average of eighteen minutes. I asked Russell for his opinion on the article. He replied: "As long as a man tells the truth, he has every right to speak his mind. I would be a hypocrite to my own standards if I said otherwise." Someone reflected as to how it looked like Bob Love, an eleven-year veteran of all-star stature, had seemed to slip pretty badly since the previous year. Someone else reflected as to how Ed Badger, the Chicago coach, would be lucky to last past Thanksgiving.

Seattle lost badly at Phoenix and then, Watts went bee-zerk the next night at home, hitting fifteen of twenty-seven shots from the field en route to a career-high thirty-seven points to go with thirteen assists and five steals. The Sonics had their twenty-eighth straight at home by the grace of undiluted luck as Wes Unseld missed two tips at the hoop as the horn sounded. What a ripper. Who needed Bob McAdoo? What a way to launch an eleven-day road trip.

14
Too Much Toward Nothing

Two suitcases. Too much to lug, but too hard to cut down to one. I feel good—eager to get out and do some good writing, to get into some good cities. Let's go see what's to do about McAdoo. Let's go see Boston Garden and the Big Apple and Zinkoff and the Doctor and let's get on down to New Ow-leeeens. Three days in New Ow-leeeens at the end of the line. All right. The players are high, full of fun after escaping with their lives the night before against Washington.

The Bullets, heading for Los Angeles, mill around the departure gate next to the Sonics. Seals and Wes Unseld stand in conversation in the middle of the wide walkway. Exactly twelve hours earlier Unseld had gone up with a shot underneath the basket—certain to collect the game-winner. Seals hadn't wanted to foul. All he could do was intimidate. Unseld had missed, gotten his rebound and tried again. The ball bubbled out of the hoop as the buzzer sounded.

"Did you ask him about those last shots?" I tease Seals as we stroll down the ramp to board the plane.

"Naw, he's too big to be askin' him those kind of questions. Besides, that wouldn't be polite." He grins.

Coming off his career high of thirty-seven points, Watts is wound up two revs tighter than usual. He's all over the first-class section as the Sonic party settles in. Players sitting next to someone, then a conversation breaking out with another, people shifting. "Come here, man. I want to talk to you." Bodies shift. Little arguments break out as to where a briefcase or a shoulder bag or a coat has to be stowed.

Watts is babbling, "I'm gonna get my shots. I showed I can score. These guys ain't gonna freeze me out." He laughs, exchanging jabs, sparring with everyone who bothers to respond to his assault of enthusiasm.

Furtado moves about the cabin, stowing gear. "We're gonna have to get Slick a headband expander," he chimes in. Watts laughs and holds Furtado's arm affectionately. "You're cold, Frank."

Oleynick, who said he set a new Pacific Coast speed record getting to the flight, not daring to incur a repeat of his fine for missing the flight to San Antonio, sits down next to me. "I think Furtado was going to sit there," I say, not really caring who does, but knowing what's coming.

"Yeah, he gave me his seat, it's cool," he replied. "You up for another backgammon lesson, B.J.?"

While I protest that there is nothing noble about taking money off a total innocent, Furtado shows up. "Get out of my seat, Frank." It's a message delivered in a quasi-dictatorial, quasi-kidding manner often used by Furtado.

Oleynick gets up, grabs his money pouch—most of the players pack leather ones with Seattle First National printed on the side. He shoves Watts, sitting on an armrest across the aisle, back into Mike Bantom's lap, easily, so that Watts really didn't have to fall.

"That's okay, Frankie," says Watts. "I just gotta shoot enough to keep 'em honest. Make you all look good."

Oleynick motions Watts's nonsense away and finds an empty seat. Green comes loping in, seven minutes after our scheduled departure time, and sits next to Oleynick. The exasperated stewardess finally gets Watts buckled in, checks around, and the plane starts to taxi. We're off to eleven days that seem like blank pages awaiting six games' worth of action with all the accompanying life-on-the-road action. All the unexpected adventure with hundreds (thousands? hundreds of thousands?) back home attentive for reports of the action.

The 747 climbs up through the fog and jumps out into blue sky and sunshine like a trout springing from a sparkling lake. (Did you know the reason fish jump is so that they can see where they are going?) Mount Rainier, looking like a big bowl of ice cream, looms on the left side of the plane.

The headphones are serving a nice bluesy song. Life is nice. Then the captain's voice pokes onto the line. "Ladies and gentlemen, comin' up on tha left side is one of tha purtiest sights in America, Mount Rainier." (Why is it that everyone who wears a uniform—be it military, aviation or law enforcement or UPS deliveryman—talks like he was born and raised three miles outside Mobile?) "Now we don't want to tip the plane ovah, but if you folks wan to peek out for a look, maybah some of yo neighbors on the lef sahd will shift sahds with you for a minute. Sure is purty, in't it?" Shore is.

We circle almost completely around the mountain. Except when there is a heavy overcast or a storm, Mount Rainier is like a lighthouse beacon for the Sonics every trip in and out. Most of the time you'll have a hard time finding even two players bothering to look out, but on this morning, even the most blasé take it in. It's as though we're just hanging inches away from the peak—the crevasses and glacier sheets looking like wrinkles and folds in a pile of laundry.

There is a wisp of cloud encircling the top. Watts says, "It's even got a little ol' headband." Seals slaps Watts's head and the serenity is lost. As if on cue, the plane pulls out of its circle and heads east.

Russell has to abandon his customary seat, left side of the cabin, second row window. I often wondered what significance that seat had. Russell once proclaimed he would die someday in a plane crash. He was a calculating sort. Did he learn somewhere that was the safest seat? Or was it the most deadly? He had to abandon it for this trip though as he's catching smoke from some neighbors. He moves back across the aisle from Furtado. We worked off a little energy discussing the inconsideration of those who smoke in public. We decided that it's not the same imposing no-smoking values on someone as it was to smoke and disturb others. We sentenced the villain to five years in a sealed phone booth.

Some of the players break out a deck of cards and cut for dollars. The game goes on and on, swearing and shouting, ego one-upmanship much more important than the money itself. The white wine is flowing. I can't recall when Russell lowered the no-drinking inflight barrier, but it is definitely down. A Wide World of Sports segment comes on the screen behind the card game. No one in first class can see over the players.

Russell hollers out, "Hey, Bantom, that's a twenty-five-inch screen and you got a twenty-seven-inch head." He laughs loudest. He doesn't gain much improvement in vision.

There are a pair of stewardesses plus a very foxy black chick seated in the front row to keep players ever on the make. Some talk quietly and patiently; others jabbing and floating like Muhammad Ali's butterfly-bee.

The meal comes, the meal goes away. Snooze, talk, listen to music, listen to the jive, tune it out.

As we near Chicago, the card game has been reduced to a drag race between two players—both having apparently sucked in all that the others were willing to donate and now trying to determine which one will walk off the plane with all the marbles. They're shouting at each other, slapping money down, slapping down cards. Talking the game, working the air into froth, trying to create a gush of vibes that will sweep the bread into the right pocket.

The stewardess has everyone buckled in, seat backs and tray tables in their full upright and locked position. All things properly stowed in the overhead racks or under the seat. Everything is battened down except Watts, who is sitting on his seat edge. Watts bops at the Stew with his energy, babbling to hold her at bay.

Russell has called out several times to stop the game, but it's like two five-year-olds wanting just one more turn on the swing before dinner. You don't get into the rush of a good gamblin' game and just turn if off.

Finally, because Watts and the Stew are close to getting into something strong, Russell gets up, walks to Watts, puts his hand on his shoulder and tells him in firmer tones than what he has been using, "That's enough. You've got to calm down now."

Watts is too bouncy to slow up, but sits in his seat and buckles up. He sulks for a minute. The game keeps going on the long reach. As Russell returns to his seat he breaks the awkward tension with, "I don't care about the game, but I don't want them to have to issue you a parachute." There's some jive back and forth, no one's hurt.

Behind Russell, Tolson and Bantom are slapping each other and play-fighting over something. Russell calls over his shoulder, "Dean, you're a Neanderthal."

Tolson turns to Bantom and asks, "What's that?"

Everyone goes crazy, slapping hands and trying out various primitive man routines on Tolson. Seals leans across the aisle, "Give me some Neanderthal man," he says holding out his hand. "You're my man,

Neanderthal man." Tolson knows it isn't the nicest compliment he ever had—he pushes Seals's hand away. "Fuck you, you fish with fur. Bark, bark, bark."

The plane lands in Chicago.

Players head for the ice-cream stand or the phones. Watts calls one of his sons. I buy three newspapers and head back on the plane.

I sit down next to Russell. We share the papers and comments. The *Tribune* has a wire service picture of Watts collecting one of his career-high points on a crazy layup. The report is an Associated Press rewrite of my story. It seems strange to have words written into a messy notebook, transcribed into type for a whole nation's readers. From such casual conversation to profound printout.

The Bulls are still stumbling. "Looks like they're going to shove Badger out and hire Costello," I muse to Russell as I read a report in the *Tribune* by Bob Logan—a hard-hitting vet of the NBA beat.

Russell frowns. "Why don't they ever rehire blacks that get fired—like Lenny Wilkens or K.C. Jones or Ray Scott?"

Russell was one of the two black head coaches (Al Attles being the other) in the league at that time. He had been the first black head coach in major sports history when he took the player-coach role in 1966. There had been five blacks among the eighteen head coaches in the NBA in 1975–76. With the merger of four ABA teams the roster swelled to twenty-two franchises and the total dropped to two as Scott had been fired at Detroit, Jones fired at Washington and Wilkens fired at Portland—and all replaced by Caucasian coaches.

"The biggest fear of hiring black coaches is the awkwardness of firing them," I added.

"I never heard *that one* before," Russell answered, anger leaping momentarily into his voice.

"Seems pretty strange, doesn't it? Why do they keep hiring the same guys around the league, anyway? A guy fired in one place and hired somewhere else the next year. Why are the owners so reluctant to try new blood—maybe find a guy who will be outstanding. They already know the guy failed somewhere when they keep hiring the same faces."

Russell didn't answer, but just gave a little shrug and kept reading his paper. It really was a question that needed no answer. The situation is that coaches are fired to give the illusion of change. Things are going badly, you can't change the whole team—unless you're Russell—so you get rid of the coach. Sometimes there are conflicts between coaches and players that have to be terminated. But the new coach mainly gives everyone new hopes. Sell a few season tickets. The guy did a pretty good job running a pro team, got the players to the game on time, knows the way to the airport, must be okay. Hire and fire, change to inspire.

I read for a few minutes. I start to say something about what a thorough and entertaining reporter this Logan is. I look over at Russell and he's sound asleep, head on hand, mouth open. Instant zees.

And just as suddenly, he's awake again, exchanging jibes with anyone within ear range. We take off for Buffalo. "What kind of coat is that?" someone asks of Russell's garment—a thick hide, white with the texture of tanned leather dulling the skin. The inside is lined with thick woolly white, maybe it's sheep or mountain goat, or something like llama. "Don't know. The guy said if you have to ask, you can't afford it." I thought to myself, If you have to ask *what* it is, then you can't *afford* it. Doesn't make sense, or does it? "Get you something to drink?" the stewardess interrupts my thoughts.

"Give me an orange juice and 7-Up mixed," Russell says, adding habitually, "It's called a Screw-Up." He laughs habitually. I've been drinking OJ and 7-Up since high school, great for hangovers. I order the same. I hope Russell doesn't think I'm just copying him.

Ninety-seven percent of the conversation on planes pertains to the discussion of women, money and the good things they can provide—materialistically and aesthetically. The remainder of the conversations cover sports, food and sometimes an occasional word, almost by accident, on world affairs.

Russell is talking about eating—something he must rate near the top of life's luxuries. Someone once speculated that he didn't throw up before games because of nervousness, but rather because he had just gorged himself and needed relief to play. That has never been proven and most accounts of his game-time posture of nerves seem to support the idea that he was just one uptight, upchucking ballplayer. His former teammate John Havlicek once commented: "He used to throw up all the time before a game, or at halftime—a tremendous sound, almost as loud as his laugh. He didn't do it as much in the later years of his career—except for an important game or an important challenge, like Chamberlain or someone everyone was touting. It was a welcome sound, too, because it meant he was keyed up for the game."

What he does now might be another thing. The amount of food he consumes at times borders on a carnival act. He has the money and the time to enjoy life as his every whim might dictate. He sticks to room service almost without exception when on the road— the hassle with the public in coffee shops and restaurants is usually just not worth the stepping out.

During the first road trip I went on with the Sonics he invited Furtado and myself to join him in a run on a little barbecue house on the South Side of Chicago. We had gotten in around eight o'clock and headed across town a couple hours later. He bought chicken wings and sweet potato pie and what-all in huge amounts. We took it back to the hotel, he departing for his room. It was very, very good.

He was now talking about a place in Buffalo that has the "best chicken wings in the country. I'm going to get me some chicken wings and then get me a lot of sleep." He didn't invite anyone along.

We talk about enjoying life, about having priorities and not cluttering them up. He says, "I have more fun now than I did twenty years ago. I know what I can do and what I can't. I'm comfortable with myself now. I don't need drugs or alcohol to make me high. I'm high on my own life."

"Didn't you ever drink?"

"Yeah, but one day I decided it wasn't worth it. What if Sophia Loren came to my door some night and I wasn't ready for her. I couldn't take that chance." His laugh was deep and strong.

Six hours of talking and eating and drinking and eating and reading and waiting, plus a three-hour time loss and here we are in Buffalo, at 7:30 P.M. One more day gone away.

We walk off the plane in Buffalo—winter hits us like a door slamming in our faces. Russell is bundled up in his coat. Johnson—who had a year earlier been playing for Pepperdine located in paradise on a hill overlooking Malibu—cringes against the wind, slips on the ice and stammers, "Man, oh man, I gotta get myself back to L.A. I wasn't bred for this." Watts, behind Johnson, calls out, "Hey, rook, that's a nice bag you got there—too bad you ain't got any decent clothes to put in it."

Most of the players have wandered off to the Executive Inn, covering the snowy quarter mile in shuttle buses, by the time the last of the luggage comes up. Russell has secured his car and disappeared— apparently for a load of chicken wings.

15

Buffalo Snow-Out

They shove a Buffalo *Courier Express* under everyone's door in the morning. The rooms at the Executive Inn have radios as well as TVs. The little extras that keep you coming back even when you don't have any choice.

The room wore a blue hue through the closed drapes. I rolled over and flipped on the radio: "This is WBLK, your black network news station. It's ten degrees, wind chill factor reads minus eleven. Travelers' warnings are up for Erie and Niagara counties with snow accumulations of a foot or more forecast for later this afternoon or evening. . . .

Turning to sports, there were no players from black schools mentioned in the top fourteen Heisman Trophy finalists, won by Tony Dorsett of Pittsburgh. In black college basketball last night . . ." I jumped up, picked up the *Courier Express*, jumped back into bed. The Braves lost at New York the night before; eight of nine down the tube. Randy Smith was benched, ending starting streak at 249 games. That must be dandy for morale. McAdoo was benched earlier in the week. Trade must be ripe, but ownership hassles between Brown and Snyder leaves it up in the air. That's the story here—when will Brown get control of the team?

A midmorning saunter wound up as a genuine scramble against a fast-building snowstorm by the time Heberlein and I regained the front door of the Executive Inn. We headed down to the coffee shop for some thaw-out soup. Tolson and Burleson were seated there. Burleson, $350,000; Tolson, $30,000. Both tall, Burleson at 7'2" like a thick cedar; Tolson at 6'9", like a willow.

"Well, guess ol' Fred won't be gettin' here. They closed the airport," offered Tolson. Brown had gone to visit a sick relative in either Detroit, Kansas City or Milwaukee. No one seemed to know.

Burleson got up, left a dollar bill for a tip.

"Sheeeit, Tommy. You got no class. Millionaire like you leavin' *torn* dollars," Tolson chastised. "Look at this." He picked up a soiled dollar bill in two pieces.

Tolson then started dumping piles of nickels, quarters and dimes onto the table. How he could hold it all in his pocket was amazing enough—why it was there was worse.

"I was makin' this long-distance call and had to keep puttin' in change," Tolson explained. "Then when I get all through, the dumb bitch pushes the wrong button and it all comes fallin' out of the machine. Sheeeit."

Tolson left some of the change for his tip and started to leave. He came back, put down four more quarters and picked up the two pieces of dollar bill.

"I know it's good money, but I don't want her to think I left it."

I read and worked on pregame notes and tried to run down some further information on McAdoo. I fell asleep staring at the darkening sky. I awoke—nothing existed outside the room window. Thirty-mile-an-hour winds and the snow flew like goose feathers. Snow sifted through the seam in the sliding glass frame and built a mini-drift against the wall. I headed down the hall to visit Furtado. Three hours to game time and he was on the phone trying to find options for getting to Boston, where the club was to play the next night. It didn't look like there was any way the airport would be open the next morning the way it was coming down then. I kept after him to outline the options.

Finally he said, "What are you so worried about? You know it'll work out one way or another."

"Frank, I'm a reporter. There are thousands of people in Seattle who will love to worry about their guys out here in snow country. It's unusual stuff. It's a story."

"Oh yeah. You know I forget about all that sometimes. Do you think they really follow it like that?"

"The *P-I* has spent a lot of bucks having me here on the contention that they do. So keep me informed, will ya, travel agent."

He threw a ball bag at me.

There was talk of taking a bus charter out right after the game. A 450-mile run through this kind of weather would take forever, if you got through at all.

If there was any doubt the Buffalo weather was hostile, such thoughts were dispatched when Russell climbed aboard the bus in the run for the arena—leaving his car well buried under the snow in the parking lot. The night was deep blue, illuminated by the white carpet which covered everything. It had stopped snowing suddenly. Cars were abandoned, noses stuck in the banks at the side of the road. Some were stalled right in the middle of the expressway—leaving a slalom course for the driver. We were the only thing moving. It seemed the world had stopped. Maybe everybody got off but us. No one could know, although it was easy to imagine, that we were part of the first hours of what turned out to be a winter disaster for Buffalo—snow accumulating steadily throughout the next month into drifts of twenty feet causing games to be canceled on many nights.

They should have started the cancellations with this one, but it did prove to be an evening of major developments.

As we pulled up to the auditorium, Russell called out, "Anybody want my tickets for tonight?" He laughed. No players seemed to be very jovial. They weren't very pleased to be facing the possibility of a long bus ride to Rochester, or maybe even all the way to Boston.

Over a cheese sandwich and a Vernor's ginger ale, Heberlein and I visited with the Braves PR man, Mike Shaw.

I checked with a *Courier Express* reporter whom I had called from Houston. He doubted anything was cooking on McAdoo.

"Heard things might be getting close," someone said.

I looked at Heberlein to see if he was taking much interest. Didn't seem to be.

I took Shaw aside. He said he felt things were indeed hot. Could come down in a couple of days. Told me a TV sportscaster named Ed Kilgore had an announcement on his show that evening. I should check with him. As I headed behind the Sonic bench while the teams warmed up—the bouncing of balls strangely hollow in the virtually vacant arena—I stopped to query Russell, alone on the bench.

"A TV guy here came on his show this evening and said McAdoo is going to Seattle for Tommy and cash. Anything cooking today?" I asked.

He shook his head.

"Still the same situation, huh?"

He nodded and stared moodily out on the court.

Enough of all this, I decided. I called Kilgore. He said he got the story from a friend at ABC in Chicago. He said the friend told him Detroit turned down McAdoo for Lanier. I asked him about the Knicks' connection. He said there was bad blood between the Braves and the Knicks' general manager, Eddie Donovan—who had done big things in building the New York championship of 1970, moved to Buffalo to get them upward bound, then jumped back to the Knicks the past year. Kilgore didn't have much more than I did, but we found the pieces we did have seemed to match up. The rest of the press in Buffalo seemed to scoff at the idea. They'd been through too many Paul Snyder deals to jump at the scent of another one. At least Kilgore had taken the burden off me by breaking the story in Buffalo. If Snyder didn't get all bent out of shape with the local announcement, why worry about it coming out in Seattle? Of course, if he blew the deal, Russell couldn't get upset with me—well, he could have gotten upset, but he couldn't do so honestly, for whatever that would be worth. What the hell, if I bent any farther, I might as well have gone on the Sonic payroll.

Heberlein had his antenna up and was sniffing around. Since I'd had the story ahead of him, it didn't matter to discuss it. He said he had heard the faintest of rumors a few days earlier, but gave them as little response as I had initially.

As they played the National Anthem, Heberlein and I divided up the stands and came up with a total of 374 bodies, including players and ourselves. The official gate rose all the way to 994—smallest in league history as near as anyone could determine. The game was horrible. Seattle was garbage and Buffalo tried to keep the aroma consistent. McAdoo had eighteen rebounds and twenty-nine points, Burleson eight and eleven respectively.

Heberlein and I talked to Buffalo coach Tates Locke after the game. In the ordinary course of reviewing the game, Locke said, "I've liked Tommy ever since we played against him in college."

Greg said, "People say there might be a trade. McAdoo for Burleson." Locke looked up sharply. "Who are people?"

Then he stared down at a stat sheet and added, "I don't want to say anything else about it right now."

I finally had a story to print:

BUFFALO—Although management on neither end would comment on the matter, news sources here last night supported rumors that have been circulating recently signaling a major trade between the Sonics and the Buffalo Braves.

Ed Kilgore, sportscaster for WGR-TV in Buffalo, announced on his show last evening that a deal was in the works which would bring Bob McAdoo to the Sonics for Tommy Burleson, another player and cash.

"I have heard some reports of this trade from individuals on several clubs, so there must be plenty of speculation throughout the league," Kilgore commented. "I know Detroit turned down a Bob Lanier for McAdoo trade earlier and there was some talk between the Knicks and the Braves over McAdoo."

What makes McAdoo, the league's leading scorer the past three seasons, such a lively market item right now is the fact he's playing out his option and the Braves are afraid they might wind up with his departing for another club next year—leaving the Braves with nothing in return.

Bill Russell, coach and general manager of the Sonics, did not comment on the matter, but Braves coach Tates Locke had a few curious words in response to a reporter's query.

"I've always liked Tommy Burleson," he said in reference to his play in last night's game between the two clubs. "We played against him three years in college." Locke was coach at Clemson while Burleson was playing at North Carolina State.

"People say there might be a deal working where McAdoo would go to Seattle in trade for Burleson," the reporter stated.

"Who are people?" Locke retorted, then dropped his head to look at a stat sheet, muttering, "I just don't want to say anything else right now."

Skies were clear at 3 A.M. I couldn't sleep, the time change finally having caught up with me. "Don't fight it. Lie back and look at the stars. Breath deeeeply." It looked like we would be able to skate out in the morning if they could get the runways cleared.

We were up at 7 A.M. The bus to haul us up the road to the airport was ready half an hour later. The sky was gray, ready for more snow, but the runway was clear. Russell left his Hertz car in the parking lot—nineteen inches of snow covering it. Bundled up in his Mountain Goat Coat, he was upset that not everyone was on the bus at the time of the scheduled departure. He said there would be a shooting practice as soon as we got to Boston.

At the airport, we sat in the waiting area, scattered around the room, reading papers. Snow was starting to fall again outside. We'd like to get on that bird right now, thank you.

"Barry had twenty-eight points, eighteen assists and five steals last night," I read aloud from my *Courier Express*.

"He's got to score for Golden State to be tough," commented Russell without lowering his own paper. "He lets up some on defense, but he still will hurt you. He's smart." The conversation rumbled along, one-liners, countercomments, filling time. Blackburn read a quote from the 76ers' trainer how no team was unified. Everyone was pointing the finger at Philadelphia because they had a busload of superstars.

"When I was with Boston we used to go to shows together," Russell said, lowering his paper to his lap. "We were always going somewhere together—different guys in groups of three or four at different times. I once went to four different shows on four straight days with a different set of guys each time. We had fun with each other. I remember one time we were playing the Hawks. We were up one with eight seconds to go. Cousy missed a free throw that would have cinched it. Everyone just laughed and said, 'Glad it was you shooting.' Everyone knew everybody was doing their best so there was no reason to get on a guy or say he choked."

I was reminded again of Costello's words of dismay during Alcindor's rookie year. ". . . Here they play a terrible game like this and now they're taking off, going their separate ways. It wasn't like that when I was playing . . . we'd sit around for a long time and talk . . . so many outside interests . . . so many things on the side. . . ."

Russell was still talking: "There's only about ten players in the league who are really dedicated to being as good as they can be. That means doing everything they can to be good on and off the court." Someone mentions the "Red on Roundball" series which features former Celtic coach Red Auerbach conducting quickie coaching clinics with various NBA stars at halftime of televised NBA games. He came across as very authoritative, almost belligerent. Was he really that way as a coach?

"No, that's not him," Russell said.

How much did he have to do with the esprit de corps on the Celtics?

"He picked the players, but I don't ever recall him trying to control a player's personality. Someone once asked him, 'Red, you've got Cousy, Sharman, Russell, Heinsohn, Ramsey, K.C. Jones, Sam Jones, how do you handle all those stars?' Red's answer was, 'Hell with 'em. Let 'em get along with me.' But he did his thing in a way that worked for all of us. There were no cliques on that team. We mixed together all the time. That's something you find with all intelligent people."

He glanced around to see who among the players was listening. Few were within ear range. Only Wilkerson seemed to be tuned in among those who could hear. "The Celtics were like a family to me. I made good friends and things were very peaceful on the team. That's why I never tried to squeeze them for more money. I'd probably have been traded several times and had to deal with all the uncertainties that go with that."

"I see Red's giving locker room lectures again," Blackburn said.

"He should be," replied Russell.

"How much of a hand did he have in the program while you were coaching?" I asked.

"I had available the best mind in basketball. I used to ask him for help. I'd have been a fool not to," Russell answered, lifting his paper again.

Someone read aloud the latest chapter in the stormy life of Marvin Barnes, who was in trouble for a parole violation and AWOL from the Pistons. He had been given a suspended sentence for assaulting a Providence College teammate with a tire iron two years earlier and gone on to play a pair of troubled seasons in the ABA—continually suspended and fined and in the wrong kind of headlines. Now Detroit had him and he had just been arrested for trying to board a plane with a pistol in his luggage.

"He's a hoodlum," a player said. "He's going to blow a great career sittin' in jail."

"Helluva contrast, isn't it," I offered. "He's either sitting in jail with nothing or outside in the limelight making three hundred thousand a year."

As Furtado came around handing out boarding passes I asked Russell if there are more oddballs in the game than there were in his generation.

"You have to remember, there were only eight teams for a long time. That didn't mean very many jobs—only a few new guys each year," he replied. "So you didn't have to put up with the malcontents or head cases. With the expansion and increased number of jobs, you had to dig deeper in the barrel. I think it'll stabilize again now that you've cut down the number of pro teams. What was there, six teams folded when the ABA merged? That's a lot of jobs right there that are lost."

We walked down icy steps, across forty yards of runway whipped by the meanest of winds, dashed by a building snow flurry, and clamored aboard the plane for escape to Boston.

"Get me out of *here*," yelled Johnson as he bundled up in a blanket.

"Good for ya, boy," replied Watts, who was wearing a single-piece jump suit open to the middle of his stomach. "Make you a man so's you can do somebody some good in this world."

Seals, who had been hiding a small snowball in his hand plopped it on Watts's head. Watts turned around in his seat and tried to slap Seals. One stewardess rolled her eyes to the other. I hated to think what a twelve-hour bus ride would have been like.

16

Mecca of the Master Mystique

Boston Bay was denim blue as we took a big turn for landing at Logan International. The streaks and dots of islands and peninsulas in the bay were bright in the winter sun, but the beaches were empty—a complete contrast to the summertime folly that historically invades the New England beaches. It felt as though the world had suddenly come on in color after the black and white Buffalo.

It was nearly 1:30 by the time we arrived at the Parker House in downtown Boston. The bus made the turn down a narrow street in heavy traffic, and stopped. We unloaded while blocking the street, horns blaring, people blaring. Quaint Boston. It was an hour later by the time Heberlein, Furtado and I ate. It was nearly 3 P.M. when I finally got through to Harvey Pollack, the publicity director of the 76ers. I wanted some update statistics for a feature I would use Friday morning to advance the game in Philly. It took three calls to three different offices before the 76ers could figure out which office was his. Then I needed three more calls to Los Angeles before I finally located Schulman at his tennis retreat in Palm Springs. He had just returned from Hong Kong. It was good to talk to No. 1 man.

"Bill really wants to make the deal," Schulman explained. "He says McAdoo would really turn the team into a winner and that he could be a good team player. What do you think of him?"

"Well, I've done a lot of research on him since I first heard the deal was a possibility. He was the rookie of the year, he was the league's MVP in '75, he's been the league scoring champ the past three years. His assists have been getting higher the last two seasons. So we know he can play, right? I have never heard too much negative about him, although I did a feature last year where I interviewed ball boys around the league about who were the biggest jerks, you know, the guys who were most demanding in the locker rooms and so on, and his name kept coming up. But I don't know how much you worry about things like that if the guy can play. His stats are certainly better than Tommy's."

"I just don't know what to think about Tommy," Schulman said slowly. "I took such a chance to get him, I spent so much money. He just doesn't seem to have it, does he? He has to be really inspired to be effective and he isn't always that way. I guess we have to try to make a deal if we can."

"What is the deal, exactly?" I asked.

"Well, dealing with Paul Snyder is not the easiest thing in the world, as you may know. And I don't know just what is going to happen if John Y. Brown gets the club. I think Brown wants to deal McAdoo to Washington for Elvin Hayes if he gets the team, but if Snyder keeps the team long enough to make the deal, he says he will trade with us. I guess we have to try to do it; we have the nucleus of a good team, but something is missing. What do you think of Tom McMillen?"

He's referring to the gangly 6'11" forward who was celebrated by *Sports Illustrated* as a high school phee-nom, was an all-American at Maryland and was now in his second year with the Braves. "Well, just last night I was commenting to Heberlein how the guy looked about as uncoordinated as a two-hour-old chick. I've never been that impressed with him."

"Well, he makes too much money, anyhow," Schulman replied. "He makes over two hundred thousand. I guess that's why Snyder wants to unload him. They say we have to take him as part of the deal. They want Tommy and Leonard Gray for McAdoo and McMillen. Plus they want cash. We're arguing about the amount and how much interest has to be paid and all that now."

"Oh, I thought it was Green instead of Gray."

"Well, this has been going around and around for a few weeks now. I was on the phone at three A.M. in Hong Kong for I don't know how many nights. This is what they want now. Bill says it's really important so I'm doing everything I can to make the deal for him. It's going to be very expensive."

"How?"

"A lot."

"How soon do you think it will come off?"

"I don't know. It's up to Snyder and Brown to make a move now."

It was 4:30 by the time I had a story put together on my conversation with Schulman. I couldn't decide whether to go run in Boston Common, just down the street, or to take a nap. Heberlein called at 6 P.M. to find out when I wanted to head over to Boston Garden. I had fallen asleep trying to decide whether to fall asleep. Wish all decisions could be made that easily.

Charlie Scott was in the elevator going up in the rattletrap corridors of Boston Garden. The elevator attendant asked him if he thought Cowens would return this season. "Don't know," Scott replied absently. "Nobody knows."

It had developed that Cowens didn't have a rare disease, but had just, in his words, "lost my enthusiasm." That seemed pretty much like a disease, anyway, since Cowens stood for hustle and desire and the obsession for success that was the epitome of the Russell-era Celtics under the obstinate, stormy Auerbach. For Cowens to lose his enthusiasm was like Farrah Fawcett-Majors losing her hair. He had been the league's MVP in 1973, and at 6'9" was the prototype of the small, aggressive-active centers. He was the heart of the defending world champions and he had just walked into Auerbach's office one day and quit.

The decision was made all the more dramatic because it had happened to the Celtics. Cowens was as much of an oddity in sports as was the team he played for, and for that matter, the place he played, the Boston Garden—the mecca of the Master Mystique. You only have to look at those world championship banners hanging in the rafters—rows of them, thirteen in all—to realize the significance of the place, of what it stands for. This is where the greatest reign of success in pro sports history took place. It was great because, unlike the Yankees of yesteryear, there were drafts which were supposed to balance the league, but it went on and on. The place became a living legend, with Auerbach's single-minded lust for exellence forging men into a myth that will only get larger in the eyes of time. The Celtic Dynasty: Every coach in every sport called upon its professed principles of pride, togetherness and determination trying to mold their own tower of achievement. Everyone wanted to bring into their own lives that smug satisfied look that would roll over Auerbach's face as he would lean back and light up his famous victory cigar.

But while he proved to be a man with sensitivities demanding their own role, there is also an apparition in the dynasty of the Celtics—like a shamrock-green cloud softening unattractive features. There was the racism of New England which kept crowds at less than capacity during all those thirteen years that Russell and a black-dominated team won eleven titles. There was the renowned lack of sportsmanship conveyed by Auerbach, whose hotheaded and high-handed arrogance bullied players, referees, press and the league itself. And there was even the distorted image of the Garden. To the national TV eye, the checkerboard court seemed like the jewel of a beautiful sports palace, when in reality, it was a warped sheet of ill-fitting boards surrounded by four tiers of grime-green chairs. The place was and is worn-out and dreary, yet emits the scent of so many exciting memories, not unlike an old jersey from which the smell of perspiration will never completely be washed.

Bob Leonard, coach of the Indiana Pacers, once said Auerbach's key to success was that "he had the strongest hands in basketball—he held on to Russell's jersey for thirteen years." Auerbach will acknowledge Russell was at the core of all that was achieved. "Of course it began with Russell. But once we developed an identity I think we did it by convincing players that they wanted to be part of the mystique. So once they got here, they usually felt they really were part of something special. Plus, look at who we brought in. Not just quality players. Quality people. How many are or have been NBA coaches? We had more players start and finish their careers with us than the whole league combined. That was all part of the mystique."

How noble was that mystique? Let's say it had its flaws.

Cousy was probably the greatest play-making guard in the game's history. He could lay equal claim to having been one of the most competitive individuals to ever pull on a jock. "On a basketball court I had that instinct. I could climb over anyone or anything to succeed," Cousy related in his book *The Killer Instinct*. Reflecting that if winning is the American Dream, losing is the American Nightmare, Cousy expressed shame at the limits of behavior he had pushed himself to in lust for success. He tells of knocking a youngster down at his basketball camp and beating on him until he was bleeding, trying to get the ball loose. "I'm no longer so proud of the killer instinct. It may be the drive that makes a superstar in sports, sells a product or wins a war. But it can do more than blow away an opponent. It can kill the moral sense, the happiness of a family, even the man himself. It is not an instinct I can get rid of. It is something I must live with the best I can."

The killer instinct, fostered in human desires, executed in bodies that can run away from their own sense of morality. Russell's description (in *Go Up for Glory*) of the final game of the 1965 championship series against Los Angeles in the Garden tells it all: ". . . Then it became frightening, more than a mere sports event. We were not just beating this team. We were destroying it. The people were screaming. They were yelling for blood. It was like the Colosseum of Rome. They were yelling for all their frustrations, all their pent-up feelings about the world. They were egging us on to destroy, to kill, to reduce an opponent to nothing. And we were responding. We were, in a basketball sense, killing them, leaving them shattered among the ashes of their pride. We were running over them like a man might run over a floundering cripple with his car. Compelled. Unable to stop. Meshing together all the years and running like a precise, perfect machine.

"It was my worst moment in sports. There was the horror of destruction, not the joy of winning. The horror of knowing you are the instrument of the voices of man calling out: 'Destroy . . . kill . . . ruin.' "

Russell has told the story on many occasions of how he knew it was time to retire as a player the night he came over to the bench during a time-out and found himself screaming: "Come on, we can *kill* these guys. Let's *kill* 'em. Let's *kill* 'em right now!"

Auerbach is credited with a "genius" basketball mind and with an uncanny ability to pick the sort of men he could mold into the awesome prowess expressed above. But he also established a tarnished reputation for cutting corners on sportsmanship—for doing anything to gain the edge. In his book *Basketball for the Player, the Fan and the Coach*,

Auerbach lists fifty-eight moves under the heading of "Team Strategy" which he claims are listed impartially, and the player or coach can decide to adopt or not.

He once offered these two tips for winning: "Question officials' decisions, especially on the home court," and "A smart team will take advantage of the home court and the home fans. In fact, they may make moves to stimulate crowd reaction in their favor." Auerbach was notorious for calculated outbursts as a coach, evoking technical fouls and ejections to inspire his team. It all sounds afoul of the Clean Competitive Ethic we are told is noble in sports, but it can be worse than that in practice. It can be frightening.

The first trip I made into Boston Garden found Seattle and the Celts locked in a rugged struggle, characterized by a continual shoving, bumping, elbowing match between Burleson and Cowens. Finally, with 7:10 remaining, Burleson suddenly went down with Cowens on top of him, fists ablazing. As the two tumbled off the end of the court, seemingly hundreds of fans spilled across the court and out of the end seats as both squads joined the melee. People surged across the press table, knocking over chairs. I jumped the table and got out to the middle of the court. It's not a very comfortable feeling to be one of eighteen individuals who could be considered "enemy" by twelve thousand natives—and to be one of the more attractive targets. Police waded into the mob. I roamed the court, trying to keep with the flow and muttering, "Bah-stun, Bah-stun" and nobody took a poke at me. Who should appear, as things were finally settling down, but general manager Red Auerbach, standing two inches from referee Joe Gushue on the center line, screaming, his face bright red. Gushue had ejected both Cowens and Burleson. Auerbach, flanked now by the contorted face of Tom Heinsohn, kept screaming, "Go fuck yourself, Joe! Go fuck yourself! Go fuck yourself!" The sight of Auerbach throwing his tantrum at midcourt kept the crowd in a frenzy, howling from all sides and tossing things onto the court. How a riot was avoided remains a mystery. How Auerbach can justify such a lack of leadership and responsibility is an even bigger mystery.

But according to the philosophy of Leonard Koppett, he did one thing right—he kept his teams intact. Koppett, a *New York Times* sportswriter, once expressed in his column in the Sporting News: "The essential element in sports from a commercial point of view, is 'rooting interest.' No other entertainment activity offers this particular set of emotional satisfactions. Not everyone wants this feeling, but millions do, and they can't get it any other way. Rooting interest means, at bottom, vicarious victory. The feeling of winning, of beating someone, can't be obtained by any recreational activity. . . . By becoming followers of professionals who can play these games intensively, many people can get the winning-losing experience—fleetingly and indirectly, but frequently. If not for this very strong craving, commercial sports would not exist. . . ."

Koppett also expressed that this pursuit of vicarious victory must be conducted in the context of a team within a league that provides the illusion of authenticity through a history and continuity. "Most people do not have exceptional pride and integrity, only an ordinary capacity for being influenced by immediate self-interest," Koppett stated.

In that theme, there is the need for people to demand those things from their heroes to carry out the vicarious scenario. One cannot overlook the need people have for a sense of purpose, something to rally around. In times of a nationalistic cause as dramatic as say World War II, there is, among all the other human drama and tragedy, a grand sense of single-minded pursuit of a goal. Now sports, more than any other facet of our society, absorbs that need. The longing of people to belong to something cannot be overrated. Mobility and expansion have fragmented the sense of community for most people and the local sports teams are the strongest magnet available to give one a sense of belonging, of being "in this thing together." The stable team—the one that keeps the same faces—best suits the fans' need to identify with the cause.

Auerbach understood the importance of player stability, even if from management's side. For years the Celtics made fewer trades and purchases than any other team. Now the Celtics had new faces everywhere. And conflicts and maybe even the atmosphere that turned Cowens off. Auerbach would reflect: "By and large, we're seeing an erosion of basic values—things like pride and integrity and dedication—and this upsets me tremendously. You can talk all you want about new breeds and changing life-styles and the rest of it, but damn it, some things should never change. They should not be allowed to change."

But the Mystique was fading from the Masters as we invaded Boston Garden in the early rounds of the 1976–77 season. Not only was Cowens absent, but Don Nelson had retired and was coaching Milwaukee, and Silas had been dealt down the road. Scott was pointing an accusing finger across the locker room at newcomer Sidney Wicks and stating, "You're not a Celtic." JoJo White was upset because nobody went through the plays he called. Troubles for the men in green.

The Garden was as rowdy as ever, though. Just into the second quarter, with Seattle making a rally into the lead, White fell over in front of me as Watts stole the ball. A fan sitting behind me yelled, "Hey, hey you! Did you see that foul?" I looked over my shoulder and shook my head. "Well, then what the fuck are you sitting up there for?" I kept waiting for a beer to go down my neck.

The game wound up a shoot-out between Brown and Scott in the final frame. Brown banged home thirty-six points; only Green shared double figures among the Sonics. Boston had six players in double figures and won by four. Seattle's fourteenth straight road loss. In theme with all the other dilapidated facilities of the Garden, the press usually has to hold postgame court with Russell in the main corridor. Kids would shove their way into the cluster of reporters, people yell pro and con statements at Russell. It is very uncomfortable. We asked Russell if we could adjourn to the locker room. He complied and a half-dozen writers encircled Russell as he stood in the middle of the room, Sonics slowly unpeeling wet green uniforms around us. Gray, who had played only fifteen minutes, lay on a training table glowering at Russell.

A Boston writer asked Russell, "You've lost fourteen straight on the road, ten this year. What do you think is wrong with your club?"

Russell, arms folded, just stared over the top of the reporters' heads, a storm cloud on his face. Seconds passed. The silence grew, everyone studied their notebooks, their shoes. It was probably only ten seconds, but it seemed like two hours. I thought of saying something like, "Er, Mr. Russell would prefer not to answer the question." But I didn't want to act like I was working as a catalyst for him. Besides, Boston writers are supposed to be so hard-hitting. I wanted to see who was going to make the next move. Russell didn't. Finally Heberlein asked a question pertinent to the game's final minutes and the interview ran a normal course.

I looked around the locker room. Gray was still stewing in the corner, Watts and Brown were both surrounded by tape-recorder-wielding radio and news men, so I scooted down the hall to the Celtics' dressing room. Heinsohn sat in a chair near the door, his large body looking rumpled. I spotted John Havlicek standing idly on the side of the room. He hadn't played due to an injury. I had wanted to get him before the game for a possible feature, but he hadn't shown up in time. I walked over, introduced myself, and asked him if I could have a few minutes. A veteran of fifteen seasons, he has a reputation as being cooperative with the media. We leaned against the wall and I asked him how much things had really changed with the Celts—were the reports true?

"We don't have the same twelve familiar faces we had for so many years, so the pressure is on the vets to keep together as much as we can. Even when Bill left we still had a lot of vets. In 1971 I went from youth to old man in one year. JoJo is going through that now. He calls a play and no one reacts like we used to. It bothers him," Havlicek commented.

A radio reporter, packing a large tape recorder, had been wandering around the locker room, never asking a question, but sticking his mike in where others were interviewing. He came across the room and poked his mike two inches from Havlicek's nose. I'm burned, but didn't figure there was much I could do. Havlicek's a public commodity.

"I've had a few conversations with Russell on the changes in the NBA since the ABA was formed and expansion became so extensive. What changes have you seen in that regard?" I asked, the radio guy shifting his mike to my nose. I was considering kicking the guy in the stomach.

"There's definitely not the intensity there was in the league when I broke in," Havlicek answered. Another reporter came over. "I guess it's hard to get hungry with the high salaries. We used to face a situation where it meant working at a summer job if we didn't go all the way. That was real motivation. I think it'll come back as the league solidifies. But it'll take a while."

I decided to wait and see what the leeches would produce. I paused. The radioman said nothing. The reporter asked Havlicek a question about tonight's game. The radio guy whipped the mike into his face. I nodded to Havlicek and left. I caught White and Heinsohn for a couple comments and then spotted Havlicek alone again. I shot back over.

"John, if you don't mind, I'd like to pursue our conversation a few minutes more." He agreed. I asked him if there is that much difference in playing skills of the players compared to say ten years earlier.

"If you really didn't understand the game and the concepts of it, you didn't make it. Physically, there are much more talented players around today, but how many really box out, really work without the ball or give themselves up as a decoy? All these little things are taught. Auerbach made everybody do it. A lot of players used to be cut that had a lot of physical ability, but didn't understand the game. A lot of guys got in through expansion. The way the Knicks played a few years ago, it was really good basketball to watch. There was so much more to the game then than just good shooting—you set picks, you moved to make the offense work, you never relaxed on defense. Those things just aren't stressed enough now."

"What about Cowens?"

"Whenever Dave does something, it doesn't come as a total surprise. I wouldn't be surprised if he walked in tonight." The radio parasite was back. I told him, "He's all yours." I waved to John and started toward the door. Havlicek was right behind me. I thanked him for his time. I casually asked him if he thought the Celtics would get it together this year.

"This is off the record, but sometimes I feel like a stranger in here. I don't know what will happen anymore."

We headed separate ways down the corridor. I'm struck again by the comments of the longtime veterans and coaches who span what apparently was a very different era in pro basketball. The league has been diluted by expansion, players are making incredible salaries, many of them guaranteed before he ever plays a pro game. There has been a complete transposition in the racial ratio. Almost all the arenas are new and shiny, the travel—if more extensive because of expansion—is at least first-class. The changes are alien to Koppett's theories of the need for continuity and stability to create rooting interest—and yet pro basketball is drawing unprecedented attendance and TV ratings. There are plenty of sketches to be made by an observer, yet the complete picture has as many different focuses as a Dali masterpiece.

I headed up the four tiers to the press room to begin writing. Previously the press room had been in the basement and I had to pay a runner five dollars to deliver my copy upstairs to the telex operator. Now everything was in the rafters. I pounded out my story, transcribed the tape of a pregame fan interview I had conducted about Cowens and pounded out my column. It was past midnight by the time Heberlein, who had been working on some "Take-A-Shot" letters, and Boston *Globe* writer Larry Whiteside and I trudged off into the night.

It seemed like every decent restaurant was always closing down its kitchen five minutes after I would get through covering a game on the road—didn't matter exactly what time it was or what city. Whiteside found a place that was five minutes from closing down and we took advantage of the service. Then it's off to another bar, unwinding, talking out the NBA from two sides of the country.

"What happened to Bob Ryan?" I asked, being surprised that the *Globe's* veteran of nearly a decade on the Celts had been replaced.

"They took him off and put him on baseball," he explained. "He blasted Heine right in the middle of the playoffs last year. Here they were on their way to the championship and Ryan comes out saying Heine is a rotten coach. He just got too close. He lost his objectivity."

We talked about race. I told him I felt there was a barrier with a lot of the guys, not just because I'm a reporter, but because I'm white. I wondered if being a black reporter breaks through that. Whiteside said he thought it helped him some—not altogether, though. He said he thought he was too close to JoJo White. He said White was really upset with a lot of his new teammates because they don't have that dedication, that old Celtic drive. He said White told him off the record that Wicks is a lazy mother. You never can use the best stuff. He said he covered all the Celtic practices. "The press knows all the plays. They know the thirty-second play is for Havlicek. We get to know what each guy is supposed to do. When we're watching a game and a play breaks down, we know who probably is at fault." Heberlein and I agreed that there is probably a real advantage to being that thorough in covering a team, but if you aren't getting any overtime or compensatory time off, it doesn't make a guy want to volunteer to blow three hours every day watching practices in addition to covering all the trades and interviews for advances and columns and the games and all the time on the road besides. "If we really wanted to do it, we'd challenge Russell on the practice ban. But it's convenient not to have to be there under the circumstances." Whiteside said Russell had a lot of tangles with the Boston media, but there have been some real arrogant writers he had to deal with. I said they weren't exactly leaping at him tonight.

I hit the pillow at 3:15. Wake-up call came at 8:45. Philly, here we come. The airport bus was scheduled to leave at 9:30. Blackburn called at 9:10 and said the bus was leaving in five minutes. I threw things in the bags, stuck my toothbrush in my jacket and split—cursing that I would have wrinkled clothes and a full week left on the road.

17
One Jump Above the Ghetto

As the Sonics' bus scurried along Philadelphia's inner-city trails of poverty, something H. Rap Brown once wrote or said seemed tragically appropriate: "Funerals are black, weddings are white. Angel food cake is white. Judas is black, Jesus is white. We ain't won one yet."

If there ever had been style, dignity, to these buildings, it's hard to imagine in what form or how long ago. Two-, three-, four-story buildings stood side by side, with an occasional weed-pocked vacant lot indicating where decayed wood and soiled brick had somehow escaped their drearisome duty. A window patched with weathered plywood would be flanked by one from which a tired black face stared. Trash not tumbling along in the wind lay in corners and along the feet of fences and steps—as if having drifted in during an all-night blizzard. A two-story building was burned wide open in the back, a black woman hung laundry on the front-porch balcony, placing it in a race between freeze-drying and becoming so full of wind-blown dust it would have to be washed again. A mid-fifties Olds sat on its wheel drums, windows punched in, hood and doors gone, engine sitting in six inches of sooty snow on the sidewalk. A black youngster, five years old at the most, bounced up and down on the car's rusted roof.

The hawk, "the almighty hawk" as Lou Rawls immortalized in song, sucked at the people scurrying along the sidewalks. Black faces—nowhere was there a white one—cringed against the wind inside of upturned coat collars. Corner visits moved quickly into little dark doorways which wore neon signs saying "Bar" or "Cocktails." Even the raw December sky seemed particularly drab, particularly defeating. The scene ached for the mournful blues of a Jimmy Reed or a Robert Nighthawk or a Billie Holiday, a Muddy Waters—someone whose voice and music convey this sort of sadness.

But there was only the jabber of the Sonics, traveling in an isolation booth. Mike Bantom continued to lecture flippantly on various landmarks. As the bus crossed the intersection of Broad and Vine, he sang out, "There it is. There's my high school, Ol' Roman Catholic High. City champs 1969. Look back there, see that old hoop—that's where I learned to do it."

The backboard, battered and bent slightly forward, was tucked into a pocket playground surrounded by three sides of Roman Catholic's brick walls. It was on that concrete playground during lunchtime games that Bantom had come to grasp his potential for basketball achievement—and accompanying escape from the ghetto.

By his own definition, Bantom was always "one jump above the ghetto," but his passage through the bitter world of drugs, gang fights and the antiproductive cultural setting of the inner city provides an insight into an environment from which few escape. Those who break through are celebrated to some degree, but more often, the stand of white middle-class America is to condemn those who don't make it out.

"I'm not a genius and I'm not dumb," assessed Bantom. "There was so much that I was not aware of—until somebody fortunately kind of showed me things and guided me along. There is so little to do and so little motivation to do anything about it—you just don't feel like you can do anything about it even if you tried. There are libraries around, but if you're not conditioned to use a library or brought up to see the value of an education, well, you get an image from the street that an education is negative. You are kind of held down by the other guys on the street—like everyone is more comfortable when you stay down.

"If you don't have someone you trust, and trust is very rare, to come in and tell you things, you just aren't going to see any way to get exposed to anything beyond the streets. I look back at the number of breaks that have happened to me and I shudder to think what might have happened. There were a lot of people in high school that I thought were pretty hip to what was going on in the world, but they ended up bad—on drugs, just hanging out. And now I see their younger brothers doing the same thing.

"I always had a strong desire to make a lot of money, but I didn't have any idea how I could go about it until I became aware of my ability to make it in pro basketball. Most guys never have a chance like that."

Bantom climaxed what could safely be called a "storybook" rise to success when Phoenix drafted the 6'9", 210-pound forward in the first round in 1973. He signed a five-year contract for $150,000 annual salary, which pretty well established his escape from the streets. He spent two seasons with the Suns before Seattle bought him just as the 1975–76 season was getting under way.

"My mother and father were divorced when I was about three, but she did a pretty good job raising myself and my two sisters. We lived in a housing project until I was about ten. There was a lot of poverty around but it was a new project and it hadn't started to deteriorate yet," Bantom related.

This was on the North Side of Philly, one of that tough city's toughest areas. Wilt Chamberlain, Hal Greer and Chet Walker used to play at a recreation center near Bantom's project house until the neighborhood became too rough.

"When I was about ten I got what I consider a big break. We moved about ten blocks further north to a predominantly white working-class neighborhood. This area was cleaner and had more open space and that's why I say I've been spared a lot of the frustrations of living in the worst of the ghetto."

However, leaving his all-black neighborhood planted the youngster in his first exposure to racism.

"The situations I had lived in before were the result of racism, but I was oblivious to that then. I was one of three blacks in my new class and had to deal with name calling and stuff like that," Bantom continued. "I developed that same kind of prejudice toward whites—sort of a protection reaction."

Bantom wasn't into basketball for anything but fun through grade school, limiting his time to half-court games among "not very good" kids in his own neighborhood. He didn't make the freshman or sophomore squads at Roman Catholic. "I was excited if I could just make a layup during the warm-ups for tryouts." Until he was thirteen or fourteen Bantom hung pretty close to his immediate neighborhood, as did all youngsters. Gang warfare was, and still is, a dictator of one's activities in the inner city.

"If you went into another area and weren't recognized you got the hell beat out of you. Kids were shot and stabbed for no apparent reason. When I got older I was kind of a risk-taker and I always felt like I could run pretty fast, so if I was careful not to walk right into the middle of something, they had a hard time catching me."

Bantom, who by this time was a gangly 6'5", started going to a playground half a dozen blocks from his home to get involved with a better brand of basketball. "I had to walk through the territory of two other gangs. It wasn't too bad going down there around five o'clock, but when the sun went down and you were coming home at ten you had something to think about. But I used to go down there every day.

When you're tall and look like you don't have much strength guys are always wanting to mess with you. There was almost no way I could make it back from the playground without somebody wanting to start something. Turning around corners was the biggest thing—if you walked around a corner into a group of twenty guys there was nothing you could do.

"There were a couple of times I walked right into it and had to deal with it from there. Those weren't too pleasant. But guys who went to public schools had to deal with it every day right in the halls. In one neighborhood for about two years every kid got beat up badly at one time or another because they had to cross through another gang's territory to go to junior high school."

Eventually joining a gang seems like the intelligent way toward survival. Bantom thought so for a while and joined the Cool World. "We came to the playground one day and these guys told us they were going to form a gang and wanted us to join. They presented it in such a way that it almost seemed crazy not to. They said, 'We're not looking to start any trouble with anybody. This is just a social club and if anyone jumps you, you at least have some friends who'll help ya out.' That sounded good to me.

"When we had our first meeting there were about fifty to seventy-five guys there and a couple of guys right away wanted to get some guns and get this other gang called the Village. This was the gang that lived in the neighborhood of the junior high school they all attended. There were some particular dudes they wanted to get and start this gang war. I said, 'Hey, wait a minute, I thought there wasn't going to be none of that.' They said, 'Well, hey man, that's what's happenin'.' So me and my cowardly buddies decided we wanted to get out—which wasn't as easy as getting in, but we managed."

That little courtyard hoop behind Roman Catholic High became the scene of lunchtime games. It was the extent of the school's physical educational facilities and, as Bantom described it, wasn't much bigger than an NBA free-throw lane. "We used to go out there after this priest started bringing a ball out during the lunch period. We'd take off our jackets and ties and really get into it. Before my junior year this priest asked if I was going to turn out for the team. I hadn't even come close to making the sophomore team and I told him I wasn't planning on turning out again. But he talked me into it.

"I had never played full court up till that time. I really didn't know what was going on. Sometimes there was only one basket up or there were too many people to get a full court. I had been playing at this one playground where the guys weren't very good. As I started to improve I wanted better competition and started to go down to this other place about seven blocks away. As the sun would go down the guys would start to come out. There were some pretty good players, a lot of them from the public schools. You'd just come down and wait your turn and then try and win so that you could stay out there.

"I really didn't concentrate on my game that much until after I had made the team as a junior. I just played junior varsity that year, I had so much to learn. Where I really got a chance to develop my game was in the summer before my senior year. I played in three summer leagues. I was playing every night of the week. I started to get my confidence. I had to go out of my neighborhood for that. There was this friend of our coach who would come around and pick me up and take me all the way out to some suburb area where we'd play. This is what I mean by getting a break.

"We'd go out and get sandwiches with the other guys after these games. That's when I first had my eyes opened as to what it means to be a person and relate to other people. When I started going off with this guy I used to get a lot of heat from my friends. 'Why the hell you gotta go off with this dude?' they'd ask. But they were just playing with the same guys on the same playground and going out and drinking a couple of quarts of beer every night—I'd come back later and catch up with them, but I rarely missed anything."

Booze gave way to drugs about this time on the streets and the scene changed. "Drugs came in initially as a thrill thing," offered Bantom. "I remember when drugs first came around our neighborhood. It was like if you smoked pot you were a junkie. It spread and after a while it became the thing to do. You get loaded and you alter your sense of where you are. You're still in the same situation doing the same thing, but your mind is altered a little bit and so it doesn't seem like the same old grind. It used to be wine and beer before dope came around. All the hoods were drinking wine and then they all were smoking dope. The scene changed on the streets then in that when gangs would get loaded on wine these guys would get in a wild mood and want to beat on people for fun. But things cooled out a little when guys got into grass and drugs.

"That's where a lot of these guys were at who I was leaving behind when I went off to play ball in the suburbs. These guys just didn't have an opportunity to see anything else and now days they're still just hanging out, getting loaded and, like they say, 'just tryin' to make it, man.' "

As Bantom approached his senior year he started to believe in his abilities to play ball. He came into his final high school year at 6'7" and suddenly found himself as the best big man in the city. "Nobody expected us to be that good, but we were really disciplined. We had a coach who demanded it, didn't ask. We won the city title." Bantom was named to the all-city team in his first and only varsity season.

"Up until that time I had no thought of going to college. I was always a fairly good student, but within the family and within the culture I was living there was never any thought of it. You had nothing to really compare yourself to—nobody else was going to college." His rapidly developed basketball prowess was the ticket college coaches were willing to offer, though. And some of Bantom's courtside associates were getting more than tuition dangled in front of them. "People were getting cars and talking about receiving cash and everything, but I didn't find anybody offering me any of this and I wondered why. I didn't want to get too far away from home so that I could still kind of take care of my mother and my sisters and I was really impressed with the spirit at St. Joseph's, so I stayed right in Philadelphia.

"I wasn't thinking of pro ball then, but I knew if I could just make it through college I would be all right. What if I hadn't made it to college? You know I really hate to think about that, because after college I felt like I could get into whatever I wanted. Even if I hadn't gone into ball, I think I would have been okay."

After his junior year at St. Joseph's, Bantom competed in the Olympic trials. "I didn't think I had enough publicity and came from too small a school to make the team, but I found out I was better than a lot of these cats and from that point on I thought I was going to be a pro." This was the squad that included other future pros like Tommy Burleson, Jim Brewer, Doug Collins, Dwight Jones, Ed Ratleff and Tom Henderson. This was also the squad that became the first Yankee cagers to ever lose an Olympic game when the Soviet Union came out of that stormy championship game in Munich with the title.

From the Olympics to the pro ranks the following year, Bantom clearly had realized achievements few even bother to dream about—especially those locked into the defeating realm of the ghetto. "There are all those people still living in the projects that I was in twenty years ago. It's just the breaks as to who gets out."

18
Finally, in Philly

Half an hour before game time in the Spectrum, I was putting together some work notes: Sonics fourteen straight road losses, ten this year . . . last win, 3/10 at Milwaukee . . . third of four games in five nights . . . at New York tomorrow night . . . Seattle won against 76ers 11/7 at home, 98–91 . . . Bantom 25th birthday. Born in Philly . . .

I sat back and relaxed while the teams went through their warm-ups with The Song soaring into the rafters. It seemed as though we had been on the road two weeks, instead of only five days. A week ago tonight we had been at home against Chicago. Forty-eight hours ago we were in Boston. Twenty-four hours ago Furtado and I had been sitting in the hotel restaurant eating dinner, filling time. Time On The Road: It hangs on humps, seemingly stopped, then it's suddenly gone in big lumps.

In my room that afternoon I had reflected on the sluggishness the road life breeds. Maybe that accounts as much as anything for the one-sided loss records most everyone produces on the road. Stuffy rooms, windows usually sealed. One's metabolism gets lulled into low gear as he lies around, trying to relax, using up the hours, keeping off his feet. And after a whole day spent dozing and watching the tube and eating, he's listless of body, even if his head is anxious to attack.

At least dinner got a guy out of his room. A couple Scotches, a salad, a steak, talk, talk, talk. The previous evening's discussions with Furtado covered the Sonic world. I mentioned how it seemed so absurd that the guys were working against each other. There didn't seem to be any positive leadership. Players were working against Russ, against each other, against themselves the way some of them live on the road. "I should be writing it, Frank. But what can I really tell the fans? I've already said there is dissension. I've already said Russ should be more open. You know how when you're involved with a group like this you want to make it come together, to realize its potential, as they say." I told him about my hallway discussion with Russell earlier in the season. He said I had a "savior complex"—trying to make everything right for everybody. A tough task, especially since it's just my opinion against theirs as to what is right.

At that point, Green, wearing his green warm-up pants and a faded T-shirt with "Adidas" on the front, came loping across the dining room. People turned their heads. He came over, pulled up a chair. He looked as though he hadn't fully awakened from a hard sleep.

"Hey, man, where's my bag?"

Furtado replied: "Should have been sent up to your room."

"Aw, well, I can't find it. Hey, man, I don't feel good."

"What's the matter?"

Green stared at him, at me, stood up and said as he started away, "Wouldn't matter if I told you. Wouldn't matter." And he walked away.

Furtado and I looked at each other, looked at the people around us, who quickly looked back at their plates. We couldn't even think of anything to say, so we didn't.

Stuffed, but not ready to face the four walls and the tube, we continued. We agreed the hassle over the playoff shares last spring seemed to have set the stage for this season's friction.

The playoff pool hadn't been as much as the players had planned on receiving, because they hadn't planned on Phoenix knocking them off in the first round. The shares amounted to less than five thousand each. Greed spilled the banks when it came time to count out the portions. Watts, Bantom and Gray had led a move to vote not even crumbs to individuals who had much more the year before. They, the team, had voted no shares to Oleynick and John Hummer and only a half share to Furtado, in contrast to a full share the previous season. Hopkins had received a full share the previous year, this season none. Office workers had received three hundred dollars each, same with the ball boys, the year before. Nothing this time around. Russell reportedly intervened and ordered another meeting to provide partial shares for Hummer and Oleynick, who had played less than full seasons due to injuries—but in Oleynick's case only fourteen fewer games than the also-injured Gray. Hummer stomped out of the meeting charging his teammates with being "racially prejudiced" and told them their selfishness would destroy the morale of the team the next season. He was right.

We ordered after-dinner drinks. Furtado said, "It didn't matter so much about the money. If they had just even said, 'Thanks for the good job,' that would have meant a lot." I reflected how I can't ever remember hearing a pro ballplayer say "please" or "thank you." Furtado adds: "These guys are something. They're continually trying to beat me on cab money. Why would guys making hundreds of thousands of dollars scramble for an extra two bucks?" We sipped our drinks. Furtado said after a minute, "They don't seem to be aware of other people, those on the fringe, as they see it. The night we were in Indianapolis, Bobby Knight came into the locker room to see Wilkerson and Russ. He was introduced to everybody in there but me."

We tried to think of something besides basketball to discuss, but the momentum of the road wouldn't let go.

"You think the club will win one this road trip, Frank?" I asked.

"Yeah, I know it sounds crazy, but I think we will win tomorrow night. If Tommy comes to play, I think we can knock off these guys."

"Can't see it, Frank. You know I figured something out about T this morning while I was lying in bed. Tommy makes just about forty dollars an hour around the clock every day of the year. Isn't that a trip?"

Furtado agreed that was a trip.

"And you know what else? The meatball was complaining to Blackburn that Russ has been putting too much pressure on him to come out ready to play every night," I continued.

"Just because a guy is making a lot of money does that mean he's supposed to rise above normal human characteristics?" Furtado asked.

"I don't know. But I think I've figured out something about

Tommy. I had this long talk with him when we were in K.C. It seemed like he was just dogging it, not giving a damn on those nights when he wasn't getting the job done. Yet he really got incensed when I suggested that some of the guys were playing without any pride. I mean, I don't think it was an act, he really wanted to have no part of this team if he was sure people weren't trying all the time. So I think what it is with him is that he's just a guy who has the physical size to be good at basketball and so he gets hired for the job, but he's really not a very combative sort. It's really not natural for him to go out and get fired up and be at the peak of his physical and mental efficiency every night. Not like a Watts, for example. So he's actually just locked into trying to be something he isn't."

We agreed that Russell must be looking at Burleson along those lines if he wanted to deal him. Seems strange, too, we agreed, to have Burleson going—he being the guy everyone figured Russell would mold into the next great center.

Furtado proved to be a prophet as the team finally found victory on the road the next night. Bantom had come out and scored ten birthday points in the first quarter. Burleson had played a whale of a game, twenty rebounds for the awakened giant. Watts had banged in twenty-seven points, Brown twenty-nine. And Brown had tied a league game mark with ten steals. Russell had gone with the veterans for the most part, except for using Bantom just that first quarter and Green a total of three minutes.

Russell came out of the locker room and began, "Unaccustomed as I am . . ." The Sonics were like high-schoolers after the state finals. It was a wild scene. The vets went out of their way to make sure we understood that the reason they had won was that Russell had gone with "the experience under pressure." Bury the kids. I went down to the 76ers' dressing room, found Erving tucked into a closetlike cubicle with ice bags on each knee. He explained how Seattle had taken control of the passing lanes and "got us into their free-lance game." McGinnis didn't think the 76ers played very well down the stretch. Dawkins was too busy stuffing pop cans into an airline bag to discuss the matter and Shue was just generally disgusted. I went back down to the Sonic dressing room to see if I could catch a couple of players who had been busy with radio interviews earlier. Russell met me coming out of the room.

"Let me ask you a question," he said seriously. "Why would anyone say, 'What was wrong with Mike Bantom?' "

"I don't know, guess that was a Philly writer," I said, trying to figure out what he was driving at.

"No, Greg asked that after the game. I thought Mike played a good game."

"I think he meant why didn't he come back in after the first quarter."

Russell said, "Oh," and walked out of the Spectrum.

I was curious myself, but something told me not to chase after Russell.

I went to work on the typewriter:

PHILADELPHIA—They came swaggering down the hall on the way to their dressing room, arm-in-arm, drunk with joy, bellowing a chorus of "Happy Birthday, Mike Bantom, Happy Birthday to Youoooooo. . . ."

The image of sailors finally ashore after a long, horrible cruise was not completely inappropriate. The Sonics had just broken a 14-game road losing streak. . . .

"The home teams wait for a break. You give it to them and that's your ass," chortled Bantom, who was born 25 years ago yesterday in this city and launched the Sonics with 10 first quarter points. "We don't give them anything when they needed it. . . ."

The team was off to New York via bus while Heberlein and I followed later in a rented car. In the myriad of topics that went down with the beer and the miles, I mentioned how awkward it was trying to figure out how much Burleson, Gray and the rest of the team knew about the trade. The players seemed to have good connections to Seattle, so they certainly would have word about the stories we had run out of Buffalo.

Heberlein said, "Tommy told me on the plane coming down from Boston he didn't think Russell would trade him without telling him first."

"Oh, Jesus. He'll be totally in the doldrums when he finds out."

"I feel like we're on the threshold of disaster," Heberlein commented, laughing. "I think a lot of things are going to come tumbling down before things get better. I don't know what, but I feel it."

"Oh, by the way, Russ asked me why you wanted to know what was wrong with the way Bantom played. When I told him you probably wanted to know why he hadn't used him anymore after the first quarter, he just said, 'Oh,' and walked away."

"He probably just forgot about him down there on the bench," Heberlein suggested. "He's sure hard to figure out."

"I know. It's funny how everybody has a tendency to accuse him of screwing up, rather than being shrewd, just because he does things different from the norm. If the team was doing well, he'd be a weird genius," I added.

"Now he's just weird.'

"Well, for publication, we might go with: 'Bill Russell is very unorthodox and highly suspect.' "

"Suspect of what?" Heberlein asked.

"How about, suspected of stealing a quarter of a million bucks a year from Sam Schulman," I offered. "But, then, he really isn't. The Coliseum is always full, the team is winning more games than half the teams in the league. Sure is crazy how mediocrity shines in the NBA." I dug through the box scores as he drove. "Look at this. Bantom gets twelve points in fifteen minutes and sits the rest of the way tonight. Burleson plays six minutes against Boston and doesn't get back in. Bantom gets eight points and four boards in thirteen minutes at Buffalo and doesn't get back in. He gets five points and four boards in a quarter against Washington and he sits. Burleson goes eleven against Chicago, doing all right, and sits the night. He gets some decent stats in fourteen against Phoenix and sits. He's a disaster in eleven against Buffalo and I can see why he left him out. He's rolling along in fourteen against Indiana and that's it. He's got fifteen against K.C. in twenty and sits. Oh, I don't know. I guess you can pick apart anybody's strategy—it just seems like the big guy needs more time to get warmed up. But maybe Russ is right. Oh, Christ! All I ever do is talk basketball."

Chewing Core in the Big Apple

"Ting . . . ting . . . ting . . ." The sound of a tiny monastery bell.

The hotel room door opened as I opened my eyes. The heavy voice of a maid called out, "Check-un, check-un?"

"I'm in here," I called out, irritated. She slammed the door. I looked at my watch. Nine A.M. Now I was really irritated. Down the hall I could hear, "Ting . . . ting . . . ting . . . Check-un, check-un . . . Slam . . . Ting . . . ting . . ." Probably the rip-off crew getting an early start. I tossed and rolled. The bed squeaked like a mouse every time I took a deep breath. A child's bed in Boston. A saggy double in Philly. A squeaky king in New York. Probably get a trampoline hooked up to an air horn in New Orleans.

Blackburn called to see if I wanted to go to a play. Sure. I hauled my tape recorder, typewriter and other valuables down to the hotel safe. The previous year's painful lesson wasn't going to be repeated. I had gone out to Aqueduct for the afternoon, came back to find traveler's checks, jewelry, typewriter and a pair of sunglasses picked off and long gone into the New York washing machine. The corned-beef-

and-cabbage hotel detective and his oily assistant said they "just about had the guys. Ran out the fire escape." Sure. How did you guys divide it up? Fifty percent for the dick, 25 percent for the assistant and the balance for the Scout Maid? Tell me about it. Malicious thoughts, but every time I saw the dick and his pal stationed on my floor, "keeping an eye out," I couldn't help wonder who was getting dipped behind closed doors. A lot of paranoia in New York—paranoia capital of the country. But remember, even paranoids have real enemies.

The matinee was packed. *The Comedians* was well done. A group of hope-to-be comedians struggling for a start in a British comic's school. Sort of a Lenny Bruce conviction. The protagonist with his message for the people, his intolerance for their hypocrisy. His message makes society uncomfortable, so, as society has a way of doing, it chews him up and buries his angry, tormented soul.

It was an unkind afternoon, dull and cold, when I came out of the theater. I was tired, but wanted to go uptown. I asked Heberlein if he wanted to go check out the old neighborhood. He wasn't interested. You can't relive memories with others, anyway. I climbed down into the subway to await the IRT uptown. Same funky smell. Same graffiti on the pale yellow tile walls—different messages, different cries for attention, different protests, different heroes. But the same graffiti. Poster ads with mustaches drawn on, eyes poked out, racial slashes. Fifty cents a ride now. What was it, fifteen cents when I was here in '64? The subway came hammering out of the dark tunnel, single headlight growing bigger, noise louder—going so fast, slammed to a stop. The pale blue exteriors of the cars were covered with Day-Glo messages, calling cards in huge swirling lines like "Aqua-Leopard 1." Where do they get the time to be so elaborate? Must be at the car barns. Distinctively New York City. Aerosol-Art.

Off at 116th. Up onto Broadway. Same background of sirens, always sirens. And the cabs, pounding along, rattling fenders and bumpers as they go too fast on the beat-up streets. Cabs swerving, blatting their horns at old pedestrians struggling to survive in a world going too fast. Onto the Columbia University campus. The Keep Off the Grass signs gone—the grass gone—the last attempts at aesthetic beauty having been trampled by the campus riots in 1968. A wave of melancholy swept into my chest as I looked at Hartley Hall—up there, in that window, that room's floor had been my bed. I had come to New York—the city, I thought, the countryside it turned out—to play ball (as opposed to attend school) at C. W. Post College on Long Island. I soon dealt with priorities, quit school, moved into my buddies' room at Columbia, played ball by day and ran the streets by night. Romantic? I saw it that way then. Such a sense of adventure, going to try yourself in the CITY. It was running away to sea, joining the circus. It was going to the big pond.

I crossed Amsterdam Avenue and looked down through Morningside Park into Harlem. The sky, gloomy and threatening rain, gave no warmth to the brown-gray buildings below. The leaves on the ground left silhouetted branches to frame my view. Winter sat like a hawk, perched, waiting to move in and make life even more uncomfortable for those who had no cushion against their environment. I felt as though I were looking across the Berlin Wall at forbidden territory.

A sweltering, sun-glow picture came before my eyes as I recalled the late afternoon three of us had walked down the steps through Morningside Park on 116th to catch an IND on Lexington Avenue up to Yankee Stadium. There had been riots earlier that summer. As we descended into Harlem the streets had been filled with noise and color—a gaiety, a carnival atmosphere with men and women sitting on the stoops, leaning against signs that read "Do Not Sit on the Stoop" and "To Be Demolished." Children ran among parked cars, played on concrete stained by the wastes of man and machine. Names and lines for games were painted over dried blood, spilled whiskey, rotted food. Squeals of little children, the music of the Shirelles, the Drifters, Ray Charles, James Brown, the Ronettes, the Coasters, drifting out of upper-story windows and out of bars. It was a picnic atmosphere in the streets. Except they didn't have anywhere else to go. Then someone spat at us from a stoop and someone else threw a half-empty pop can and people were calling names. One of us was from New York. He said to just look down, don't say anything, keep moving, hope they let us through. They did.

I was wounded. I was crushed. This wasn't the way it was supposed to be. What about the Apollo Theater on Saturday night? What about all those Friday and Saturday nights out in Seattle, standing around the kitchen drinking beer and listening to the black radio station. Hey, we knew when Pat Boone and Paul Anka and Frankie Avalon and the rest of those safe-as-milk honkies were making all the money recording your songs that it was wrong. We bought Fats Domino and Chuck Berry and Little Richard and James Brown. Hey, James Brown, that album of his: "Saturday Night Live at the Apollo," hey, we knew. We knew. We listened to that album, man. We wanted to be there, up on 125th Street on Saturday night when they lifted the movie screen up and King Coleman, in his raspy hype, stepped out on the stage and wailed: "And now, ladies and gentlemen, the star attraction on tonight's show. Mr. Dyno-mite. Mr. Please, Please, Please Himself. Lost Someone. The hardest working man in show business. Mistah *James Brown.* . . ." And his band was thrusting like a stud at service and the girls were screaming. Man, Negroes even sound like music screamin'. And then He was there shouting, moaning in that torn, tortured voice.

We heard you hollering and screaming as he would glide around on the stage and act like he had fainted and get up and fall down and get up and the band was just pounding on and he kept singing and sweat was pouring off him, flying like a boxer's. And you were all sweatin' and drinking Southern Comfort. We just wanted to be there, too.

But they didn't want Whitey there. This was theirs. White man uses and abuses. Even if he invites you to come play ball for him. He's just using you. He don't want to give you nothing, just takes. Fuck Whitey. Kill Whitey. Slay the oppressive pig. Say it loud—I'm black and I'm proud.

The cold wind was collecting smoke out of chimneys and sending soft sooty clouds southward over the rooftops of five-story-deep Harlem. And down across 110th into another neighborhood, down Manhattan—a concrete honeycomb with the greatest of culture and commerce, the most famous of people, pocked in among the worst of depression, crime, human anguish. It scares and it consumes.

I walked back along the south end of the campus—past massive churches, their huge wood and iron doors beckoning as refuge from all the noise and torment outside. I walked along Columbia's Greek Row—worn buildings with battered ironwork. What isn't worn and battered in New York City? I turned the corner, where thirteen years earlier, coming the other way, I had stumbled upon a mob filling the streets. I had waded through, wondering what the occasion was. Suddenly I was standing next to Bobby Kennedy, afloat in this sea of people. Grinning, shaking hands, saying, "Thankew, thankew" to all those who wished him well in his bid to become state senator. I reached out, shook his hand. People were jostling and he was bracing himself and smiling and being plowed slowly toward a waiting limousine. He reached it, stepped on the hood, climbed onto the roof. He stood there, waving, arms raised over his head as the limousine moved slowly through the mob, flashbulbs popping in the evening dusk. He was just a man, but there was a grand pageantry in his presence. I now looked down the vacant street. I shook Bobby Kennedy's hand right there. I felt on the verge of tears.

I retreated into the West End Café and leaned over a beer, trying to get the tightness out of my throat. The West End had been a college hangout in the mid-sixties, the back booths adorned with pictures of the few glorious moments Columbia had enjoyed in football. They were old, faded pictures. Now the place was void of any college connections. They were putting some good jazz in there. Restored by a couple of drafts, I swung back onto the streets. It was getting darker, colder. If those clouds opened up it might be snow as well as rain. The vegetable trays in front of stores, newspaper stands, pyramids of garbage stacked in bags and cans—everything out on the streets. A painted plaster statue of Jesus poked out of a box of trash, its head busted off. I picked it up and set it on a stoop ledge. It fit.

I swung down Riverside Drive. People walked toy poodles and killer shepherds for their nightly deposits on sidewalks and the scrubs of grass that refused to die in Riverside Park. The Hudson River was across the park and the West Side Highway. Used to be beautiful up here. Exclusive neighborhood. Not anymore. Still costs incredible rents for apartments with three locks on the door and bars on the windows. I checked to see if a friend was in. Not there.

I headed down Riverside. There's the playground. The park playground scene has almost become a cliché. I guess New York has almost become a cliché. But beneath all the prose, both are real. They were real when I was first here. Not much was written about the playground then. It hadn't become vogue to talk about the guys who learned their game on the blacktop, to celebrate those who escape with hope from the world of wine and dope, to immortalize those who didn't escape. For me, that first Saturday morning in this park was a living dream—a love affair with the self-image of playing on the street with blacks—they were called Negroes then—in the Big Apple.

That day was the first time I heard someone say, "Basketball is poetry." I don't remember the guy's name. He picked me up in a yellow Olds, this guy who lived up by the George Washington Bridge. I'd met him at Post. We would have been playing somewhere up in Harlem, except my white ass wouldn't have been worth a bag of rags if we went up there, he said. He'd said he'd be down at 10 A.M. if it wasn't raining. It wasn't. In fact it was one of those rare days in New York when the sea breezes somehow muster enough courage to come in past the Verrazano-Narrows Bridge and rout out all of that smog. As we got down to the courts, I was struck with two things in such a contrast to the gyms I hung out at in the West. In addition to the cracked concrete courts, the rims were all bent downward—thanks to all that slamming and dunking that everyone over 4'9" seemed to feel compelled to do. The other thing was that I, being the only white there, also was the only guy in shorts instead of sweat-caked Levi's. It didn't take me long to realize how sweat-caked Levi's protect one when sliding on cracked concrete.

There were two balls on hand, one a lopsided rubber beauty and the other an old leather globe, pounded slightly out of shape and worn smooth as a baby's butt by the concrete. It felt slippery and uncomfortable to me, yet some of these guys had no trouble palming it for one-handed stuffs through the netless rim and putting all sorts of wild English off the old steel backboard—which rattled and resounded with a hollow *ker-bang* on every shot.

We played three-on-three, half court, and nobody passed the ball unless they got stuck in the air with six hands all over them. Connie

Hawkins was the hero of the playgrounds in that day, the Hawk. A basketball in his hands was like a grapefruit for the normal man. Everybody on the playground, it seemed, was holding the ball out in one hand (shoe polish and bowler's stickum were popular with playground fingers) and trying to take that big stiff-legged step to the hoop. Everybody's game was patterned after a player. Dave Bing, then a junior at Syracuse, was big. Chamberlain was averaging about forty a game in the NBA with the Warriors, but no one could identify with his size. Lew Alcindor was a senior at Power Memorial. I heard talk about this 7′6″ kid who was going to be better than Wilt, but I didn't see him. There were a couple of Gus Johnson fans who animaled the boards. But beside the Hawk, Elgin Baylor was the man. All his characteristics were emulated, mainly the quick-shuffle travel he usually committed before taking off the hoop. His head twitch was pretty big, too—the guy bringing the ball down one side or the other flinching his head to the side. That's the ultimate of superstardom when people imitate your idiosyncrasies.

The player's GAME is the man. "Bring you GAME." He stands for his action. What can you do—who are you? Up in the Paawk. In your face, mother-fucker. It ain't who wins. It's whose move is the coolest, whose move puts the other man down. Come on, try me. Come on, you ain't got shit. Take me. Try me. It's jive, it's talkin' shit, it's laughin' and slappin' hands. But it's as serious as a man's first love affair. He's rocking back and forth, pounding the ball, backing in Oscar Robertson style. Come on, man, try me. Shoot through, shoot over—in your face, mother-fucker. He works for hours, days on new shots. There's a ticket out of here if he gets good enough. But mainly it's just the best thing to do with time. Playing ball is some recognition. He's broke. He's black. He's got nothing else going. But he can play ball. He can play. He's somebody. And when he goes off to college and the coach wants him to Sacrifice for the Team, he says, No, man, I can't give up *me*. And if he gets to be *me* through college, then he can't give it up for no pro coach. Maybe he'll be one of the guys who *can* play, but who wash themselves away because they never get past being on display. There might be as many guys who wash out that way as there are to the sea of drugs and crime and inability to show up somewhere on time.

After we had played for a couple of hours that Saturday in '64, everybody but us trooped up the steps and disappeared, chugging their OJ and Coke. I stayed to shoot with Yellow Olds. We rapped as we shot. The sky seemed like it was very clear and blue, hard to imagine a clear sky in New York, as it is. The old leather globe coming off the fingers, floating, spinning against the blue and then banging off the board or dropping silently through the netless rim. He said it was poetry. It was the motion of man's body and his inner music, he said. The man's on his game. He's got rhythm. If there had been a net and a nicer ball and a tighter backboard, it would have been finer, but that day in the park, Yellow Olds planted a precious seed of appreciation in me for basketball's poetic beauty.

That is never purer than when you are shooting alone. Moving, shooting smoothly through the net. Swish. Swish. The net dancing softly like a hula skirt. Pure poetry. There is a ballet in the team game, in the running the court and the flying to the hoop. In the delicate fadeaway jumper. But it begins to become cluttered with bumping and hanging and jarring as a team game. And then there are plays and execution is disciplined and defined and you set picks and you make sure you don't get called for being too long in the key or not getting a shot off against the clock. It becomes something different—still beautiful to patrons of the court—but not the essence. No other sport has as its heart an art form. Those who learn that on the playground always resent giving that up—some can't.

It was dark and starting to drizzle as I left my reverie in the park and trudged against the wind back to Broadway to catch the IRT to the hotel. As I climbed the stairs to the street and walked to the hotel I ran into Watts, coming out of a cheap-o clothing store with a fake fur cossack cap. He had it pulled down to eye level, the yellowish-brown synthetic fur sparkling with the drizzle.

"Hey, B.J., check this out," he called eagerly. "You gotta check this place out. Man, they got coats and boots and look at this hat. And this stuff is really inexpensive. Get yourself a hat, man. Beat the hawk." I looked in the window, decided I didn't see anything too appealing and we walked down to the hotel. As we hit the door, Seals was crossing the lobby in his green warm-ups. There were eight, maybe a dozen, autograph hounds patrolling the lobby. They jumped on him as he waited for the elevator. They had twenty-dollar books like *The Pro Game*—full of color pictures of the players in action. Those books, and collecting cards and programs and souvenir pictures, wore autographs of nearly everyone who mattered in the league. One had a magazine with Seals checking Erving from the ABA days.

"Hey, Bruce," one adolescent called out. "Bruce, how'd you like playing in Utah? Whatta ya think the Doctor will do in the NBA? Hey, sign this, will ya?"

Another young teen-ager, who must have been over six feet, thin as a rifle barrel, handed Seals a paperback that profiled each player in the league. He had Seals sign across his thumbnail sketch.

"Who you?" they asked me. "Who you with?" I didn't fit any pictures in any of the books. Probably a nobody, but gotta check. I told them I was just a writer and they immediately had some uses for me:

"Hey, could you get Russell to sign this? He never signs nothin'."

"He doesn't, you're right. Not for me. Not for nobody."

"Shit. Hey, where do you think Tommy Burleson is? Think he'll be comin' down this elevator or the one on the other side of the lobby?"

"Don't know."

"Hey, where's Slick? You seen Slick around?"

"Yeah, he's around," I answered, wondering what the hell was taking the elevator so long, and knowing that Watts must have found someone attractive to discuss the weather with, since he had borrowed 25 cents to go into the newsstand for a paper. Seals patiently signed away as the youngsters kept producing more and more items to be autographed. Watts came trooping around the corner. His cossack-hat threw the pen gang off for a second.

"B.J., what's happenin'? Bruce, what's happenin'?" He handed me a nickel's change and flipped through the paper.

"Hey, you Slick Watts?"

"Could be," Watts answered, flipping absently through the *Post*, handing it to me, somehow all disheveled in ten seconds flat. "Yeah, I'm Slick. What's happenin' with you fellas?" He was grinning and taking pen in hand. The elevator finally arrived and the kids piled in to keep contact with Watts. "Think you'll get McAdoo for Burleson?" the tall one asked. Seals shrugged. They no sooner stepped off on their floor when the oily assistant house detective jumped out at them. "Hey, I told you kids to get out of here. Now get in that elevator." The kids dropped their smiles and fell back into the elevator. "Hey, Slick, give me my book!" Watts handed it to him as the door closed. "Shit, he didn't finish signing his name," *The Pro Game* kid said. "Gettem later," Tall One answered. I was pleased they weren't intimidated by the oily dick.

I flopped down on the bed to read the *Post*. The Knicks had stunk it up in Buffalo the previous night. A group of Braves fans had unfurled a banner that stretched across a good portion of one side of the balcony. It read: NO MORE BUM DEALS THAT STIFF THE FANS AND MAKE THE OWNERS RICHER. NO BURLESON! SIGN MAC AND RANDY NOW! McAdoo had told a Buffalo writer, "If I don't get the deal I want here, then I guess I've got to be moving." Poor Tommy.

A quick shower and I was ready to go. I encountered Tall One by the main entrance of the hotel lobby, trying to keep an eye on the side door as well, lest a player slip out and jump into a cab before he could intercept him. I asked how he found out which hotels each team used. He said it was easy, most teams stayed at one of three places and they'd just check them out. If someone threw in an odd one, an older-sounding kid would call the Knicks and tell them he was a representative from a shoe company or whatever and had to make some deliveries for player X.

"Hey, man, I'll give you five bucks if you can get Russell's autograph for me," he says.

"He doesn't sign. There's no way. Sorry."

"I know," he said gloomily. "A friend of mine's dad got one of Russell when he was first up in Boston. Guess he used to sign then. Never get Russell now—he wouldn't give his autograph to his father."

Watts came into the lobby with Brown. Tall One joined his cronies in the middle of the lobby. There were a couple more than had been here an hour ago. I looked out into the street. It had stopped raining. The streets were black and shiny, reflecting neon and car lights. Burleson appeared from around the end of the hotel, wearing a raincoat that seemed designed for the Empire State Building. He looked up the street for a cab. I walked out. Almost told him about the banner in Buffalo. Couldn't do it. Asked him what he thought about the trade rumors.

"I haven't heard anything from the people who count, so I'm not going to worry about it," he answered, seeming a little perturbed that there might be a deal going on without the courtesy of his being informed, perturbed that pro basketball didn't seem to worry too much about a guy's feelings in such matters. "You heard anything? You think I'm goin'?"

"Don't know. I've heard Snyder wants to make the deal, but it depends if he can get a million or two out of Schulman."

"A *million or two*," he said, plainly upset. "He ain't *that* great." A cab pulled up, Burleson ran for it as the autograph fleet came whirling through the revolving door. "I'll talk to you down there," Burleson said, ducking into the cab and pulling the door shut as the kids pulled to a halt at the curb's edge. "Fucker. Fuck you, Burleson," a couple of them called out. I started back into the lobby. Tall One called after me: "Thanks for telling us he was out here, you bastard." I started to plead that he had just gotten there, but left it. The crew almost ran me over as they plowed back into the lobby.

The players' entrance at Madison Square Garden was fronted by more autograph hunters. They peered in our faces, not concerned with politeness, just making sure a Somebody didn't get past. "Nobody, just writers," one with a visor splitting his Afro into two clouds said for all of them as they glanced disdainfully at the briefcases and typewriters. We flashed our Pro Basketball Writers passes at the security desk, climbed into the elevator and headed up to the press room mezzanine. The feeling among the local (that somehow doesn't sound appropriate to New York) writers was that McAdoo wouldn't be going anywhere, nor would the other high-priced holdout, guard Randy Smith. Someone mentioned that Snyder was calling a press conference Monday morning to clear the air on his dealings with the two athletes and possibly to announce the sale of his share of the Braves to Brown.

I wandered down to courtside to leave my gear on the press table. I put my probing tape recorder in my pocket and whistled around the end of the court. Wilkerson and Johnson were shooting.

"You get around town today?" I asked.

"Naw," Johnson said, "oh, I went out and looked around a little."

"First time in New York?" I asked, grabbing a rebound and tossing a shot off the front of the rim.

"I played here in college," Wilkerson answered. "It's his, though. The cabbies scared him to death," he added, bouncing the ball on the back of Johnson's legs, laughing.

"Oh man, I don't care if we ever come back. They're all trying to kill each other. Can't even cross the street. Get me out of here," Johnson said, his boyish face wearing a look of disgust.

"Give me one more," I called for the ball. "I never leave a gym without making my last shot." I took a step to my left, rose for a little jumper and dropped it through, not clean, but in. A cop came around the side of the court, told me to get off it with my street shoes. I headed off through an aisle and rode the escalator up, up to the very top of the Garden.

From the court, the cheap seats in Madison Square Garden look like a thin blue ring painted on the rim of a huge bowl. From the cheap-seat perspective, the court is little more than a laminated cutting block on which dollhouse figures dance around a tiny ball. There weren't many patrons in the blue seats the night I circled the upper concourse as the Seattle Sonics and the New York Knicks warmed up for their Saturday night date.

Whenever on the road I tried to allow the time before a game to climb to the farthest reaches of an arena—partly to clear the claustrophobia that develops after too many hours locked into contact with seventeen traveling companions; partly to deal with the nervous energy that builds in anticipation of the job ahead. It also helped to get the feel of a place—to partake of the accents and the local topics of discussion. There was the desire to remind myself that there were people paying money to see a basketball game. They didn't care about all the intimate intrigue active inside the heads of reporters, coaches and players. The game should be evaluated, at least in part, for the performance.

I also wandered the arenas to gaze upon the lovely ladies. There was one that night, a dark-haired girl in sweater and teen-tight slacks. Her face was especially pretty—the sort a traveler hopes he can frame in his mind to savor behind closed eyes during the next long wait along the road. She was snuggled up to an amorous lad who leaned against the concourse wall stroking her nicely rounded tail. It was hard to tell if he was doing it more to indulge her or himself, but they looked not to stay for the whole game. While the love pigeons cooed, a thirtyish fan and a cop trampled on the pregame serenity of the Madison Square Garden rafters with a harangue that was typically huff-and-bluff New York City. They had drawn a line of confrontation at the front row railing of Blue Section. The fan wanted to sit one row below and the officer wanted him to stay in the seats he had paid for. It didn't matter where they had drawn the line or what the issue was—it was a time-killing exercise which had become swept up in bravado.

"You know I'm right, but you won't back down. You aren't man enough to back down," the fan bellowed down on the cop, who stood below the railing over which the fan leaned. "There's no fucking reason why I can't move down a row so I don't have this fucking railing in my face. There's no one here . . ."

"You bought those seats, you stay in 'em or I'll throw your ass out of here," interrupted the cop, who seemed to be both scowling and laughing behind a face that said: Whatever this comes to, I have the hole card. I wear the badge.

"You're just putting me down because you don't have anything else to do."

"My job is to see that everyone stays where they're supposed to and doesn't make any trouble. And you're makin' some, friend."

"If I come over and kick your ass will you let me stay?" the fan shouted, looking around at his companion for applause.

"If you come over *you'll* get your ass kicked."

"By you?"

"By me and I'd love to do it."

The fan leaned so far over the rail it seemed certain he would flip forward onto the cop. "You can't talk to me like that. You're a tax-supported . . . you're a public servant and you can't talk to citizens like that."

"And you can't break regulations."

"They don't make any fucking sense. They're an insult to the paying customer. Do you think Eddie Donovan wants you to insult fans? If he knew what kind of trouble you were causing he'd fire your ass in a second," the fan continued, referring to the Knicks' general manager.

"What do you want me to do? Just let everyone go down there and sit where they want? You want to go sit with Holzman? What about the rest of these people?" The cop was asking questions, but he was wrapping up his case.

"Well, faaaaaa-uk," the fan bellowed, sagging back in his seat, resigned that he'd pushed as far as he could. The cop gave him an authoritarian look, as if to say, "It's settled now. Understand?" and walked away—not too cocky, but refreshed as though he'd just taken a brisk walk along Battery Park.

The fan, the flush of confrontation fading from his face, slapped his companion on the shoulder with beer-commercial macho-gusto. "I love it up here. This is where all the crazy shit happens. I sat down almost at courtside once and everybody seemed too big, you know, like on a movie screen. Ah, I could get off being a little closer, hearin' them talk their shit, you know. But this is where it's at. What the fuck I wanna see the Pearl sweat for, man? I can see him shoot it up here and I can drink my beer and fuck with some fuckin' cop. Nobody takes anything too serious up here, know what I mean?"

I moved out of the row I had occupied behind the blustery fan and covertly flicked off my pocket tape recorder—I didn't want him to get any ideas about lobbing the Lanier Microsette 60, all $261 of it, off into space. I looked down, seemingly from nine miles above my chair at courtside.

After some timeless period of reflecting on the NBA as it appeared from up here compared to the perspective of my courtside seat, I looked at the Knick bench. In street clothes, injured, sat Bill Bradley— the Oxford scholar, "the brains" of the NBA's brawn fleet, the man above prostitution through commercialization. If he had any faults it was that he was too perfect to be tolerated—so said the image. Suddenly I realized there was an interview sitting there. I reproached a desire to remain on this cheap-seat station of reflection and moved down out of the blue seats—down, down into the bottom of the bowl as the Haywoods and the Russells and the Monroes became larger, took on features and became people to be dealt with again.

I swung around the end of the court where the Sonics were taking their final warm-up shots. I felt the presence of the court as a stage. A ball bounced off the endline. I picked it up and flipped it back to Oleynick, who was standing just inbounds. "I thought you had some people coming down from Bridgeport? I don't hear 'em," I said. "They're ready," Oleynick replied. "I just hope Russ is." Oleynick was loose. This was one of his first runs in the Garden. For a kid who grew up in Connecticut and played "in the city" all the while he was developing his game, this was the time to feel like you've made it.

In the five seconds it took to exchange words with Oleynick, a handful of adolescents scurried up with their bubble gum cards, programs, books. "Hey," they called to Oleynick. "Later, gotta shoot," he replied, spinning away from the endline, curling his upper lip in his particular pout-sneer and snapping off a twenty-footer.

"Whad he say to you?" a boy of about fourteen asked me, trying to figure out where I earned any edge. "You know him?"

"Yeah, I cover him for the Seattle paper," I said as I walked toward the Knicks' bench, realizing I had blown too much time.

"You know all these guys?" You travel with 'em?" another youngster asked, trailing me.

"Yeah."

"Sheeeeeit, what a job," he gee-whizzed. About time somebody gave me some respect.

As if to make sure I didn't relax even in the ardor of a New York adolescent, I tried to rush a conversation with Bradley despite an instinctive warning that this wasn't the time. I had asked him a few questions after previous Sonics-Knicks games and found him to be terse, not anxious to talk—but articulate if cornered. Having just read his book *Life on the Run*, I felt I knew him better. In the book he had painted a picture of the reporter role as being mainly absurd:

> "Basketball players and politicans have at least one thing in common. They meet the press almost every working day. In basketball the interaction leads to a charade. Reporters try to lead players to statements which will confirm the reporter's own preconceptions and players try to avoid saying things that will make them look bad. So every game must be followed with explanations of the self-evident. . . ."

I agreed there were far too many times when there was no meaningful essence to the questions or the answers. I wanted to ask Bradley under what circumstances he felt meritable dialogue could be conducted in the ineluctable review of a game.

The cop patrolling the Knicks' bench didn't want me there and most of the Knicks had finished their warm-ups and returned to create a flutter of conversation which surrounded Bradley when I leaned in to introduce myself. With the cop trying to ease me away and my taking three clumsy starts at trying to frame my question, I realized I had created a situation for myself that was leading to increased embarrassment and there was no chance of anything good coming of it.

But I was stuck. After forcing Bradley to furrow his forehead trying to figure out the question that I couldn't fully develop, I finally mumbled, "Do you think it's possible for a reporter to ask an intelligent question?"

The cop was tugging on my arm and babbling about me having to leave the area. Bradley paused as if he wasn't sure he had heard the question, decided there wasn't anything else there and stated flatly, "Yes."

"You mean," I murmured, "if a reporter can get it out of his mouth." By then I was ten feet away, sweating with discomfiture, feeling like a buffoon, and steaming that I had been so imprudent as to start an in-depth philosophical discussion with an Oxford scholar—especially when he had only time for a one-word answer.

I got to my seat just as the National Anthem was starting. I vowed not to let Bill Bradley retire without my coming back for at least one intelligent interview. And while I fulfilled that by season's end, that moment was one of those times when I wished the blue section was all the closer I ever got to the NBA.

Watts did an elaborate Ali shuffle at midcourt as the teams came out for the jump. The crowd loved it. Russell cackled and set his coffee on the end of the table—six inches from my notebook. "I hope this isn't an exciting game," I told him. "Why's that?" Russell asked, looking over curiously. "Because I don't want to wear your coffee the rest of the night." "Oh, ha, ha," he replied in laugh No. 22 (the one that is only slightly more cordial than his No. 20, forced chuckle). He left the cup there.

And, for the first half, it was an exciting game for Seattle. Watts was at his chaotic best, throwing up ridiculous shots that somehow went in around the peeved expressions of Frazier and Monroe. The Sonics were running out of control, totally free-lancing. But they were up by twelve in the third quarter. Then things fell apart. New York started taking the chaos out of the Sonics and leaving them groping for desperation jumpers against the shooting clock. Haywood caught fire in the final frame and led the Knicks to their first win over Seattle since he had been traded more than a year earlier. Russell didn't spill his coffee.

There must have been fifteen journalists clustered around Russell as he emerged from the locker room. Archie Clark popped down the hallway. He had played his next to last year in pro ball with Seattle. Russell greeted him warmly, told him sure he could go into the locker room. Reporters edged close, radiomen leaned across notebooks to stick mikes in Russell's face. I shrugged my shoulders to get a little breathing room. Somebody shrugged back. I could just see a fight breaking out among the press corps. I'll bet Russ would be rolling on the floor with laughter. It would almost be worth it just to hear him really, really laugh—kind of like, well there really isn't anything like Russell's wide-open laugh.

"Are you going to deal Burleson for McAdoo?" a New York microphone-holder asked.

"Now, you know I couldn't tell you that even if I was," Russell answered, arms folded across his chest, easy smile on his face. Somehow it didn't seem as though the game even happened. At least not that the Sonics had just lost.

"Would you say that you are less than satisfied with the development of Burleson?" the reporter persisted.

"I don't want to talk about anything like that," Russell said, still casual.

"Just touch your left ear twice if it's yes," I interjected. Russell laughed. So did a few writers. Ho, ho, ho.

"No, I've got too much to worry about with my team to discuss anything else," Russell continued, his face sobering. "I don't know if you're aware of it or not but we haven't done very well on the road."

Now, ain't that a bitch, I said to myself. Heberlein and I exchanged shakes of the head. Here he was bringing up a subject that drove him to frozen fury three nights ago in Boston.

"And I blew the game tonight," he continued. "If Red Holzman had said, 'Bill, this is what we'd like you to do to help us win,' we couldn't have been more completely cooperative. And it was my fault that happened. I didn't take charge early enough. We were ahead and I let things go that I knew would get us into trouble. We didn't have any discipline. I got our substitution out of rhythm and I didn't insist on the things I should have."

Thinking that was a rather interesting approach, I wandered into the Sonic dressing room. I asked Bantom if Russell had taken credit for the defeat when he met with the players after the game. He looked at me rather quizzically. I explained. He said, "Well, gosh, I guess you can't argue with the coach. Naw, we played pretty poorly. Even at the end we were just floating around looking for a shot without really working inside."

I started down the corridor toward the Knicks' dressing room. Spencer Haywood, here I come. I felt rotten all of a sudden. I had written a commentary critical of his playing style when he was traded to New York and he had refused to talk to me the next couple of rounds between the Sonics and the Knicks. I had finally gotten a nibble of communication with him in his second visit to Seattle last spring. Well, they had won the game, that ought to help. Such a discomfort, though, to wonder if the guy would snub you or get nasty or embarrass you in front of the rest of the Knicks. How unfair that *he* could dictate the situation. I could rip him in the paper, but I still had to feel at the mercy of his mood if I wanted to tune in to him. This isn't so much of an overt thing as an inner tension. I don't want to spar, I just want to get his thoughts. I ain't lookin' to lock or sock or knock you up, all I really want to do, is baby get an interview. I wonder how Dylan would have covered the NBA?

I walked into the room. Haywood was sitting in the booth directly across from the door, peeling tape off his leg, which had been wrapped to the knee. He looked up.

"Hello, Blaine. How're you?" he asked, a tired smile on his face.

We shook hands the Rotarian way.

"Howya doin'?" I replied. "Finally got the old boys, huh?" I hoped he didn't take "boys" the wrong way.

"Red switched me onto Seals in the fourth quarter. He was having a good game and I was able to get good position and help cut off their inside game," he commented in a strange mixture of diction which sounds like equal parts northern street/southern country/Bahamas classroom. "We needed this one and it feels good for that more than just me beating the Sonics."

I knelt down. It hurt my knees, but I never like to loom over a person I am interviewing. I want them to sense me as something comfortable, casual, unaggressive. I asked how things were working out for him. Was New York delivering the things he came seeking, other than the victories, of course?

"Last year was sort of a history-making year for me. Perhaps I was a bit negative and yet, I guess I figured I could speak out on certain things without having all the bad effect that it did." He had all the tape and elastic wrap off his legs. His sweat-soaked Knicks jersey came off over his head. He seemed relaxed. "I made a mistake in that I judged a whole group of people by the attitudes and actions of a few. It just became like a war between me and the city, but that's not there anymore in my mind." A couple of New York writers listened in, but didn't seem very interested in the trend of conversation. They didn't care what a New Yorker's hassles were with outsiders. As I feared they might, one asked something about the game. Haywood answered tersely and made a point of looking back at me. He wanted to get something into the Seattle papers.

"I regret what was said, and yet, I guess that if I was back in the same situation, feeling the way that I did, I'd speak out again—and wish things were different a year later. I just felt like they didn't respect me as a human being and that I had put in a lot of myself. Oh well, now I'm in New York and things have worked out well for me—financially and many other ways. I've gained the things I wanted, in and out of basketball, and I just want to accomplish a winning record with the Knicks this season."

I shook hands again, thanked him for his time, wished him luck, said I'd see him in Seattle, stood up—my legs felt as if they had been tucked in a small box for forty days—and looked around for Bradley. He was long gone, maybe hadn't even come in here. I hated to leave that pregame debacle hanging like that. Humiliating. Heberlein moved over to Haywood, having been in the other room with Holzman and Frazier. I asked Holzman a couple of nonprovocative questions and got a couple of nonprovocative answers. He seemed so Big Time. I guess it took me a second to remember that he wasn't therefore going to necessarily be great copy. He looked just like a tired, rumpled version of the Championship Coach of yesteryear. So many interviews after so many games. How long could a guy go through the dance?

I pounded out a feature on Haywood and the game story. Heberlein and I grabbed a cab and shot back to the hotel. Haywood and Brown and Clark were going up in the same elevator. They were quiet in the ascent—as if we had interrupted a conversation they didn't want media ears to hear and couldn't think of another one to get started as a front. We bid them good night and they continued on up. Old friends briefly together again, the way it had been every night on the road for whole seasons.

20

Hurricanes and Bigger Storms

We were riding the bird from New York to New Orleans, via Atlanta. Three evenings in New Orleans—couldn't ask for more than that. Sunshine and the French Quarter ought to make the road soften up considerably. I was sitting next to Watts, behind Russell, in front of Bantom and Gray. No sooner had I settled into my seat than Bantom leaned forward and asked, in a voice only slightly aggressive, "I heard you quoted me as swearing in the paper."

"Huh?"

"You had me saying, 'that's your ass' in the Philly story."

My first thought was, good they didn't edit it out. My second was, jeez, these guys have good contacts back home. I turned in my seat to address Bantom and whomever else might pay attention. "I don't want to embarrass you and I obviously wouldn't use anything that I thought would. I just want to give 'em a little reality. Earthiness is good for everyone. You agree?"

He just shrugged. He didn't seem to really care. I turned around and waited for someone to take up the attack. No one did. Watts was going through a datebook, checking out social engagements and appearances. Notes were scribbled across several dates. It's no wonder he has a hard time getting to the right place on the right day, let alone the right time. He was telling me a raunchy story about himself. He went on and on. Russell looked back with a scowl. Watts continued on in his jive. It was entertaining. Russell looked back twice more. Glowering. I figured it had to be a pride bit—don't degrade yourself. Watts aimed a scowl at his back and rambled on. I laughed. Bantom piped up with a story about some legendary NBA groupie who called him in New York and said she would fly to New Orleans from wherever in the hell she was if he would buy her a certain six-hundred-dollar coat she had her eye on. He apparently was opposed to supporting the killing of small animals for adornment and told her he couldn't accommodate her terms. I finished with a pile of *New York Times* and looked around to see if anyone wanted it.

"I don't read the paper," Gray offered flatly.

"That hurts my feelings," I replied.

"It's nothing personal," he added, smiling.

"What you got there?" asked Norwood, sitting across the aisle from

Gray, his thick, round face peeking out from under his ever-present gray cap.

"Just some papers I picked up at the airport. Some of it is from today, some of it is about a week old, I think," I said as I handed it over to him.

"That's okay, I'm a week behind, anyway."

People read and snoozed. I came across a quote by Eric Sevareid in a magazine. I held it over for Watts to read: "Better to trust the man who is frequently in error than the one who is never in doubt." Watts said, "I hear that," as he pointed a finger at the back of Russell's head, and mouthed the words, "He ain't never had a doubt."

As we're getting off the plane for an hour's wait in Atlanta, Norwood pulled alongside me. "Hey, I've got a good story for you. I want some more playing time. It worked for Bobby, sheeeeit," he said, half laughing, nudging me with his hand. So that was it. The night before, during the game at the Garden, I had caught his eye as he sat on the bench and he had shaken his head in an expression of disgust. He had survived on hard work, hustle was his game—learned under Hopkins at Alcorn A&M. The six-year veteran didn't like seeing kids go past him.

I was sitting beside Russell for the jaunt over to New Orleans. I flipped open a page of *The New York Times*. There was a picture of the rafters of Boston Garden, the championship banners hanging like Monday wash. Eight large numbers that stood for retired jerseys hung on a banner. There was No. 6. Human being to the left of me, a number in the rafters. A number—the ultimate in symbolic representation. I showed it to him. He glanced at it for a minute, handed it back. "What if everybody went through life with a number on their back?" I mused. He wasn't in a muse mood. "Heh, heh," he replied. I read on for a few minutes. "I did an interview with some fans in Boston asking them what they thought of Cowens quitting," I offered. "I was really surprised that everyone thought it was okay." Russell looked out the window for a minute, then turned back to me, his face on the verge of anger. "You think if JoJo had done that they would have accepted it. Shit, if I had done that when I was there they'd have thrown me in jail."

I started to say, "Yeah, maybe so," But I just nodded instead and put my eyes back on the *Times*. I had taken a focus on a subject and imparted it as a reporter. But it still wasn't the full picture, so there was deception. I know why it has to be this way. I can't write the history of modern man every time I go to the typewriter. But where do you start and stop? How can you sort out all these people and all the different things that sports means to all fans and readers of the sports pages? So much to contemplate if you choose to burden yourself with it—or can't seem to avoid it.

I ordered a beer. Russell had a Screw-Up. I hauled out the Atlanta *Constitution* and came across a long article titled: "Hawks' GM Says Press Hurts Atlanta Basketball." Bud Seretean, then president and general manager of the Hawks, was accusing the local media of "negative writing." This was all the more interesting since George Cunningham, president of the Pro Basketball Writers Association, had recently been pulled off the beat by the *Constitution* editors after Seretean griped that he was being overly critical of the Hawks. Seretean contended: "The writers are doing a brilliant job of keeping the fans away. The press can do more to kill or sustain a franchise than anything else I know of. . . . They continue this totally negative reporting and the bulk of the Atlanta population reads it and couldn't care less about the Atlanta Hawks."

I handed the paper to Russell, who had been reading over my shoulder. "I think he's overstating the role of the media," I offered. He finished the piece. "No, the press can have a tremendous effect on whether the public supports a team or a player. A negative writer can hurt a team internally, too. If the players pay attention to what's written, or if they hash out their problems in the press instead of in the front office or the locker room, it can be damaging. A writer knows if he's being honest, though. Every man knows inside himself if he's really being honest. There are people who don't let that stop them, though."

"You want to be behind an organization," I said. "As a person with this group I want to feel like I'm doing a part to make it successful. I want to live a positive life and believe in the things I'm working at. So, in a way, that makes me a fan. I care that the team does well because it's more fun to be a part of it. Everyone is more enjoyable to be around when things are going up instead of down. I suppose when I write a commentary like I did early in the year, or come and talk to you about what I saw was wrong with the communication and attitudes on the team, I'm being a cheerleader in a sense. I'm not sitting back and reviewing—I'm trying to shove them in the right direction. Furtado calls it a Savior Complex." Russell chuckled in agreement. "But when I see things out of line and stand up and take my shots at whomever I see is at fault, I am maybe hurting the team, at least as it sees it. It's so easy in this long grind to find fault with effort and performances. I don't like to harp and harp on the negative. But I think a lot of writers, especially those who are now in their forties and fifties, who grew up in the real hero-worship era of sports, are judging today's teams and players against myths that they accepted as boys. I don't know, it's tough to draw the line. But I don't think a writer can control the attitude of a whole city. Fans are easily led, but they aren't totally blind. They know if they like the product or not, don't they? I can't buy Seretean's claim that the media has that great an effect."

"Well, I think you're wrong," Russell said quietly. I was surprised he had let me speak at such length without interruption. I was surprised now when he didn't say anything else. I was sure he had been listening. Lord, Russell could be exasperating. So hard to communicate with, yet seemingly so full of attitudes and observations that were worth hearing. He put his hand to his face, leaned against the compartment wall and dozed. I ordered another beer.

The Louisiana air was like a delicious kiss—warm, sweet-scented and moist—as we inhaled our first breaths off the plane. The sun was bright and spirits were loose, buoyed by the kindergarten birthday party behavior of Watts. He was back home where he and Seals had played college ball for Hopkins at Xavier. He was going to see old friends and relatives. Home again the conquering hero. He hadn't come home a loser that first time when he headed off to Seattle and each time he came back he was just a little bigger. He went off to a car rental counter while we awaited the luggage.

After an hour, our luggage was assembled and we loaded the bus. Watts came back in the tow of Norwood. Watts was carrying on as though he'd just had his horse shot out from under him in the stretch drive of the Kentucky Derby. He had planned to rent a car, had forgotten not only his car rental credit card, but also his driver's license. He had called Seattle to get confirmation on the credit card, but couldn't drive away without the driver's license.

"He say he know me, right?" Watts said to Norwood, turning back several times while Norwood kept him advancing toward the bus. "He say he *know* me and he won't give me no car. They know I got a license, but they won't give me no car." He was beside himself. Norwood got him on the bus. He sat there for about ten seconds. He jumped up, ran off the bus and headed back for the counter. Norwood shook his head. Seals went after him. They came back five minutes later. Watts was still riled.

"They gotta have a driver's license because they don't know that you haven't had it taken away," someone tried to explain to Watts for the twentieth time.

"Yeah, but he know me," Watts kept insisting. "Be different if they didn't know me. But he said he know who I was, didn't he?"

Half the team and both the coaches had long since departed in cabs or cars when the bus finally moved out onto the expressway for the long run to town. A police car passed the bus, siren blaring.

"My heart starts beatin' whenever I hear sirens down here," Watts said, once again displaying his amazing ability to change moods and subjects with the time it takes to snap a finger.

"I hear that," someone chimed in.

"When I drove my Mercedes down here this summer I 'bout had a heart attack every time I heard a siren. I came through Memphis and a cop is on my front and a cop covers me from behind and they keep me like that all the way to the Mississippi line," Watts continued, jivin' and slappin'. "I took more buses than I took in eight years."

"Cops see nigger drivin' big ass car and he wants to *tawk* to *you*," another voice came out of the back. Might have been Seals.

"You jus' a watermelon-chicken nigger, boy. Where'd you steal that car, nigger? Get outta the caw, nigger." Watts was rolling wide open. They're laughing. But what pain and bitterness underneath.

The bus rolled along in heavy traffic. "Hey, looka there, Bruce," Watts said. "Ain't that the motel we was swimmin' at where the little boy said, 'Daddy, is them niggers?' He says, 'Oh, no no, now you don't talk like that.' I say, sheeeit. He learned him that and now he's tellin' him to shut up. Little baby ain't even hardly big enough to know no words he says, 'Daddy, is them niggers?' " Watts was still giggling, shaking his head in mock bewilderment at the human race.

"That's some deep shit," he added after everyone had fallen quiet for a minute or two. "Ain't no place to be drivin' no black Mercedes up no rural road by you'self on a Saturday night."

"I hear that," someone added.

We pulled up in front of the Hyatt Regency, adjacent to the Super Dome. A grand place—probably the nicest in the circuit. The rooms, located off balconies which encircle the hollowed core of the building, allow you to look down twenty-five stories on the courtyard-like bar and restaurant. Elegant. The rooms are beautiful, certainly a step above your basic modern motel motif. Two huge beds, attractive decor. I was on a corner with a 180° view of New Orleans from the fourteenth floor.

That evening the Jazz were hosting Denver. Watts, Oleynick, Johnson and I wandered over to the Super Dome. Night off, go to an NBA game. We sat in the section that is pulled up adjacent to the court opposite the main side of the stand, which towers in multi-tiers to the Dome roof. The place is so huge that even close to the court there is a hollow ring to the sound of the crowd. When 25,000 are on hand, the place has a fuller roar, but even 7,000 to 10,000 feels lost in the place. It is a terribly extravagant facility—carpeted aisles and ramps, plush lighting on every level. All the rumors of political deals and private rip-offs reek in the splendor of every detail. It's a facility to behold, if you don't bother to think about the public's price.

After an entertaining shoot-out, the Jazz fell. Oleynick and I jumped in a cab and headed for the French Quarter. We got out in front of Pat O'Brien's, an always crowded bar in the heart of the Quarter. We occupied the last two stools at the bar and ordered a pair of hurricanes—an exotic mixture of rum and whatever else goes into dynamite. They're pink, they come in glasses shaped like the wick shield on an old-fashioned hurricane lantern, and they simply blow away the mind and body. I have been to the hurricane well before. I wanted to go slow. But Oleynick kept gulping and buying at a merciless pace. I felt myself starting to slip down that slide and it was too late to stop. It seemed there was an overlay of hammering music, but it might just have been the crowd. Oleynick was making mean eyes at some guy standing between two attractive girls at the end of the bar. I tried to humor Oleynick into some distracting conversation. Somehow the conversation wove its way onto, of all things, basketball.

"How do you feel playing in the Garden," I asked, sipping greedily on my third hurricane. "You talk about playing in the city, building your game in New York. Is Madison Square Garden The Place for you in basketball?"

"I tell ya, man, it was. I always thought that was The Big Time, you know what I mean? Playin' in the Gaw-den was *it*. The first time I played there last season was a thrill. Do your shit in the Gaw-den, man. Yeah, I felt it." He took a strong sip at the last inch of his third hurricane. "Now, it's just another place where you're out there trying to figure out what the fuck you are supposed to do to please Russ, please your team and yourself. I'll tell ya, man, I'm glad I'm gettin' paid for all this, because my love for basketball ain't there no more. They beat me down, man. They cut my love for basketball all to pieces right now."

"You think you can get it back?"

"Under the right circumstances, I think I can. Where I'm gonna find it is a good fuckin' question."

Six-eleven Rich Kelly walked into the bar along with 5'7" Monte Towe and a couple other players from the Jazz-Nugget affair. Byron Beck came in a minute later. We talked and got another round of hurricanes—their first, our fourth. I reminded Beck of the interview I had done with him at the start of the previous season when Seattle was in Denver for an exhibition game. Beck had played high school ball for a tiny school, Kittitas, in Washington and then had been one of only a couple of players to play all nine seasons of the ABA's existence. I reminded him of how I had talked to him before the game and that sure was lucky because Burleson put him in the hospital with an elbow ten minutes into the game. He laughed. I was glad. You say the most careless things when you've had four hurricanes. I was numbing up. My face was starting to get those tiny twinges of alcoholic caress. Novocained out.

The dude who had been standing between the two fillies at the bar was gone somewhere and I wandered over. It always seemed like an obnoxious thing to do, to use the pro basketball image, but I mentioned what had brought us to town. I asked them if they wanted to go to the game Tuesday night, go have lunch tomorrow, go for a walk now— anything. They said they were from Biloxi. One of them seemed more interested than the other so I leaned on her for a while. She was as blown away as I was. We decided that I should come down to Biloxi with her that night and since she didn't have to work Tuesday I could hang out on the beach tomorrow, we could have a good time tomorrow night and then have all day Tuesday to play around before I'd jaunt back up to New Orleans to cover the game. Awwwwwwl right. That's a helluva deal.

Oleynick came over and put his arm around the other one. She didn't like that. He got a little antagonistic right back and when the dude returned I thought it was going to be an over-the-ropes battle royal. But everybody seemed content to just glare at each other and make threats and we went back up to the other end of the bar. Oleynick ordered another round and decided we should take a hike about the Quarter. I protested that I had a date. He said we'd be back. I checked with the lady and she said they'd be there another hour and you'll sure come back heah afor we go. Yes, ma'am.

Music flowed out of every doorway—jazz, rock, blues, disco-stripper, all mingled in a mixture about as confused as my head. We hit a couple more bars, dropping a beer down the hatch in one place and a shot of Bourbon in another. Somewhere along the way we came up with a pint of MD 20-20, or whatever the rotgut sweet wine is called.

"Ain't this some shit, B.J.?" Oleynick crowed as we sauntered up Bourbon Street, arm in arm, weaving among other weaving bodies. Macho mindlessness. "We walkin' the streets of New Ow-leens, drunk on our asses and who knows what shit we'll find by tomorrow morning. Hangin' out on the great NBA way, man."

We headed upstairs to some sort of an establishment. I hadn't caught the sign on the front door before we climbed the stairs, so I didn't know if we were in a brothel, a massage parlor or a fortune teller's pad when we came to a desk at the top of the stairs. A heavy-set girl asked us what we wanted. I waited for Oleynick to answer. The prices sounded pretty high for a fortune teller. They were arguing, getting loud. She said something about ringing a bell. Oh no, come on, Frank, we don't need no trouble now. He was telling her to ring the goddamn bell. All of a sudden there was this big horse of a guy standing in the room, telling us to pack up our cares and woes and get the fuck out of there. Oleynick started to challenge him and the guy shoved him against the wall. I knew my stomach was in no shape to get hit, so I grabbed Oleynick and we tumbled down the stairs. He sure seemed to be in a pugilistic mood this evening.

We avoided being enticed into those seamy dens of debauchery where nearly naked women dance on tops of pianos and they charge you three bucks a drink, five drink minimum. That's the debauchery. We listened to some nice jazz for a while. I reflected that I have gone and gotten drunk as I promised myself I never would again. And then, about 3:30 A.M., we were in some dark, dingy dive on the fringe of the Quarter. My numbed instincts told me this was Trouble City, as they say in the movies just before a guy gets shanghaied down some trap door. But there was this chick there with this low-cut red blouse and such a lovely chest and Oleynick was negotiating with another darling little specimen by the door. The place was almost completely black, except for the greenish glow off the jukebox and a ten-watt bulb over the pool table. I couldn't make any progress with Lowcut Lady and finally, shortly after 4 A.M., I decided to hit the road. Where's Frank? I looked around, checked outside. Oh, there he is, standing among a couple of guys and the chick. He was arguing about something. Something about a chick. Oleynick said if she wanted to go with him, she ought to have the right. I went back inside and chatted with Lowcut. She said something about twenty-five bucks. I said I didn't have any intention of paying for anything. Oleynick came up and said he was splitting with the chick. Cool. I finished off a beer and made one final plea with the jury on her leaving with me. Some guy grabbed my arm and ushered me outside. I contemplated shoving back as soon as I pulled myself to a stop, fifteen yards from the doorway. But when I turned around and saw that there were two platoons of creeps waiting for me, I just turned on my heel and started walking.

I knew I wanted to go in the opposite direction from the Mississippi River. I came to the Mississippi River in a short while, turned around and started in the other direction. Well, at least Oleynick wound up with some action. Wonder how he pulled that off? It was close to 5 A.M. by the time I found the hotel. I contemplated walking around the Dome a couple of times to really sober up, but decided I was in pretty good shape after all. I lay down on the bed. I barely made it to the bathroom before discovering I was far from in good shape. I was up several more times in the next hour. I kept confusing this place with the bathroom in Buffalo, turning the wrong way and hitting my head on a towel shelf. I desperately needed some fresh air, but all the windows were sealed. I turned up the air conditioner and, as the morning pasted a light-gray silver against the overcast horizon, I collapsed—fighting for a mental hitching post to halt a spinning world.

I was in the heart of hell—a molten-hot spike having been driven through the top of my head—when the phone rang. It's Kilgore in Buffalo. You know, the TV sportscaster in Buffalo . . . the McAdoo deal. Oh yeah, heh, heh, ahhhh, *oh yeah!* How ya' doin'?

He said Snyder had "spilled his guts" at a press conference. He said he would entertain bids for McAdoo and he'd said the Knicks are offering big bucks, maybe $2.5 million plus John Gianelli. He said Seattle had offered Burleson and Gray and $2 million. Snyder said he was getting all the details out in the open so that people would realize he's not trying to screw anybody—just make the best deal.

I said, "Oh my," thanked Kilgore profusely for getting in touch with me, promised to get back to him as soon as I got any more info on this end, hung up the phone, set my head very carefully back on the pillow and thought it terribly ironic that I was going to die just when all the action was starting.

It was early afternoon by the time I could blink my eyes without feeling as though I was breaking off chunks of crystallized gray matter from my brain. I figured it must have been around eleven that Kilgore had called. Maybe earlier. I wondered if Heberlein had gotten anything. Oh, this is no time to get competitive. Just survive. I called Schulman in Los Angeles. He was upset that Snyder had laid all the details out on the table. "That puts me in a poor bargaining position. I don't understand what he's doing." One of the biggest concerns is how the $1 million the Braves owe McAdoo in deferred payments would be paid off. Snyder wanted Schulman to inherit that obligation. He had been given the impression the Knicks were out of the running.

Still later in the afternoon, I stumbled out for some nourishment—afraid to leave the phone for fear I would miss something. I ran into Tolson, Oleynick's roommate. He said Oleynick got sick at practice that morning, couldn't go. He said Oleynick was mad at me for abandoning him in a harrowing predicament. What? I ate some soup and crackers, went up to my room and called Oleynick. Seemed he had almost gotten into an alley brawl with a couple of dudes who didn't like him talking to the chick outside the dive. I told him I figured he had left with no regard for my safety and welfare in the bar. We agreed we didn't feel very well and that we sure were careless and crazy and, no, we didn't want to go to O'Brien's and start all over tonight.

I talked to Kilgore that evening. He had talked to another reporter and learned that McAdoo's agent, Bill Madden, had supposedly promised to deliver him to the Knicks. He said Brown had cooked up a three-way deal between the Braves, and Knicks and the Bullets. If Snyder despised Donovan, who had jumped from the Braves to be GM with the Knicks, as was alleged, he would never deal with the Knicks and besides he wouldn't want Mac in the same division. But would money rule out over rivalry?

Bob Walsh showed up that evening. He said he was in New Orleans to check out some things about the Super Dome. I figured he wanted to be on deck when the deal came down. Things were perking. I checked with Schulman again. He said to check back with him in an hour. Olga Korbut was performing in the Dome that evening. But I couldn't go over. I got back to Schulman, who thought he could make a deal, but was worried that he might not be able to sign McAdoo and would wind up in the same position as the Braves were presently in, that being that he would become a free agent the next year and could go anywhere, leaving compensation in the hands of the league commissioner.

I called in a story detailing what seemed to be all the particulars: Schulman has made an offer, Burleson, Gray and $2 million for McAdoo; the Braves have offered McAdoo a five-year contract of $500,000 per year, $350,000 in cash; McAdoo, whose wife is in law school in Buffalo, wants to accept, but Madden says no; Madden wants to deal with the Knicks; Snyder would prefer to deal with Seattle because of the player help he would receive immediately; McAdoo reportedly wants to play for Russell; Schulman says today was supposed to have been the deadline, but there have apparently been four days in a row that were the deadlines. If Brown comes to an agreement with Snyder and gains control of the Braves, consider A through E as being pure fiction.

The day was long gone. Over eight hours spent working the phones. Nice way to spend an off day. It had been raining all day. At least it wasn't inviting to be outside running around. I didn't feel much like moving, anyway. I chatted with Heberlein for a few minutes. We compared a few notes and found that his sources weren't completely compatible with mine. He thought there was a real good chance New York would get McAdoo—all the wire reports coming into the paper had indicated that. I decided that was just the arrogant New York perspective.

The next morning the New Orleans *States-Item* carried a big headline: "McAdoo Expected to Sign with Knicks for Millions." The story quoted a "Seattle source" as saying, "We thought we had a deal all worked out with John Y. Brown but then Snyder stepped in." I wished I could figure out who was dealing with whom. The Knicks were planning a press conference later in the day to announce the signing of McAdoo.

I called Schulman. He had finally gotten permission from the Braves to talk to McAdoo. He had called Madden. Madden said he had to have Snyder call him to confirm that. By the time Madden called Schulman to confirm that it was indeed all right for Schulman to talk to McAdoo, McAdoo had disappeared and Schulman couldn't get in touch. He still didn't know if McAdoo even wanted to come to Seattle and under what conditions. He still was under the impression the Knicks were really not in the running. Brown (or is it Snyder?) was leaning on Schulman to commit himself to a deal immediately. Schulman said he needed time to know what McAdoo wanted to do.

I called Kilgore. He said an AP story just moved that said McAdoo had signed with the Knicks. I called Mike Shaw, Braves PR man, who said McAdoo was at the moment practicing with the Braves and he certainly wouldn't be doing that if he belonged to the Knicks. I called

Heberlein and asked him what the hell he made of all this. We had joined into a struggle for some semblance of truth and while we each wanted to break the story that McAdoo was Seattle's, we were tossed together in somewhat of a team effort—partly to use each other for a sounding board on information and partly to just have somebody to clutch onto in what was fast becoming a bedlam of reports, opinions and projections strung together on a mounting phone bill connecting Los Angeles, Seattle, New York, Buffalo and New Orleans.

Heberlein had gotten in touch with Madden. He had said to him, "I don't want to be rude, but I understand you to be the ogre in all this." To which Madden replied: "If my getting for him the money he has coming to him makes me an ogre, then I guess I am." Madden had detailed a few more facts, not necessarily compatible with the rest of the reports, but more spice for the stew.

The game seemed like an afterthought, like an inconvenience to what was unfolding. There was so much intrigue and action to the McAdoo thing. So little reason to get excited about the game. I made another call to Schulman before I headed to the Dome. Schulman had talked to McAdoo. "He said he didn't know if he wanted to come to Seattle. He also said he didn't know if he wanted to go to New York." Russ talked to him. "I don't know where we stand on that issue. I don't want another Haywood. I've got to know if he will be happy here and that he will agree to a contract we can live with."

I called this mystery man Madden. He indicated Snyder was balking on the payment of the $1 million deferred. Madden wanted it put in a trust fund to guarantee the start of payments in 1988. Snyder didn't want to do it that way. He said Schulman seemed agreeable to such terms and that he didn't think they would have much trouble in agreeing to terms. "But what if Sam and I come to terms and Bob decides he wants to go to Seattle—we still don't know that Snyder or Brown will make the deal, do we? We shouldn't lose sight of the fact that at three this afternoon, New York time, after he told Sam he could negotiate with Bob, Snyder opened the possibility of our still signing with Buffalo. I said okay, here's our figures, give us the compensation and we'll sign. He just stopped." I asked Madden about the Knicks' pitch, what about the lure of big dollars from Madison Avenue? He replied: "Bob's not that photogenic. He's pretty much of a country person, a retiring type. He's not brassy like Walt Frazier or Joe Namath. I don't think that would mean that much to him. Perhaps they would make him into a legend along the lines of Willis Reed or Dave DeBusschere, but I don't know if that is so important to him in the final analysis." He said he was supposed to talk to Schulman later that night. He gave me another number for McAdoo. I got hold of him. "I'd like to stay in Buffalo, but it's a matter of the deferred compensation. There's not a team in the league that I would rule out playing for."

I scurried over to the game. It was a terrible first half. Neither team had an ounce of life. Watts had whirled in some early goals, delighting the seven thousand fans whose voices echoed weakly in the big-as-all-outdoors Dome. But then he stopped tearing around and Seattle simply looked like pure junk. There was the Third Quarter Act revisited by Jazz forward Aaron James to liven up the second half. Having collected twenty-two of his team's twenty-four points in that frame against Denver on Sunday (it seemed like a month ago), James went nuts again—hitting nine straight New Orleans baskets to completely destroy the fragile Sonics. Russell kept the locker room closed for twenty minutes after the game. When he stepped out he wasn't in a talkative mood. I waited for the rest of the media to go into the locker room, then asked Russell what was going on with the trade. He said he didn't know. He would let me know when something happened.

I walked into the locker room. Players sat sullenly in various far reaches of the large room, peeling off tape and socks slowly. Oleynick gave me some heat about Sunday night. No one else was talking above mumbles. It was something you could sense immediately. If you weren't familiar with the team, you would have thought they were just down after playing so poorly. But there was something else. Finally, I cornered Watts. He said, with a whipped dog look, Russell had jumped all over them. "Don't quote me on this, but Russ told us, 'You're all assholes.' Then he bent over and said, 'Kiss my ass.' I just hung my head, man. But I'm not going to do that forever. I'm not going to let him drag me down. I hit five straight shots at the start of the game and he called me over and said, 'Quit going off—you're just showing off at home.'"

In the New Orleans dressing room reporters crowded around James as Maravich, who had sat out the game injured, walked by singing: "Press conference, eight A.M. to announce Aaron James for Bob McAdoo, straight up." James injected, "Naw, naw. Plus about half a million. Don't cut me short now." I started to write down the exchange. Maravich said, "Oh, look at the reporter write it all down. Stories, stories everywhere." Fuck you, Pistol, I said to myself.

I called the paper and told them the game story would be coming in the immediate future. I would also be sending a couple of takes on the day's trade talks. I would check with Schulman later tonight and call in a lead before deadline. McAdoo has gone crazy in the Braves' loss to Indiana, forty-two points and twenty-nine rebounds.

There must have been twenty people clustered in the Hyatt lounge, friends of Watts and Seals, sitting among the paths of indoor yellow flowers. Watts and I stood to one side talking about how everything was collapsing with the team. He said Gray and Russell had gotten into a hassle at shooting practice that afternoon. Tolson had been bumped down the ladder for getting taped and finally had to wait until the end and wound up being sixteen minutes late. Russell said he was going to fine him one hundred dollars a minute. Tolson tried to tell Russell what had happened. Russell said he didn't give a damn. Furtado said Tolson was telling the truth. Russell said he didn't care. I couldn't get any details on the Gray bit, at least not then, but it seemed Gray had shown up late and Russell had told him he was going to fine him, too, and Gray told him in so many words that he wasn't going to do anything of the sort. Seattle wasn't the happiest team in pro basketball that evening.

I had dinner, a late date at the plate, with Walsh. He said that nothing was going to happen that evening that he knew of. I sensed he was trying to stall me from going up to my room to call Schulman at the time I had stipulated. I didn't know if he was. I didn't know much of anything at that time. I reflected how Walsh and I had been on the verge of being close after two years of shared escapades and shared thoughts. Now it seemed as though a wedge of roles had been driven between us.

I called Schulman. He had a deal. He had been given the green light. "I have reached an agreement in principle with Paul Snyder to obtain Bob McAdoo. I am willing to take the calculated risk that we will be able to reach a contractual agreement once the deal is made. Snyder's lawyer will be flying to Los Angeles tomorrow morning to sign the papers. I talked with McAdoo's agent and I found him to be very understanding. I really do not anticipate any problems in our reaching a fair agreement and that is why I feel confident in going ahead with the deal under these circumstances. Madden will be flying out to negotiate a contract." Schulman said McAdoo would undergo a physical sometime Thursday and provided everything checked out, the exchange of players would be made in time for the Braves' superstar to be playing for Seattle Friday night against Golden State.

I had ten minutes to get a story called in for the final edition. When I finished dictating the story it was 3 A.M. on the button in New Orleans. I felt like shouting in celebration. Then I felt angry with Walsh. I called up his room and yelled at him for lying to me about the deal not being imminent. We ranted at each other. For the first time in my memory. I hung up on someone's words. He called back ten minutes later and told me Russell had told him he didn't want anything in the press and that he would fire him if he didn't sit on it. Both teams had games tonight and he wanted to hold off until Friday if he could. He said Russell was furious that Schulman kept relating everything to Heberlein and myself. We made apologies, brittle ones, and hung up. I lay on the huge bed, lights out, sipping a whiskey sour I had acquired on the plane. The lights of New Orleans were wispy through the drizzle. I started to make a list of the articles that would have to be put together: why Schulman went after McAdoo, why Russell felt the trade was necessary, what changes there will be in the offense, player reactions, interviews with Burleson and Gray and McAdoo, a fan-in-the-street reaction piece when we get back to Seattle. By the way, Russ, thanks for thinking of me getting the story.

Just before 4 A.M., I called back to the office to see if they had been able to get everything into type in time. Yep. The headline read: "Sonics Get McAdoo." I was euphoric. After a month of swirling in this deal, I finally had gotten that big headline right out there in front of Seattle's face. "Sonics Get McAdoo."

Suddenly I wondered what happened to the Biloxi Lady in O'Brien's.

21
Capital Chaos

Brown was dressed all in black, right down to his gloves. Goateed, close-cropped Afro. He looked like a New York producer. Or maybe a middle-management mobster. We were awaiting luggage at the Baltimore airport. I was reading a report in the New York *Daily News*, headlined: "McAdoo Trade Held Up by Smith." It said, "The Knicks were left waiting alone on the platform yesterday when Bob McAdoo failed to arrive from Buffalo. It seems his departure was delayed for at least a day because the Braves ran into contractual problems with another player, guard Randy Smith. Before the Braves were willing to deal away McAdoo, they wanted to make sure they had Smith snugly tucked away with a long-term contract. . . ." It went on to say that McAdoo was expected on his way to New York before noon.

"Randy's smart," Brown was saying. "This is a game you can't control—you are at the mercy of others. If you have the power, you use it when you have it or you get lost. Randy's just making his play while he can."

I found it humorous that New York still thought they were going to get McAdoo. Heberlein was facing a deadline. I had already had the story in this morning's paper that McAdoo was Seattle's. Would he be confirming it or introducing still another confusion? He called Schulman. He reported that Snyder was making another attempt to sign McAdoo. Mac apparently didn't want to come to Seattle. But Schulman said he was confident he would be able to make the deal. I felt just the slightest trace of nervousness about my latest headline.

On the forty-minute bus ride to Largo, most of the players were

Ears Up to Heberlein and me. We hadn't had such friendly conversations all year. What's happenin'? they want to know. It was a nice, if somewhat ridiculous, turn of roles. We told them the deal may be off or it may come down today. Don't anybody buy a house for a few days. Green was asking me about horse racing in Seattle. Norwood was asking about the house I am restoring. It's great to be popular.

As soon as we checked into the hotel, I was on the phone to make my circuit of calls. Schulman said the Braves were leaning on him. They said they couldn't wait any longer to make the deal or they might have to deal with the Knicks. He said Snyder told him the deal was having "a debilitating effect on everybody." I hear that. Kilgore said he thought Seattle would still get McAdoo. Madden said he was going down to Philadelphia to meet with McAdoo, who was playing against the 76ers tonight. "We'll just sit down and have a cup of tea and make a decision that will affect his whole career."

And still another round of calls late in the afternoon before we prepared to bus off to Capital Centre brought the message that Schulman was trying to get a hold of Russell to talk to McAdoo. He said that Snyder had agreed to give him forty-eight hours to be sure he could sign McAdoo and also to be able to check with the league to determine what sort of compensation he might be due if he couldn't sign him for the following season. "I could have made the deal today, but my lawyers put the fear of God in me that we might be leaving ourselves in a very vulnerable position," Schulman said. He hoped to put the deal together in time to have Mac in uniform for Friday's game. He said Snyder was insisting he take Tom McMillen as well. He figured he'd be willing to do that if he had to.

Watts, Oleynick and Norwood were standing by the door of the hotel lobby. No one wanted to make the twenty-yard run for the bus through the sleet until everyone was ready to go. Oleynick and Watts were wishing they were on the trade block. "Trade me, *anywhere*," Oleynick said. "I hear that," Watts agreed. "I don't care where I go. I'm ready to get outta here. Russ has taken all the fun out of it."

"You've got it made in Seattle," I told Watts. "There's no way you can leave. You own that town. Make a stand. Come out in the paper tomorrow and say, 'Russ goes or I go. This town ain't big enough for both of us.' Then we'll have a vote—for A.M. release, of course, and the people will decide who has to go."

"You full of shit, B.J.," injected Oleynick as Watts slapped my hand. "You got a bullshit rap. Why don't you use your talents to do something useful, like sell cars. Get outta my face with that shit." He was punching playfully on my shoulder.

"I oughta do it." Watts laughed, probably giving it some serious thought.

Norwood shook his head at Watts and Oleynick. "You guys are

fucked. You don't even know what you talkin' about. I been on three clubs and there ain't no difference—same gripes, same problems everywhere you go. If it ain't the coach, it's the players. If it ain't the head trips, it's just losing. There ain't no place like you think."

"Well, you can bullshit yourself if you want, man. But I don't want to stay and take any more of this shit," Oleynick retorted.

Watts added, "Yeah, you stay with yo' daddy."

Norwood told them they were all fucked as we ran for the bus.

I asked Gray what he made of all the trade talk as I slipped past him on the bus. "Don't make any difference to me. Makes me no mind whatsoever. I go where I'm told and do what I'm told to do. I ain't got time to worry about none of this talk. I'm just here to play a game tonight."

I sat in the back of the bus as we drove through the dreary evening. Everyone was especially quiet. Burleson was just in front of me, his long overcoat draped over the arm and into the aisle. Gray's camel overcoat spilled over his armrest. This would certainly be their last trip with the Sonics.

I had been trying to get Madden until the bus departed and immediately upon arriving at the arena, I scurried for a pay phone. Heberlein joined me. We called the hotel in Philadelphia where he had said he would be. "Do you have a Bill Madden registered there?"

"No."

"Son of a bitch. Er, ah how about McAdoo?"

"Yes, sir, room 1611."

"Wonderful. Would you ring, please?"

"I'm sorry, it's busy."

"Okay, I'll call back in a minute."

I called back. There was no answer in the room. Son of a bitch.

"Could you page the lobby for a Bill Madden, please?"

"Yes, sir." In about a minute Madden came on the line.

"I haven't heard from Snyder all day, so I can reassure you there are no negotiations going on between us. I can tell you that New York is definitely out of this thing. I hear they have called a press conference again for tomorrow to announce signing him. But it's not going to happen. I don't know what we will do. I will spend an hour visiting with Bob after the game tonight and then we'll tune in for Chapter 148 tomorrow."

I trotted up to the press room and, around gulps of dinner, batted out the latest report. I used as my kicker: "If this reporter was called upon to guess what the results will be of 'Chapter 148,' it would be: McAdoo to Seattle before the Sonics play another game."

A group of reserves, Norwood, Green, Johnson and Wilkerson, led by a rampaging Gray, went the final seventeen minutes to run past Washington for a ten-point victory.

I was interviewing Norwood, when Green, dressing rapidly, leaned in and said, "Hey, man, you don't have to talk to no reporters. They pay us to play ball, not to talk to the press." He wore a sneer on his face as he wrapped a long scarf around his neck and headed out of the locker room. These sorry bastards, I reflected. Six hours ago he wouldn't have been nicer if I had been trying to decide who should receive a million dollars. As I was finishing with Norwood, Gray came into the locker room after doing a postgame show with Blackburn. I stepped over to him.

"Nice game, Leonard. What enabled that second unit to get rolling so well there at the end?"

"I don't have any comment," he stated, grimacing as he pulled off a shoe.

"Well, you were just on the radio. What difference does that make?"

"Well, let me think about that for a minute," he said as he picked up the twenty-five-dollar radio check and waved it in front of me. "There must be some reason, but it just doesn't come to me right now."

"Money is the root of all evil," I tried.

"You got some you want to give me, then?" he asked.

Heberlein and I walked away.

Back at the hotel, it was too late to get anything to eat so I did the only thing left—drank. Burleson and NBA publicity director Matt Winick and some overbearing character who markets champion-ship rings shared a table.

"Russell is a greater man than the league commissioner, because he knows the game and he wears a championship ring," Ring man said. "Alan Ameche is a greater man than Pete Rozelle, because he played the game and he wears a championship ring. The ring is what sets men apart. There is something magnificent in a man who has been crowned a champion—he is a different sort of man." The orator was insuffer-able. It wasn't a credit to the rest of us that we sat around and listened to him until 2 A.M. There just wasn't anything else to do, except go up and face four walls. Sleep apparently has its own schedule—one disre-spectful of the wake-up call.

Even though I knew we had to be up in barely three hours, I couldn't get to sleep. I called the paper. I was pleased to hear the phones had been ringing steadily as Seattle citizens tried to find out what was up with Bobby Mac. The desk man made the mistake of telling me they didn't have room to get the kicker of my McAdoo story in the paper—the one that predicted he would be a Sonic before their next game. What's the point of going out with bold and insightful statements when they won't even make sure it gets in the paper? The guy on the desk said I sounded as though I'm a little emotionally spent and to get some sleep. He was right. I felt close to being classified as a blown fuse.

The bus left for the airport at 5:45 A.M.—2:45 Seattle time, which we would be plugging into about noon. It was the first time the bus had gotten away on schedule the whole trip. Anybody glad to be going home?

The sky slipped out of predawn blackness and grew a face of salmon-pinkness, a spectacular winter sunrise. Burleson, sitting across the aisle from me, looked out the window and said, "We get up about now to go fishing back home during the summer." The bus was quiet, except for the unsquelchable Watts, who roamed the aisle, talking about nothing, singing, keeping everybody else from the shut-eye they so desperately sought. Traffic poured along the expressway in both directions—people off to jobs and schools and endeavors in a world that we seemed to have no connection to. Seals was talking quietly to Norwood behind me. "Should have been unbeaten this trip. That hoop got smaller and smaller at New Orleans. We could have won 'em all out here."

Heberlein called Schulman from Chicago when we stopped to change planes. He said Schulman was getting the squeeze from Snyder to make a deal right away, but that he figured he could hold him off until he was sure the deal was sound. Looked like the same old runaround from every side. I couldn't figure out what it all meant, but it seemed that if things stayed the same—i.e., McAdoo hadn't left the Braves—maybe that would be the most likely result to all this. I cringed when I thought of that headline. Naw, it would all happen. McAdoo would be Seattle's today. We headed west. Someone asked where Green was. Russell said he stayed in D.C. to handle some business matters.

I headed directly home, scooped eleven days' worth of papers off the porch, scooped a pile of mail out of the box, checked to see if my plants had survived, popped a beer and phoned a fine lady I call Lebanese Lily. We flowed into bed in pursuit of the indulgence, warmth and tenderness so hungrily sought after too many miles and too few smiles. I was in bed twenty minutes. The phone rang. I didn't know why I answered it, except I was living like Pavlov's dogs in response to a phone. It was my editor. He wanted to know if I was going to have a column for Sunday. I assured him I was. I climbed back in bed. The phone rang fifteen minutes later. It was my editor again. A story had just moved on the wire stating the Knicks had made the deal for McAdoo. It had been confirmed with both wire services. It looked like the real thing this time. I felt as though I had just been run over by a logging truck.

I staggered back to the bedroom. I wanted to get back in and crawl to the bottom of the covers and never come out. I told Lebanese Lily I had to go to work. She said I had just been working on the road for almost two weeks. I told her I would try to explain it someday and headed for the office. Stories were flying in from the Knicks' camp about how excited they were and from Buffalo about how they were glad it was finally over. I called Schulman. He was home in bed, exhausted, his secretary said. I was beyond being courteous to the sick and wounded. I called his home. He sounded sick and wounded. But he was bitter enough to talk.

"I had a deal twice with Snyder and he balked both times. He called and said I had to make the deal right away or he wouldn't be able to wait any longer. I told him Madden was on his way out here to discuss the thing. We've been having conversations since Hong Kong. Why all of a sudden do we have to make a decision this minute? He says, 'Oh, the press and everybody is after me and I just have to do it right now.' I told him to just give me until this evening. But he said he couldn't do it. It got awfully fishy to me. I believe he never wanted to make the deal, he was just using me to get more money out of the Knicks, which he succeeded in doing. I regret this whole frustrating experience. I feel used. But I have absolute confidence that it is all going to work out for Seattle's best interests. At no time did we mention any specific names of players offered in the McAdoo bid, but insofar as the rumored names of Burleson and Gray seem to become a fact through repetition, they both have my assurance and Bill Russell's that their value to our present team has in no way been diminished."

Polish up those damaged goods, 'cause we is still stuck with 'em.

I called up Kilgore. He was as stunned as anybody. "This is incredible. McAdoo doesn't even know about it yet. He's up in Toronto shopping for Christmas presents. The Knicks were completely out of this thing twenty-four hours ago, as much as anybody around here figured. There is no way to figure out what Snyder was doing."

I called Burleson. He seemed to be rolling with the punches. "I figured Sam Schulman and Coach Russell were trying to make a deal they felt was important for the team. Bob McAdoo has been the leading scorer in the league the past three years and Seattle just went all out to get him. I guess I was part of the deal because I play center, too. I don't feel betrayed by this. I knew it was a cold business and you never know when you can be traded." I called Gray. He said he hadn't been disturbed by the rumors. "I never read the sports pages so I didn't pay any attention to any of it." I called Russell. He wasn't around. I didn't blame him for being lost.

We went with a banner headline: "Sonics McAdon't, Knicks McAdoo."

It was pushing midnight by the time I finished my column and an advance for the next night's visit by Golden State and an advance for Sunday's visit by Houston. I was too tired to sleep, too weary to weep. I thought of calling the lady again, but decided I was also too weak to go to the well. I headed to a bar and ordered a beer. Been pushin' too hard, wound up too tight. I felt really let down that the deal had fallen through after all the drama. I felt burned, but in no rational way, that New York was the victor after all. I felt depressed that the club was going to be a disaster now, what with the deterioration of attitudes. And I felt so consumed by my job. No one in the office seemed to understand what I had been through. But how could they? Why should they? I won't get any overtime for all those extra hours worked, because that's not part of my deal. But what difference would a few bucks make? I remembered Furtado's comment on not getting a playoff share, "I don't care so much about the money. I just wish they'd say, 'Thanks for the good job.' " I sat and doodled on the tablecloth and had another beer and listened to the jukebox. Waylon Jennings was singing some appropriate words about cowboys sadly in search of their slow-moving dreams. I wondered if I wasn't looking for things in this job that were not there? I wondered if I wasn't making it into a competitive arena which in truth was impossible to survive as a winner? Every time I relaxed, though, seemed like something got away from me. I watched a couple talking quietly by the window. They seemed to be breaking up their relationship—not in a huff, but in a quiet, sad resignation to the fact that they weren't happy together. I wondered if I wouldn't come to that point with this job eventually.

I put up with editors who can't say, "Thank you."

I put up with players who say, "Fuck you."

I put up with fans who say "Who are you?"

I closed my eyes and started to put my head on the table. I remembered a state law: You can't rest your head on a table in a bar. You can't sleep. You can relax—but only so it looks presentable. Soften up. Soften up. Forget the work and the hours that have gone down. Forget that the deal fell through. Forget the hassle with Walsh. Forget the tension with Russell going all the way back to San Antonio. Forget the road. Forget the hours without compensation at the pay window. Forget you've got another game tomorrow night and another one Sunday. Forget, forget, forget. Let the music and the beer go through you. No, don't look at that chick. Stop the hustle. Get off the muscle. Forget.

I fell into bed just before 2 A.M.—almost twenty-four hours since I had rolled out into that Salmon Sunrise on the other side of the country.

My editor called the next morning as I languished over breakfast and reread the papers from the past two weeks. He said a story had just moved on the wire out of Washington, D.C., about Green. He had been arrested early in the morning after the Sonics' game against the Bullets on a narcotics charge. Seemed he was stopped by police in the company of two other persons. Seems there were small amounts of marijuana and cocaine found in the car. Oh, for the love of a dull moment. I told him I'd be right in to see what I could dig up.

I finally got a statement out of Walsh on behalf of the Sonics saying that Green had a long talk with Russell and that he felt he was a victim of "guilt by association." A court date had been set for March 16 in Washington—our next visit there. I was pleased to note that when I completed the story and tossed it on the copy desk, I still had almost five hours before tipoff against Golden State.

I dialed Lebanese Lily.

22
A Stoned Grounded Perspective

Color spills off the TV screen, invading the darkened room to cast diluted rainbow hues on expressionless faces. The Lakers are playing the Nets, but the sound is off, replaced by the ice cube coolness of Freddy Hubbard's trumpet filling the room from oversized stereo speakers. The players look like fish in a tank, taking beautiful dives and swoops. A flick of the tail, a scoot forward—Lucius Allen executes his customary little stutter step, then flashes by Al Skinner for a layup. Kareem is like a rare exotic fish, his goggle glasses and long limbs freakish. It is a scene of abstraction, made so by the absence of an announcer, the intoxication of the jazz, the mellowness of the marijuana floating across the consciousness of the five TV viewers.

Among those faces, three NBA players from two different teams and a pair of sportswriters, there is a familiarity with everyone performing on the screen. The score is meaningless—it is the art form of the movements, the ballet of a game loved by everyone there. Beyond that, there is an involved understanding of the match-ups, the execution of skills and expression of emotions. These are colleagues perspiring in performance, locked into the intensity of a battle, actually. Yet the observations from the darkened room are casual. There is an in-crowd feeling, a snobbery.

"Williamson's got the body, man. Strong mother-fucker."

"He can play."

"I hear that."

Silence, except for Hubbard's trumpet.

"Oh, Foxy, don't go in there. Sheeee-it, Jabber inhaled him. Nobody goes in on the big fella. Foxy oughta know better."

"He's the best there is."

"Who, Foxy? You fucked."

"Pull your mind out and give it some air, man. You know I ain't talkin' about no Foxy. You stoned or am I?"

"I don't know, man. But I heard that when you get this far you don't take notes."

"Who's takin' notes? Reporter takin' notes? Sheeee-it, leave me beeeee, paleeeeese."

"Give us some credit. What do you think . . ."

Someone turns up the sound on the set.

"Hey, no, man. No, no, we don't want no Cousy. Turn that off."

The announcing voice of the former Celtic great is gone, leaving only the ballet. There is a knock on the apartment door. Everyone stiffens for a second.

"What's there?"

The door opens. Another player stoops and comes in.

"Hey, what's happenin'? How ya doin', bro?"

He spots me. "Hey, what's happenin'? I didn't know you hang with these fellas. What's happenin'?"

"Well, I believe everything is happenin'," I respond, having adopted the attitude that since I don't know if "what's happenin'?" is wanting to know about my head, or my job, or the two of us, or the team, or the world condition as a whole, it's best to be obscure right back.

"That's cool. Yes, sir, it's nice to know you can hang with a reporter." He deposited himself in a soft leather couch, sinking back, his knees stabbing his vision of the TV set. Someone lights a joint and hands it to him. It is quiet for a minute. Then the out-of-town player, sounding mostly asleep, offers:

"Thing is with reporters you never know when they're workin' and when they're not."

"Well, you can check a guy out. Everything seems cool once you get to know the guy. I'm not worryin' anybody."

"Sure, but the thing is, why risk it? You don't need to hang with a reporter so much that it's worth maybe gettin' in trouble."

Others enter in.

"Press is all management anyway."

"I hear that. Press won't fuck with Russ. Press is definitely management."

"How do you figure we're pro Russ?"

"Shit, you know what's going on with this team, yet you don't write it. You just quote Russ after every game like he was some god."

"Well, fuck, I take more shots at him than anybody else. I take shots at everybody and I sugar everybody when they do good. Besides, how can I write all the negative shit unless the players tell me the tales. I don't have to use names, but I got to have details. I'm not a mind reader."

"Sheeee, you can see what an ego trip he's on."

"Yeah, but I can't convince fans of much if I don't use some examples, some details. I'm not in the locker room. I'm not at practices."

"Why don't you come to practices?"

" 'Cause Russ doesn't want the press there."

"So you just accept that. See, you won't fight the fucker."

"Come on, what am I supposed to do? I challenge him and I lose all communication. He quits talking about all the little everyday shit that the fans want to read. I gotta worry about tomorrow, too. Russ can be a bitch."

"I hear that."

"You're management, man. All press is management."

I am surprised by this. Hurt, actually.

"Help me take him on then if there's so much to tell."

"I ain't gonna fuck up my career. He'll plant my ass in the streets like he did Brisker. I don't need that."

"Well, there are ways to bring things out without getting shot down. Remember last year in the playoffs when everyone was pissed at Russ and you had that meeting and Russ said he wanted to hear any gripes anyone had and only a couple of guys said something?"

"Yeah, what good would it do?"

"Well, at least the fans found out some of the hassles because guys talked to me. Remember, I wrote that story quoting a bunch of the players without using any names?"

"I don't read the paper. It's all management."

"Fuck you."

"Ah, you're all right, man. I know there's some guys on the team that don't know where you're at. They think you and Greg are just out to get big stories all the time. Most of the guys are about seventy percent sure you're okay. But seventy percent ain't a hundred. So, like he says, why risk it?"

"Hey, turn that up," someone interrupts the debate as Elton John's face jumps on the TV screen—the game having ended without notice of all but a couple of faces which had kept staring.

"Hey, fuck it, man. We got music. Leave it."

"How'd the game come out?"

"Lakers got it?"

"What was the score?"

"Don't know."

"Hey, turn that shit off."

Elton is prancing around the stage, neon bubbles dancing on his electric glasses. A cape flows behind him as he surges shirtless back and forth like a caged leopard. The TV sound goes off again. A joint comes around. The records are changed. A strong sax, the scrape of a snare drum, cymbals, ball-bouncing guitar. It's turned up loud. The bass bounces inside the room, creating a fuzzy *thum, thum, thum,* inside my chest.

"Herbie Mann, awwwwwl right."

"What's that song?"

" 'Sunrise High.' Nice."

"Hey, man, turn that down."

"Well," the man at the stereo responds in disgust, "if you just want to hear it."

"I can hear it lower."

"Like I said, if you just want to hear it, that's okay. I thought maybe you wanted to get *into* it."

"You're fucked, man."

The room falls silent except for the music. The glow of a joint brightens with an accompanying *esssssssph* inhale, then moves to the next hand. There is an occasional murmur as the passer tries to get the attention of a laid-back passee. Social sedation. Minds step inward to play with ideas, schemes and free-form dreams. Mine is wrestling with the words left from the conversation. The reporter is a partner with the athletes, yet against them. The players are rivals with those on the screen, yet they are cohorts. To most of these who watched that game, players and writers and management are all part of a tight group. Yet we are obviously fragmented. One role doesn't seem to fit anyone.

My imagination steps to a mental blackboard and draws three circles as in the design of a target.

"Hey, check this out," I call out to one of the players, one who might be most receptive to this. "Picture in your head a target, three rings. Got that?" No one says anything. I go on.

"Here are most of the fans. They seem to be the most limited in seeing what is going on. They know so little, only what reporters give them. They want what? Escape. They need intensity, involvement, commitment for that. They want you to get them off every night—what an impossibility, to get off for them *every* night."

"I hear that," someone says.

"To do that a fan must accept sort of a worship of the team, its players and the importance of getting wherever the team is trying to get. The writer can understand the powerful spectacle of this enthusiasm, but does he function there? Do the players and coaches? Do all fans?"

My eyes have been closed, trying to keep the target image. I open them. A couple guys are staring curiously at me. The rest have their eyes closed, sailing on thoughts of their own or mine. No one interrupts.

"If one draws this target with three rings, the bull's-eye would be what I just referred to. Call this the romanticism ring. This is the religion of sports, the autographs and the shaking of a hero's hand. This is life on the baseball card mentality—players reduced to objects. This is community rallying around team against other cities. Nationalism, on an international level. Players can live on this level, as well as reporters. This is the player overflowing with his own importance, just because he's in the NBA. This is the reporter as jock-sniffer."

"What you call this?" a voice asks.

"Romanticism."

"No, I mean your target?"

"Bull's-eye."

"Sheee-it. Bull's-eye. Man, you're ripped."

"Let me go on with this," I insist. No one refuses. "We drop outside to the next ring. This is the workaday level. This is where the reporter interacts with the players for interviews, where the game is analyzed. This is the competition for starting berths, the pursuit of victory for playoff shares and the satisfaction of beating a rival. This is skills and strategy. Call this the functionalism ring. The emotional influences in a job well done. Was the crowd entertained? Was the story well written? Did I play well? Friendships, true friendships, are in the next ring out. This is working relationships. You enjoy a time together because you are on the same plane. You wouldn't be together if you could choose time with others. This is a level of mutual respect. Players respect a rival's ability, a player or a coach respects a reporter's attempts to do an honest job. A person asked for an autograph here gives it as part of the job, his role, not because he really thinks he's so special that his name means anything on a piece of paper. The fan who is in this ring is a student of the game, not just in the "we won" thing. If he asks for autographs or a picture of his favorite player, he's on the romanticism ring."

"Fuck them autograph assholes, man," interjects a player.

"I hear that. Those mother-fuckers use your name for toilet paper and come back for more the next night."

"Hey, let me finish," I beg.

"Finish, man, finish."

"Okay, in a sense, each ring looks in, or down, on the inner one. And the outer one is obviously superior, for it is the integrity and self-identity of the individual. This is the egoism ring. Not like conceit, but like where a relationship goes beyond the roles and becomes a genuine friendship between a player and a coach or a writer and a general manager, say. It takes a sense of detachment from job titles and a great deal of trust to achieve. It's almost impossible. A fan could be on this level, but he can't get mindlessly in love with a team out here. This is where you see how fucked up sports can get. This is where a Dave Cowens quits. This is where asking a bunch of fucking questions after a game seems absurd. This is where you think Russ is fucking with you because of his head trying to rule yours, instead of him just coaching and you being a performer."

I pause, trying to hang on to the picture and the words.

"You finished, man?" a voice calls with genuine politeness.

"Yeah, you finished?" another asks, more impatiently.

"Yeah, I'm finished."

"Good. 'Cause I can't handle too much deep shit and you are definitely deep shit, man. Sometimes I think you think too much for your own good. Gotta be loose, B.J. Have a good time. Life takes care of itself."

"I hear that," someone adds.

"Just shoot the rock and fall back," sings another.

"I hear that, too."

"Yeah, you got some good shit, B.J. But I'll take some of this other shit here instead if you don't mind," one says as he draws flame onto the end of a new joint.

"I'm glad somebody around here knows what's happenin'," says the host as he puts on some new music. "But seems like it don't do anybody any good even when you do know."

"I hear that," I murmur.

23

On the Midseason Seesaw

Another sellout in the Coliseum. Another victory—this having been the twenty-ninth consecutive at home in regular season play. Golden State fell reluctantly by four and Seattle had equaled the second longest home streak in league history, Minneapolis having garnered twenty-nine in 1949. Sunday evening the Sonics go for No. 30 in pursuit of Philadelphia's league mark of thirty-six set in 1967. When there are no franchise-shattering trades, middle-of-the-night drug arrests or other such trials of the headline market to discuss, it's nice to have streaks to play with.

That gimmick ran out Sunday as Houston rolled in and over the

Sonics. Gray had been the best Sonic performer over the past three games, which came across as somewhat strange when I found out on Monday the details of his New Orleans encounter with Russell. Hopkins, rapping in conversation off the record, said: "When Leonard came late to practice, Bill asked him why he was late and Leonard just shrugged. Bill said he was going to fine him. Leonard told him to flush it up his ass. Bill told him to take some laps. Every time he came around, Leonard kept mumbling something at Bill. He hasn't been at practice since." Before I can pursue the story any further, Walsh calls me and says Gray has been traded to Washington.

Walsh later reconstructed that event: "Bill called me at the El Gaucho where I was having a late lunch. He said, 'I've traded Gray to Washington.' I got in my car and drove back to the office. Bill was gone. I can't reach him at home. I don't even know who we've traded him for. I'm supposed to put in a conference call to the league, where each side repeats the terms of the deal with each side on the line at the same time so there is no chance for mistakes. You have to tell them that you know of no physical disability or health problems with your player. Then you send a telex message saying the same things to the league and the other club. Then you make an agreement as to when the deal will be announced—that part never seems to work out. Well, here I am not even knowing what the deal is. I called Bob Ferry, the Bullet's G.M. and say, 'What kind of a guy is, ah, ah, you know. . . ?'

" 'Spoon?' Ferry asks.

" 'Yeah, Ol' Nick Weatherspoon. Slipped my mind for a minute.'

"So I called the league to get the details on his contract and now I've got to get a hold of Leonard. The six o'clock news is going to be on in an hour and I've got to find him before then. We've agreed to break the story then. I went over to his house. He wasn't there. I sat on the steps. At six I gave up, left a note and went back to the office. He called me a little while later, about two minutes before it was to go on the sports news. He said, 'Where do I send my bags?'

" 'Washington,' I told him.

" 'Great.' "

Gray contained his enthusiasm, barely, when I reached him that evening. He didn't want to say anything about his conflict with Russell. "What are my thoughts on the trade?" he repeated my question. "My thoughts are that I'm gonna get up and go to Washington, D.C. I have no emotional response except I will miss my friends here." We exchanged a so long and good luck. I called Russell. He refused to acknowledge the details of the New Orleans hassle. He wanted it left alone. Inasmuch as Hopkins had stipulated that the details were off the record, I just alluded to the fact that Gray and Russell had traded words and I decided I wouldn't take sides.

So, just like that, a mighty force in the Sonic camp—a man who had thwarted my desire for communication, a man who made life uncomfortable for me as a part of the media—was gone. I felt relieved in a way. And yet cheated out of a chance to possibly build an understanding of each other. Even though Sonic fans knew there had been a debate and maybe Russell had been dealt some harsh words, they seemed to finally be drawing a line after three and a half years and more than two rosters' worth of players dispatched. They were drawing the line and saying Russell had stepped over it. Signs rimmed the Coliseum as Seattle hosted Denver two days after the Gray trade:

"Heil, Herr Dictator."

"Der Führer Strikes Again—Russell's Next."

"Only One Thing Wrong with Sonics—Trade Russell."

"Who do you get along with, Russell?"

Russell stroked his beard and glanced around the perimeter at the signs. I leaned across the press table and told him it might be good public relations if he did a little goose-step walk down the court with his hand in a Sieg Heil salute. He laughed fairly soundly. I never was able to determine whether Russell or Walsh issued the order, but the signs were removed by tipoff. Something of the Pious Perch, which journalists are frequently guilty of, came into play here. I found myself making a judgment—that the Sonics were petty to take down those signs. I wanted to challenge them on it, maybe embarrass them by making an issue of it in the paper. I asked Walsh what the story was. "We have a policy of no signs in the Coliseum," he explained. I asked him why they never took down the "Freddy's Fans" and the "Slick the 76ers and Teach Them Watts For" signs. He said it was a flexible policy and that as long as there were no distracting characteristics to the signs, they could stay. I made a point of mentioning the signs and the boos Russell received during the introduction when I called in my halftime story for the first editions. But by the time I had rewritten my story for the final, relating how awful Seattle looked as Denver ran over the Sonics by fourteen, I got around to mentioning it only at the end. I was disturbed that I had buried it when I read the story the next morning and was more disturbed when I saw that Heberlein had it in his lead. I wondered if I was subconsciously holding my punches, or maybe I was subconsciously being a nonsensational journalist. Truth was, I was just poorly organized in my postgame notes on that occasion.

Prior to the Buffalo game that next Sunday, Russell read a letter as he sat on the bench during warm-ups. He flipped it over in front of me. It was from a fan and imparted disgust with the trade of Gray: ". . . The trade that should have been made was Burleson and Oleynick for a good backup center. . . . What have you done to that kid (Tommy)? The added fifty pounds has made him sluggish and it appears as though it's an effort for him to play ball. . . . The Houston game probably could have been won if you had started the second and third quarter team sooner or kept them in longer. . . . Let's get with the program, Bill. . . . Maybe Schulman ought to make the next trade: Russell for a coach who's not a prima donna and one who can communicate. You shouldn't let personal conflicts enter into professional sport. . . . The communications problem you appear to have may be within, look in the mirror once in a while."

After reading it, I said to Russell, "Some people have to pay for advice like that, you know."

"Yeah," he replied. "I've been getting it wholesale, lately."

Following a one-point loss to the Braves, I gambled that Russell would be in the locker room for a while and shot over to the Braves' locker room to interview Zaid Abdul-Aziz. He had been with the Sonics the year before but Russell wouldn't invite him back to camp. Abdul-Aziz had caught on with Buffalo and now came back to almost single-handedly beat the Sonics down the stretch. Abdul-Aziz was very happy.

Tolson was very unhappy as I encountered him walking out of the Sonics' dressing room. He told me, "Off the record, Russ said we didn't have no intensity. He said he was sorry that some of us were upset over his having traded Leonard, but we are here to do a job every night and those of us who can't deliver are gonna be looking for a new home." Tolson looked like a whipped puppy, scared. The rest of the locker room scene was a match as players dressed hurriedly and said little. For the public's consumption, Russell would only acknowledge, "We need to improve our concentration and poise under pressure. We have been playing with a lack of interest at times in the past few games. I'm not worried that we can't get it together." I asked if the spirits among the Sonics had been this sullen at any time during the previous season, even during lengthy losing streaks. "No, but I think you'll see things improving soon."

I used Tolson's words, without attribution, in my lead. I found out later Russell was upset and didn't want what happened or was said behind the locker room door winding up in print.

Two days after a double overtime loss to Chicago, Green and Brown jumped on an afternoon flight out of Denver and headed home. Blackburn related at the start of his broadcast that Brown had an injured leg and Green had the flu. I had remained in Seattle and it wasn't until the next day, via the *Times*, that I learned that officers of the law had come to the Sonics' shooting practice and tried to serve Green with a subpoena involving a child support suit. He left town for fear they would catch him at the game. The Nuggets destroyed Seattle by twenty-eight. And without any warning, it was Christmas.

Russell had wanted to fly to Portland Christmas Eve to keep the players' minds on the next night's game, but relented and headed down the next morning at ten. I could think of a whole lot of better ways to spend Christmas Day than sitting in a hotel and didn't head down until

180

two hours before game time. I walked out to courtside in the Portland Coliseum and sat in a chair as about half the team warmed up in private shoot-arounds and games of one on one. It felt as though I had been away from them for a month. They reacted the same way—cordial greetings. The Christmas spirit or a search for allies? They trooped by, some sitting and dropping off a load of discontent—Watts, Oleynick, Wilkerson, Johnson, Burleson—and moved back out onto the court. Nobody wanted to be quoted, but they all wanted to spill their guts to me. B.J. the Confessor. I figured I've got to listen now and try to talk them into some public statements when I can.

Burleson came back over and sat with his hands folded across his chest, staring out at the court as he talked in a monotone. "Russ says I'm never in shape until January. I need to be pushed, but he never goes hard in practice. Russ puts us down. He acts like he's made us what we are. Like none of us ever did anything till we met him. You'd think he picked up a bunch of construction workers to play for him. He gets on us because we're the worst free-throw shooters in the league. He says we're not concentrating. We're weak. I'd go to management, but he's too powerful. I'm just glad there are some people on other clubs who think I'm okay, that still want me. If Russ had gotten Mac, he would have carried the load and been the core of the team—can't blame Russ for wanting to trade me for him. Mac would have covered all Russ's weaknesses and carried him on through. This is all an embarrassment right now." I asked again and he declined again to let me use his sentiments in a feature.

Herm Gilliam trotted by with a Christmas greeting for his old mates. Russell had sold the guard at the end of last season, sold him out of misery and into the cat bird's seat. They were doing everything Walton's flashing eyes had promised on the eve of the campaign. They were currently the winningest team in the league. After six years in the basement, they were making dreams come true. It was a dramatic contrast to see the expressions conveyed by Walton and Gilliam and their crew compared to the sullen Sonics. The fun was all theirs right now.

Heberlein and I headed into the press room for a little Christmas feed. I informed him he did a helluva job on the road trip. Mr. Green had just informed me at courtside that he wasn't talking to the media "because that stuff about the arrest and the child support got nothing to do with basketball and shouldn't be in the paper." Heberlein said he had also been so informed. Oh, let's see, what else shall we talk about? Basketball, maybe. He said at Chicago some reporter had asked Russell in the postgame interview how the Sonics had fallen apart at the end of the double O.T. Russell had asked him what paper he was with. The guy had named some surburban paper. Russell had just turned and walked away—end of interview. I asked Heberlein what Santa brought him. He said a transfer to cover the Blazers.

Seattle was feisty for a half, leading by seven at the intermission. Oleynick was playing for the still-injured Brown and filling it up. Walton took over in the second half and Portland went on its merry way for an easy win. Seattle dropped its sixth straight and bounced into the Pacific Division cellar.

The next night a sellout crowd in the Coliseum booed itself for showing up (well, I assume that's who they were booing) as the Sonics dropped into a 24–12 hole. Portland missed six fast-break layups or it would have been worse. Now, in case we haven't established the fact that Seattle was playing erratic ball at this juncture of our tale, get this: That 24–12 was Seattle's lowest quarter of the year. In the second quarter the Sonics put together their highest frame with thirty-seven, while holding Portland to thirteen. They went on to win by two. Fans who were booing left drooling. I confessed that evening, in the privacy of a day-after-Christmas party with close friends, that I did not know how to figure out the team I was covering.

As the team chugged off to another little stint on the road which would ask them to visit Atlanta, the New York Nets and Cleveland on successive nights, I was content to sit at home with the radio and the incoming mail. A late-arriving Christmas card just about summed things up: "May the coming year bring more unanswerable questions, more doubts, more thought, more soul-searching, more highs and lows for both of us; because, after all, that's what it's all about. God save the Sonics. Merry Christmas, a fan."

I wrote a comparison study as to what Gray and Weatherspoon were doing for their new teams since the trade. On the morning it ran I got a call that brought me out of a comfortable sleep:

"This the Blaine Johnson who writes for the *P-I*?"

"Yeah."

"Did you write that article comparing Weatherspoon with Gray?"

"Yeah."

"Well, I think you're full of bullshit." Click.

So here I was office-bound as the Sonics headed out for three games in as many nights. I didn't feel I was apt to miss too much—until I walked into the office to monitor the Atlanta game and saw a banner headline in the *Times*. Oleynick had opened his soul to Heberlein. Christmas night he tells me how upset he is, "but I'm not ready to print it, yet." He got ready in a hurry. My New Orleans friend-in-fun, my running road mate. How could you, Frank?

"... I'm disillusioned. Things just haven't developed totally the way I expected. I really can't say the opportunity has developed. . . . I'm not saying I should be third guard or not fifth guard. . . . The only thing I question is why he has me hanging around. He traded Herm Gilliam before the season. He told me he traded him so I could play. But I haven't. It's hard for me to grasp what his motives are. . . . Sometimes I go four, five games without playing. Then like he played me in Washington. He put me out there three-four-five minutes. I was tired. I hadn't been playing. He told me I was out of shape. Any fool knows that. What did he think? I was out jogging? . . . He has told us those who aren't playing will be lucky to be around by the end of the season. . . ."

I called Oleynick at his hotel. He said he was sorry that the story had gone to Heberlein, but that he had just been talking at dinner and decided to get it out in the open. He was real sorry, he repeated. So was I.

I received a memo from my editor the next day:

"I know you are very conscientious about your beat, but two of the more interesting stories that have come out lately have been the UPI story on Bob Wilkerson and the Oleynick story by Greg. I have also had people ask me why the boos that greeted Russell at recent games were in the *Times* lead and headline and in the last graf of our story. I'm not worried about this except that I don't like to see good, controversial player profiles come from other sources. We want to be first and best in every beat."

My first inclination upon reading the memo was to ask, "Where were the thanks for all the extra work on the McAdoo piece? What about all the little anecdotes that come out of the road trips that you aren't seeing anywhere else? Who else is getting in-depth interviews with Walton? Who else is writing commentaries while covering a beat in this town?" But the painful truth was that I had been beaten on a couple of good stories. I may be batting well, but perfection is the goal around here. I walked into his office and explained my approach with Russell and the players. He said I was probably too close to the players—unable to approach them as a reporter and ask simple questions. I was getting involved as a confidant rather than a reporter.

I thought back to the Three Ring Perspective I had conjured earlier. I wasn't being a fan, was I? I wasn't letting the team's lack of success disturb me? No, I didn't think I was bogged down in the romanticism—wanting everything to be rah-rah perfect. It was, I decided, a confusion of functionalism and egoism. I wasn't able to separate the two. I was trying to extend the workaday relationships into personal relationships—ones with meaning and mutual interest. I was trying to be what I would want Blaine Johnson to be if I were in their place. It wasn't working to the fullest extent, apparently, because while I was getting a better rapport with some of the players, I wasn't covering the beat to the satisfaction of my editor and I wasn't really satisfied with the relationships, because there wasn't true mutual respect. I had to try to look at the players and Russell more as subjects and less as people.

Two wins in the three road tries set up the evening's match. It was the first game at home since Oleynick spoke out in the article. How would the crowd react for his having challenged Russell's judgment? The fans booed Oleynick. They booed Russell. The fans didn't appear to be very happy with anybody.

Early in the game Russell called out to Gushue, "Hey Joe, I remember when you came into the league. Guess I'm an old man, huh? Ha, ha, ha." Gushue smiled. Soften 'em up, Russ. That certainly was a lot more palatable than the way Gushue had been treated by Russell's former mentor when Auerbach stood at midcourt in Boston Garden, screaming at Gushue. It's all psyche—just different styles. The referee sees them all.

The referee—the lonely warrior of pro basketball. They have all the travel and yet no companions. They have all the pressure, and yet no side to turn to for approval. The most they can hope for is being ignored—that means they are doing a good job. The league had kept, and still does, a pretty tight muzzle on officials. So it was a bit of a challenge, as much as a curiosity, to want to gain an interview with one of these men in gray. Earl Strom proved to be a perfect companion for my aspirations. A rebel in character, he had proven to be outspoken and full of entertaining insights during the several conversations we had in pregame sessions at the Coliseum and during a couple of airport encounters along the way.

When I sat down to write the story, I tried to find some way to lead into it without using what I knew had to be the most provocative angle. I didn't like to mark him as a spectacle in a circus act when what he had to impart was actually the reflections of a man much more sensitive than the screaming maniac he had been that one wild night in the Coliseum. But I had to go with it, the reference to the night he had become involved in a verbal—and more if he could have gotten it— battle with Brown at the end of a Sonics' game against the Rockets.

In February 1975 the horn had just blown on a one-point Seattle victory when Strom started to exit across the court. Archie Clark's girl friend grabbed Strom on the arm. He pushed her away. Suddenly he was standing toe to toe with Brown. Russell stepped between them, they continued to yell at each other, leaning around Russell. Strom's partner, Hubert Brown, was barely able to restrain Strom. The crowd was on the verge of being worked into a riot. I was halfway up in the stands. I told a friend at that time that "that is inexcusable conduct by an official. They should never let him work another game." I'm glad now he was kept in the league. In my opinion he's one of the best officials in the NBA and his attitude has to be respected for its honesty. At the age of forty-seven he was completing his nineteenth season as a pro official. He called that incident in Seattle "the tensest situation I've ever been through as an official."

The next morning's paper account had quoted him: "A broad

came out and grabbed me by the arm when the game ended. I pushed her away and then some other fan grabbed me. Then Brown got into the bleeping act. No, Brown didn't swing at me. He just grabbed at me. I'll fight that little bleeper. I want him. Look at this (he holds out arms red from being grabbed) and this (pointing to his beer-drenched uniform). Is this what you get for a tough night's work? Kind of like old times," he had added with a rueful smile.

It wasn't just that Strom had gone into such an outlandish fit in front of all those fans that made this incident so startling. This was compounded by the fact Strom had exposed the unspoken. It was suddenly obvious that NBA officials could talk, or think, or have their feelings hurt, or do a lot of unpredictable things besides blow a whistle that nobody wanted to hear. "I've always maintained that if you can work a game and have people saying as they leave, 'Gee, that was a good game. I wonder who those officials were?' you've done a good job as a referee." Strom commented as he pulled on a knee brace in the small official's dressing room and commenced with some stretching exercises and push-ups.

"Some guys think they get an edge by complaining and beefing, but on the whole, I think that has improved over the years. I don't think you have the Red Auerbach type coaches who start at the opening whistle trying to get the edge. In the old days Red wasn't alone either. I guess it was expected of coaches. Guys like Al Servy, Alex Hanum, Red Holzman. Now, Holzman has mellowed over the years. But all those guys felt they got the edge by intimidating officials—and maybe in those days they did." Strom agreed with the observation that it seems ironic for former Celtics like Russell, Cousy, Sharman, K.C. Jones, Nelson and the like to have spurned Auerbach's courtside manner when they took up coaching. "Tom Heinsohn is the only one who in any way has resembled Red. I will say this, Russell seldom said anything as a player or a coach unless he felt he had a valid objection. There certainly are some who don't wait to feel they are being truly unjustly treated before you hear them start peeping.

"I'd have to say that Brown is probably the greatest shooting guard in the game right now. I think a lot of times that these guys are seeing the ball so often that they don't realize they are often creating the contact by jumping into people on their shots. He'll shake his head at the official or the crowd because he didn't get the foul he thought he had coming, or he'll wave his hands. He's trying to embarrass the officials when he does that. We hope that we wouldn't become petty in trying to get back at a player who has tried to embarrass us, but I suppose subconsciously it happens. You have players who give a choke signal, grabbing their neck. Rick Barry is a good one for that, walking along clutching his throat, generally behind your back so you can't do anything about it. Hanum was particularly bad when he was at Syracuse, where they didn't need much encouragement to turn the place into a riot anyway. If a call went opposite the way he thought it should, he would just turn to the crowd and hold his hands on top of his head, as if to say, 'What's he doing to *us*?' Well, the place would just come down.

"Bill Walton was giving a nod of agreement or a shake of his head on every call during one game. I quietly told him I didn't need any of his agreeing or disagreeing on the court. He stopped. Mike Newlin is a good one for that. If you make a call in his favor he'll come over and say, 'Good position, good call.' I told him, 'I'm the ref, you're the player. I'm getting paid to have good position and make good calls, knock it off.'"

Strom works a game with physical authority, giving the impression of strength, a degree of toughness, as he clasps a hand on his other arm to indicate holding or hacks his forearm to indicate a hacking foul. Manny Sokol is called a "stargazer" because he supposedly protects the superstars. Richie Powers has some cute little hops and expressions he employs when calling a foul. "Every official has his own idiosyncrasies," says Strom. "We are told to keep the showmanship down. And I think that's a proper philosophy. People aren't paying money to watch some official put on a show." The no-foul-out rule has long been considered by the NBA, primarily because people pay to see the stars play and basketball happens to be the only sport where a player is disqualified from the game for ordinary infractions of the rules. It is true that most officials tend to favor the established stars. One reason is that the stars know how to make the other player look like the guilty one, and also because there are a lot of calls that could go either way and the official is bound to go with the established player over a rookie or reserve. There should be no doubt that officials favor the home team. There is a noticeable shifting of gears when it gets near playoff time and an official realizes the importance of the game to both teams. But through most of the regular season, human nature is going to prevail. It's my contention, after watching the facial expressions and actions of officials, that making the call that favors the home team and therefore brings a thunderous roar of approval is fun to make. No official is going to be doing this purposefully, but subconsciously I have to believe it is a factor. Another factor in relation to the home court is the help an official receives from the fans—who will call out when an opposing player is in the lane, yell when a local is being held and so on.

Strom, without agreeing in detail, admitted the reality of human emotion and its role with officials. Human emotions—such a foreign element in the image of an official. Their life is almost subhuman for the duration of the season. Strom, married and the father of five, gets home about five days a month. Required to have minimal contact with the players and the writers and any club management, he, like all officials, must stay at separate hotels and take other flights when at all possible. It's the life of a loner. Often the partner official is even on a separate schedule.

In the eyes of the league, the closer an official is to existing as a nonbeing, the better. That anonymity was violated in the opinion of the NBA by our communication. Some of Strom's observations were enough to stir up the men in the big tent at NBA headquarters. John Nucatola, who was then superintendent of officials and always a strong proponent of the mum-to-the-point-of-meekness stature of referees, called me shortly after the article ran. I found out two things. Apparently a lot of teams read the *P-I* and apparently a lot of people can't stand honesty. Nucatola said the Warriors had called and were very upset that Strom had made those statements about Barry. There had been other complaints saying that Strom was implying he was out to get certain players. Nucatola said Strom had been pinned down on the matter and said that I had misquoted him.

Instincts, nothing else, told me Nucatola was trying to get me to sting Strom. I said we had enjoyed several conversations and it's possible I might have picked up something that was meant to be off the record. He said Strom shouldn't be saying those things to anybody. I told Nucatola I thought it was damn good for basketball and that there was nothing wrong with acknowledging referees are just human beings with human responses. He said that wasn't the league policy to take such an approach.

Later in the year I encountered Strom on the road. I told him about Nucatola calling. He said he was pleased I hadn't backed down. He said he never even implied that I had misquoted him.

The Sonics knocked off Chicago for their fourth win in five outings. Weatherspoon survived a head-on collision with Norwood to put in the winning shots. The Sonics continued to confuse even the closest of followers. There had to be something to account for the turnabout, right? It turned out Russell had a little heart-to-heart while the team was in Atlanta.

I had gone to the Sonics' office the day after the Chicago game and wound up talking to Watts, who was there collecting some appearance moneys from the club. We sat on the leather couch in Russell's office. Russell wasn't around, but there were those various pictures of him— including a poster of him clad in a full-body riding suit and helmet, riding a motorcycle over a jump, airborne. I had intended to ask Watts about his current status as second-leading vote collector in the fans' balloting for the All-Star game. He figured if he and Brown could get back there, to Milwaukee, that he could get the MVP award for Brown. "I could set him up all night long." He happened to mention there had been some heavy things said in Atlanta. I thought that at least there was something that happened on the road that Heberlein hadn't consumed while I was absent.

"Russ told Tommy he cared about him and that he can be one of the best centers in the league. Tommy has just been feeling down because Russ was going to trade him—that's hard on a guy, like a divorce, you know. Russ kind of opened our heads up and showed us the position he was in. He sounded sincere and I could feel the vibes change in the dressing room. You hear the truth, you can feel it. I think the new fellas should be getting a little less playing time because me and Fred done paid our dues, but I ain't gonna be sullen about it. We got to run. I'm quite sure Russ wouldn't argue with that because you know I told him when I was a little kid I used to watch him play in Boston on the TV and they ran. He said they worked plays. But I said they didn't because when they worked plays they used to get the shit whupped out of them. But they had him to get the boards. I get angry with him sometimes when he wants to keep me on the bench. I want to cuss him out, talk about him, want to shoot him. But I gotta just do what he says and help all the fellas keep the faith. Faith is all about people believin' in the same things together. I think if we all keep thinking those good vibes and keep having fun and drinking that white wine and playing with each other we'll be all right. I think Portland has a good team, but I don't see how Walton can make it all the way through the season without steppin' on a sprinkler head or something. He's so big and he plays just like me, runnin' all the time. And my knees be hurtin' and I'm healthy and little. We'll be all right as long as Russ uses me most of the time and you know I ain't gonna ever wear out. Frank Furtado will tell you there are times when I shouldn't be out there, but I just say I ain't gonna pull up and miss no games. We gonna be all right now."

It made a good off-day feature. I was sure there were some holes in the Second Coming philosophy, but most of the fans would probably like to hear a little encouragement along about now.

The next evening Boston visited. Midway through the first half Charlie Scott was crying to Sokol in front of the Sonic bench. Russell called out: "You're on the road, Charlie. You don't get anything. You been in the league long enough to know that."

"Tell 'em, Russ." Sokol laughed.

Scott looked at Sokol and then at Russell. "Tell 'em, Russ? What do you mean by that?" Scott looked as if someone had just told him there was no Santa Claus.

An aftershock of Christmas generosity seemed in evidence by game's end as Seattle pulled off one of the real fluke finishes of modern basketball history. Burleson lumbered up to double-team White in Boston's backcourt with ten seconds left and the Sonics down by one. Watts lunged for the ball, White wheeled away from him and right into

Burleson. The ball kicked loose, Burleson grabbed it and bounced once toward the hoop. White cut him off. Burleson pivoted and stepped to the hoop for a two-handed stuffer just before the horn sounded. Seattle had it by one. Heinsohn was flirting with a cerebral hemorrhage as he left the court howling at the officials who interpreted the play as having been without either foul or excessive steps. He was raging as he faced reporters. Were you upset about the last call? a reporter asked. A dumb question, but it received a helluva answer.

"Yes, I was upset about the last call. Hell yes, I was upset about the last call. Burleson kicked the ball, he fouled JoJo and he took four steps going to the hoop. You think I'm upset? Hell yes, I'm upset about the last call." He was pounding the training table with his hammy fist. His voice was thick with the injustice of it all. "That was our game tonight and it was taken away from us and there was nothing we could do about it in the end. What we wanted to do in the end was spread the floor and let JoJo try and dribble the ball for the remaining ten seconds. But then Burleson fouled him and then kicked the ball and then took four steps going to the hoop. What a terrible way to lose."

In the Sonic camp the quotes were of a different flavor. Norwood: "It seemed illegal because he's seven feet tall and covers a lot of area. You just don't expect a seven-footer to make a move like that." Burleson: "I just charged up there and I think I startled JoJo." Russell: "Did he walk? They didn't call it, did they?" After all the quotes were gathered, I headed for the office stuck with a tough decision. I felt he had traveled. I had been sure they would disallow the basket the second it went through. The game had been televised locally. The TV people had obviously rerun it a dozen times and come to a decision. But I couldn't get in touch with anybody who had seen it. If I said he had traveled and the TV had shown through a replay that he actually hadn't, I would look a little foolish. Conversely, if I said he was safe and the TV had shown otherwise, well, it was a predicament. I concluded the Sonics had won it in a "walkaway."

Meanwhile, the Sonics were homestanding tall. San Antonio showed up two days after the Boston walk-a-thon and showed the folks what good ol' shoot-from-downtown basketball was like in the ABA. Denver and Indiana had offered their versions of active basketball, but the Spurs were the class of the showtime fleet. With Larry Kenon and George Gervin firing away from all over the court, SA took a 45–34 first-quarter lead over Seattle. The Sonics rallied, claiming a 131–124 victory. Fun, fun, fun. Maravich brought the league's leading scoring average in on Sunday and stunk it up, collecting only twelve points against his usual thirty-two. Seattle set a new defensive low, 92–76. The Sonics had won seven of eight.

Everybody was at ease in the Sonic camp—winning seems to provide a direct influence on the reduction of bitching. Winning may reduce some of the reporter's opportunity for discussion of human drama, but the smiles and relaxed atmosphere are worth it. Three days later Detroit fell by twenty-two. Seattle's bench was playing up a storm. Eight of nine wins. The Knicks had a few days off awaiting Friday's date with the Sonics. McAdoo came to the Detroit game. Gee, the announcer plum forgot to introduce him. Don't suppose Sonic management was worried that the fans might be discourteous and boo him for not coming west. Even in victory the fans can be hard. As Russell sent Oleynick into the rout of Detroit with four minutes left, a loud voice called from above: "Russell doesn't smoke cigars, so he sends in Oly."

Haywood apparently didn't have anyone he particularly wanted to see in Seattle, because he was forced to fly home from Los Angeles to New York with an ailing leg. This was to be the only visit by the Knicks this season, so much for any chance for Seattle's fans to pay their sentiments to Woody. The Sonics incurred boos with a sloppy start against the Knicks, then mowed them down by twenty. Nine of ten. Ho-hum, business is booming. Whatever happen to all the hassles? Did Russell's Atlanta talk really turn things around? And so instead of gripes and dissension, I was left to work with quotes such as this offering by Watts after the Knicks' victory: "New York's all a bunch of smooth, high-class ballplayers who don't like to sweat. We ran and made them sweat and that's why we won."

Schulman stopped in Seattle to announce he was establishing a ten-thousand-dollar scholarship fund for female basketball players attending the three local universities. The guy knows his public relations.

Denver popped the bubble with a narrow Sunday afternoon decision in which Seattle reminded a national TV audience which team was the worst free-throw shooters in the league by missing twenty-two of thirty-nine attempts. It was so bad that when Paul Silas was given a technical foul in the second quarter someone along press row asked if the Sonics could have the seventy-five dollars Silas would be fined in lieu of the shot.

While dishing out twelve assists as Seattle made it ten of twelve wins against Indiana, Watts took a nasty fall. It is maybe the most impressive of all their skills, the way pro cagers are able to protect themselves when they trip or fall. Watts didn't have a chance this time. Sandwiched on a drive down the lane, he flipped forward and came down on his knee. He jumped up and glared at official Norm Drucker, who called traveling. Watts told him, "If you want to end my career, just keep lettin' them hit me like that." He went into a tirade on defense, chasing the ball all over the court like a kitten batting at a string. After the game he said his knee was sore, but went off into the night to a dinner appointment.

In the middle of the night he was struck with pain enough to cause him to call a policeman to whisk him to the hospital. "I thought it was broke. I was just bitin' the pillow till I couldn't take it no more."

The X-rays failed to disclose a fracture, but when I encountered Watts the next day at the Sonics' office—hobbling around on crutches and wearing an old woman's robe—I learned he wouldn't be flying out to Denver with us that afternoon. His spirits were up, although he expressed frustration that his Sonic record of 223 consecutive games would be eclipsed.

Even in retrospect, there was no indication then of the forthcoming changes in Watts. Even a Watts-watcher such as myself had no anticipation that he was about to come face to face with the reality that he, too, was merely mortal.

24
A New Nod of Negativity

The Sonics took their hot act, winners in ten of the past twelve, on the road for a little western swing. First stop was Denver, where the matter of Green's availability to play due to his conflict with the law there remained a question mark as game time approached. The game was to be televised back to Seattle and the TV crew joined reporters and Walsh in the lounge a couple hours before tipoff. Pete Gross, the play-by-play man, wanted to know what to tell the viewers if Green didn't show up.

"Well, maybe just say he's ill," Walsh suggested.

"I don't think that's really right," said Gross.

"Well, then, just say he has personal problems," countered Walsh.

"You can say what you want," I stated, suddenly incensed, "but they're going to read the truth in the paper tomorrow morning."

"You know I've never tried to tell you what to write, have I?" replied Walsh. "I'm not asking you to gloss over anything. TV is different. The press and TV have different roles."

"I don't see it," I continued, "except that TV has to make a contract with you to even have the rights to cover the games."

"People don't expect discussion of things like this on TV," Walsh continued.

"I don't know, Bob. It seems like I've been holding my punches and rounding off edges all season. I'm getting tired of straining to decide what to use and what to hold. I go along with Russ on the McAdoo thing and he turns around and tries to completely squash the papers getting any information on it. He tells Sam to quit talking to us. Where's the reward for going along on your schedule? I don't see it anymore—all I do is get upset. I go along with the players on their gripes and I get burned. It's all getting to be a big pain in the ass."

The debate was without a resolution, however, as Green showed up, all smiles. There was no law on his tail. He apparently had straightened out his problems. Flu-bugged Oleynick would have been happier if he had been tossed in jail rather than having made it to the arena that night. He committed seven of Seattle's eleven turnovers in the opening nine minutes before being benched. Seattle managed to hang close through a half, but thirty-three turnovers eventually did them in. In the locker room I was asking Bantom about any possible effects of the altitude when Green, at the adjacent locker, started talking. I almost fell over. "It gets ya, man. This thin air gets 'em all. When I was playing for Denver in the ABA we used to get them guys running and they would just wilt. They would just fade away. They should never lose a game up here. It's no psychological thing, it gets you right here." He laughed, thumping his chest.

I didn't know what to think at the time, but the next morning when Russell casually asked me at the Denver airport why I was being so negative lately, I should have guessed it was probably prompted by my statements to Walsh the previous evening. I never did find out for sure, but the timing in wake of my comments about how I was going to handle the Green absence certainly was suspicious. He caught me so by surprise I didn't have a chance to relate just what had brought me to a feeling of negativity. It was surprising to have him even acknowledge he paid any attention to what my emotional stance was. He said it was my way of asking questions, like I didn't believe anybody. I wanted to go on with the conversation, but it was time to board and there was no chance to pursue it. Later I told him how I felt put off by the McAdoo events and a lot of other little things, such as their taking down the signs in the Coliseum. He didn't say much more. Sly guy. So sly I still don't know where he was really coming from—whether he was just plainly interested in what I was thinking or if he was worried I might become a nuisance to the image of his operation. The worst part was something I didn't see until much later. I was letting my emotions get in the way of being an objective journalist.

The next stop, in Phoenix, produced a game that possessed all the finesse of a pair of tennis shoes banging around in a clothes dryer. Seattle was never really in it and Brown took himself out of the game with five minutes to go, complaining of fatigue: "Without Slick I have to do everything. He usually directs and I score. I was trying to do too many things out there and just got tired. We need Slick." There were a couple of substitutions that made no sense to me. Bantom went in early in the second quarter, hustled, got down on the floor for Seattle's only recovered loose ball of the day, scored the Sonics' only three points in those four minutes and came out to never see action again that afternoon. Tolson went in at 10:38 of the final quarter, came out at 9:44 and went back out at 8:14.

I asked Russell, how come? "You've got to have a mix of offense and defense. It doesn't take more than a few seconds to see that a certain player isn't the one who should be in there." But don't you know these guys well enough at this stage of the season to know what kind of blend it's going to create out there? "Sometimes I see immediately that I've made a mistake," Russell answered. "It's not necessarily anything he did wrong, just that we don't have the right mix. I don't like to embarrass a guy by pulling him immediately, but there's a responsibility to have the most effective unit out there." I put together a little sidebar and concluded it with this statement: It may take Russell only a few seconds to make a reversal of a substitution decision, but the second guessing is sure to go on over the remaining months of this season—and probably the next.

Do you think that's a little too negative?

The Sonics were positively atrocious two nights later in Los Angeles, getting down 21-2 and never recovering. Afterward, Russell held a loudly worded confab in the locker room. I went down the hall to catch some comments from Jerry West, keeping an eye out for a signal from a guard as to when Russell would emerge around the corner. It was an effort for Russell to shift into his "Everything's under control" face after the diatribe delivered on the other side of the door, but he tried. Did they throw something at you that you weren't expecting? I asked. "Yeah, basketball," he laughed. But you could tell he was angry. I asked if he might consider some different starters for the next evening's rematch in Seattle. He said there was a possibility of that. Any chance of a trade before the deadline at the end of the week? "I shouldn't make any rash statement when I'm upset."

I went into the locker room. Heads hung. I felt like I was in New Orleans. I kept digging until I found out Russell had said, "You bastards ain't got me yet. There can be some changes if you guys are trying to bring me down."

The next night the "bastards" played much better as the Lakers visited Seattle. Burleson was the most dramatic twenty-four-hour turnaround one could imagine.

There's a rumor in the NBA that Kareem Abdul-Jabbar doesn't have any use for Burleson. They say that stems from a game in which the Sonic center, as a rookie, fired home a shot over the Laker postman and yelled, "In your face, Kareem." Abdul-Jabbar reportedly went wild at both ends of the court for the remainder of that game and has been out to make Tall Tommy pay on every subsequent meeting. That may be true, may not be, but when Lakers and Sonics met the next night in Seattle, he made the mistake of pounding Burleson out of a season-long lethargy. Burleson, who had been decked with a poke in the eye earlier in the game, was backing into Abdul-Jabbar when the latter hauled off and dropped him with a right cross. The goggled Laker center then danced on his toes, fists raised for more action. But the punch had the effect of hitting a mule over the head with a two-by-four to get his attention. Burleson rose to slam home the balance of his twenty-six points, Abdul-Jabbar getting half his season average of twenty-eight. Seattle pulled away for a fifteen-point win.

Of course, Burleson getting hit on the head wasn't the sole reason for the Sonics' dramatic turnaround from the previous night. Watts was back.

Two days later he received the disappointing news that he had not been picked up as an addition to the West squad for the upcoming All-Star game. That news was followed about an hour later by the announcement that Russell had traded Bantom to the Nets and picked up Bob Love, who had been waived by the Nets.

Russell didn't want to explain the deal other than to say, "Mike did not perform as consistently as we needed. Love will give us consistent outside shooting." I doubted anyone waived by the lowly Nets was going to offer much, even though it was a player of Love's former stature. Frankly, I was miffed that Russell kept making these deals and leaving the commentary to the media's guesswork. It was another in a long line of dismissals due to Russell's quirksome evaluation of player personalities. I decided to stick the facts out there and let them paint a picture that Bantom really didn't have much of a chance: "The ominous signs had been there, like the darkening of clouds on the horizon. Mike Bantom had to suspect something was wrong as the playing time became less over the past half-dozen games. Bantom, who came to Seattle a month into last season from Phoenix for $225,000, moved into the starting lineup earlier this season—then was replaced in that role when Nick Weatherspoon became a starter eight games ago. Seven games back, Bantom came off the bench to hit seven-of-nine from the field. He played 30 minutes that night against the Knicks. 'Russ told me that was the best game I had played since I came to the Sonics,' Bantom recalled as he learned of the trade. 'He never said anything to me since then,' continued Bantom, who played 12 minutes in the game following the Knicks' outing, then three, then none against Denver—that being a game in which Russell lamented he did not have enough fresh troops at the end. When Bantom gave what appeared to be an enthusiastic account against Phoenix, but was jerked in less than four minutes, the warning signs were obviously growing. Eight minutes and then none over the next two games led up to the trade. . . ." A departing player can be the best of all possible candidates for provocative evaluation of what a team is doing. Seattle had been sending them down the road all season and Bantom, like the rest, would only say "good-bye."

25
Uprooting Russell

The Coliseum crowd accorded Gray a warm welcome as he returned in a Bullets' blue uniform in early February. It seemed the boos for Russell were stronger than ever, but it was hard to separate the boos for having traded Gray from the boos for having traded Bantom.

Gray played well and the visitors took it by three. I was running late for no particular reason and yet I wanted to get something from Gray—although I feared there might be just another one of those rebuffs that had become so familiar at the opposite end of the Coliseum earlier in the season. I wove through piles of jocks and socks and sweating bodies and toweling-off bodies and reached Gray. He smiled, held out his hand. I shook it. Wiped the perspiration off on my slacks. He said, "What's this, no soul tonight?" I shrugged. We shook hands with all the moves. I wiped my hand off on my slacks again. He said he was happy with his new team and yes, they looked like a bona fide title contender and yes, he missed his old mates but that was the business, you know.

Georg N. Meyers, sports editor for the Seattle *Times*, wasn't at the game that night. He was at home. Forgetting there wasn't a University of Washington basketball game that evening, he flipped on the radio to catch the broadcast. Wayne Cody's *Sports Talk Show* was on instead. What was this? Schulman was his guest and he was offering a comment in matter-of-fact language about how he couldn't rationalize renewing Russell's contract as both coach and general manager when his present five-year contract expired at the end of the season after the current one. It is very likely that if Meyers, or another newspaperman, hadn't heard that statement that evening, the matter wouldn't have surfaced until maybe next year when I, or someone, would have repeated that question he had been so worried about during our interview at the start of this season. That is, unless Schulman had developed a plan and wasn't fully candid when he later said this comment "had just slipped out."

It must have seemed very casual, because it wasn't really acknowledged until Sunday morning when Meyers unleashed the story. As Meyers noted, it seemed safe to assume Russell would hold his Sonic post unto perpetuity, if not longer. But here was Schulman saying "Russell is too expensive. I have told Bill that I'd love him to continue as coach, but he's too rich for me. There are two things I don't like about the situation, which I compromised with when I asked him to come with us. One, I think the coach and general manager should be two individuals. Secondly, he's just too expensive for me." Was there any possibility Russell would not fulfill the final year on his contract? Meyers quoted Schulman, "None whatsoever. My relations with Bill have been excellent. Maybe I have spoken too much, and I don't know if he wants this in the press, but when I am asked questions, I usually, unfortunately, answer very frankly. I just wonder how Bill will regard it, but I'll face that."

Russell's own long-range intentions might have been reflected in his handling of a block of stock he had been given the opportunity to buy when he came to the Sonics. As Meyers stated, Russell had purchased fifty thousand shares of First Northwest Industries, for $200,000 with payment deferred until his contract would expire on July 1, 1978. Schulman had guaranteed him his money back if it dropped below the purchase price. Russell had unloaded the stock the previous spring, costing Schulman sixty-two cents per share.

That evening, prior to the Sonics' game with Milwaukee, I cornered Schulman and asked him why he had made such a statement at this time. "The matter probably wouldn't have come up if Bill hadn't wanted to talk about it the last time I was up here [two weeks earlier]. I might have made a mistake in discussing the matter on the radio but I guess the public has a right to know what's going on." I had heard a rumor that there was a $500,000 penalty clause in Russell's contract if he was fired before his contract ran the full five years. Schulman assured me there was no such clause and that there was no chance he wouldn't be there through the following season.

Following the game, a ho-hum win dramatized by eleven assists on the part of Wilkerson, the small postgame interview room was crowded with twice the normal six or seven reporters. Russell strolled in, sat down on the little couch at the end of the room, hooked his fingers around a knee and waited for the questions. I wanted to see who would wade into the Schulman matter first. I didn't want to be the one because I didn't want him to think I was being negative. Huh-uh. Someone asked about Wilkerson's play. Someone else asked about when he might consider starting Green ahead of Burleson. There was a pause that grew to five or six seconds. Such pauses can be very loaded moments. I fondled my tape recorder, looked around at the rest of the press. No one was making a move, just scribbling notes, waiting. I looked back at Russell and said, "Moving over to other matters, do you think Sam's statement compromises your position and the things you are trying to do?"

He gave me a little stare—or was it just my paranoia?—paused two counts and replied, "I don't think so."

"Were you surprised that he made such a statement?" I continued.

"No . . . I guess, I guess it only proves one thing. That I've done too good a job." His face was contemplative.

"At what?" I asked.

"My ambition was when I came here . . . well, when I came here this franchise was a mess. They needed me and I wanted to make it so they didn't need me anymore. That means that I've done what I wanted to do."

There was a long enough pause for someone to jump in. Everyone just wrote in their notebooks. "Well, you haven't accomplished everything you wanted to do, have you?" I continued, trying to be conversational, but sensing I was on the prowl for a bold statement of some sort. "You haven't put together a package that you want to tie a string around and say, 'that's the lot,' have you?"

He was leaning back against the couch, relaxing. "No, I ah . . . there's only one thing that bothers me. And that's that Sam said I was too expensive. But, then, I guess that's really a compliment that I negotiate well. That's about it."

"How do you look at the year after next, after your contract expires?" I asked.

"I shouldn't do that. As I've said to you many times, I always play the hand out."

Heberlein finally led the rest of the troops up to the front line. "Is it conceivable you would coach without being the general manager?"

"Now, you know I'm not going to answer that," Russell replied amiably. "Why do you even ask a question like that?"

"Well, because the guys at the office will say, 'Did you ask Russell if he would coach without being G.M.?' and I wanted to be able to say that I had," Heberlein countered, his smile being kissed by Russell's powerful roar of laughter.

"Greg, why don't you let your wife dress you? She does a much better job of picking things that match," Russell said as he continued to laugh. Heberlein didn't answer, but smiled at what had become a frequent tease between the two.

The master had squirmed back into control once again.

A midweek date with Atlanta failed to enhance the stature of either Russell or his Sonics. The smallest home crowd of the season, 10,593, saw a tight finish—but it wasn't exactly the thrilling wire-to-wire act that is supposed to provide entertainment en route. *Sports Illustrated*'s cage writer, Curry Kirkpatrick, was following the Hawks on their western swing. With twenty seconds left, he came from the other end of press row and knelt down by my chair, looking beyond me to Russell five feet away. The latter stood and stroked his beard as the players looked at the floor, called for juice and toweled off during the time-out.

"He's just *standing* there," Kirkpatrick gasped, shaking his golden locks from side to side. "Can you believe this? He's up by three with twenty-five seconds to go and he's just standing there during the whole time-out."

Ten seconds later, Kirkpatrick was back by my chair. Seattle was up by one. It was another time-out. "My God, I can't believe this. He's fighting for his life and *he's just standing there*. Is he like this all the time?"

"Uh, yeah," Heberlein and I offered simultaneously. "Oh, not all the time. Sometimes he says something or even draws a play on a napkin," we added simultaneously.

Seattle couldn't get the ball inbounds until it was right on the brink of a violation and when it finally did Atlanta double-teamed and stripped the ball from Watts. The Hawks pulled it out by one. Kirkpatrick went off to listen to the rapid-fire account of Atlanta coach Hubie Brown and I went the opposite direction to listen to the interpretations of Russell.

"Whew, this one hurt bad," Russell offered, dejected.

"How bad was it?" a reporter asked.

"Thanks," Russell answered around a forced laugh. "No, what really hurts," he continued, shifting instantly into a quiet, tired voice, "is that they didn't play an exceptional game and they still beat us. I think where we lost it was in the second quarter when we came into the half with a three-point lead. It should have been twenty. We just played too much one-on-one basketball tonight."

"Wasn't that one of Slick's worst games?" another reporter asked. "He must have caused half your turnovers."

"I don't like to talk about individual players in a negative way except to them personally and privately. I don't like to criticize players on an individual basis except to their face."

"It seemed like there was no flow. You say the players keep going off into one-on-one play. Can't you do anything but keep wheeling new people in there?" I asked.

"You just keep looking for someone who will pass the ball. You just keep looking for five guys who will play together—trying to get a tempo."

No one wanted to ask why he didn't say anything during those final time-outs. I couldn't bring myself to do it. I asked, instead, "How can you, with two thirds of the remaining games on the road, go out and hope to win when you're getting beat by some of the poorest teams in the league at home? How can you improve things?"

"Well, hopefully we'll just play better than we did the last two games."

What else could he say? Here was a team, average talent, poorly organized, plodding along in the middle of the pack, still with a shot at the playoffs. I didn't feel the team was working hard enough nor was he. They weren't paying the price of success. They weren't particularly entertaining and they weren't winning.

Two nights after the loss to Atlanta, the Sonics needed an overtime session to get past the Warriors. By the time I got to the Golden State locker room Rick Barry, who had gone a cold three-of-fifteen from the field, was in front of the mirror, working out with a hair dryer. I was going to ask a couple questions about the game, but first was genuinely curious if the bitter crowd response Seattle always gave him was typical of what he received from every crowd he faced on the road.

He jerked his head away from the mirror and snarled at me as the question left my mouth. "We lose a game and you come in here asking me a question about the crowds getting on me."

"Well, not even Kareem gets the treatment you get here. I just wondered if it was particularly Seattle or if you get it everywhere."

"They don't like me because of what I said in an article three years ago about Haywood. I said Wicks was better than Haywood. Ask Seattle fans what they think about Haywood now. It started then," he snapped, whipping the dryer through his hair in obvious agitation.

"I don't remember the article. You figure that's it, huh?" I continued, still not sure what kind of treatment he got elsewhere.

"Yeah, they boo me and it's like adrenaline to me. I love it. I'm a professional player. What do I care what the fans do on the road?" He was surly now, cocky.

I didn't have the energy to ask him about his three-of-fifteen night. I thanked him for his time and heard him saying to Clifford Ray at the next mirror as I walked away, "Can you believe that? The guy's asking me if crowds get on me like this everywhere we go."

I still didn't know.

26
The Geni's Grab Bag

It was All-Star time in Milwaukee. I wasn't attending because no Sonics were attending and because the *P-I* didn't think it was worth the price of freight to and from. Seattle was heading off on another eleven-day road trip, starting in San Antonio two days after the All-Star break, so it would have made sense if I was going on that trip. But the budget director was "saving it for the playoffs." I sometimes wondered if the *P-I* decided to be an A.M. paper so that it's staff would be working in the evenings—when you get reduced phone rates.

The Sonics had been on the road with games at San Antonio and New York when I walked into the office Saturday afternoon, planning to monitor the game at Buffalo. The desk editor handed me a piece of UPI wire service copy. It read: "NEW YORK (UPI)—Seattle guard Slick Watts, expressing dissatisfaction with his long-term contract with the Supersonics, said Friday night he would like to be traded to the New York Nets. 'I'm concerned with getting paid more,' said Watts, his team's high scorer with 19 points in a 93–88 triumph over the Nets. 'I've got to get what I'm worth. I've got three more years on my contract and $78,000 is less than what a guard of my caliber should be getting. I wouldn't mind being with the Nets. I'd love to play here with Tiny (Nate Archibald)—I never have before, but we could do a lot with this franchise.' . . . Nets coach Kevin Loughery said of Watts, 'He's a fine basketball player who could help anyone. He's a great defensive player. Any team in basketball would like to have him.' "

I said, "That crazy SOB has really gone off now." I prayed he hadn't left for the game. One of these days the *P-I* is going to realize you can't cover major sports with one foot nailed to the front door of the paper. But I caught him in his room and we came out of another possible embarrassment in good shape. Poor Heberlein was back there in the snow, hitting five cities in six nights, and I had an equal shot. Watts was spilling over, gushing with thoughts and words that rushed from his mouth as fast as his brain could stoke it. He was a man who had been holding back his emotions, and now they were loose on the world.

"It's been somethin' that's been gnawin' at my guts all year. I told you before the season even started there was a lot that had to be said and there would come a time. I thought I could sit on it. I thought I could make it through the year and keep my mouth shut on this, but it just been eatin' me up. I lay up here in my room and I'm too scared to sleep because I realize how quickly my career could come to an end. When I got hurt in that Indiana game I saw then that I could be through tomorrow. Kareem and Bob Lanier could stick an elbow out tomorrow and end my career like a boy squashin' a bug on a log. I play hard and I do the dirty work and for doin' the dirty work I want to get compensated. When I hurt my knee I knew I had to do somethin' about gettin' what I deserve. There's seven players on the Sonics makin' more money than I do. I talk to Bob Lanier and Paul Silas and they laugh and tell me to get out of their face—they think I'm lyin' about my salary. There's a joke on the team that says, 'Slick is the man, he's got everythin' but a contract.' I been told all along that I'm a free agent and I'm lucky to be gettin' what I'm gettin'. I can't help it if people were so dumb they didn't know know I could play. Now I've showed I can and I just want what I deserve. When I came here I had to take it, couldn't do no better, was happy to be here—now I know what I can do and they know what I can do. Let's get things to where it's fair.

"Sam Schulman is very considerate and helpful. He's done a lot for me. I respect him as a man and as a friend. He's been good to me, but as far as the business part of it, they got me on the contract so I just have to speak out. I hate to put it into words like, 'Slick Watts says pay me or trade me.' Seattle's where I want to live, to raise my family. Even if I went somewhere else, that will always be my home. I know most people think I'm makin' good money and I am. But I bring people into the Coliseum. I'm popular in the community—that isn't just for me, that helps the Sonics. Sam is gettin' compensated, Russ is gettin' compensated, Tommy's gettin' very compensated, Fred is gettin' compensated. Me and Norwood get the same salary and he's been in this league a long time and he's on his last legs. There's a lot of guys in this league makin' over a hundred grand a year and they don't even get off the bench. Russ told me to be patient and I'll get mine when I'm older. But maybe I won't be around. Maybe things will change. Maybe I'll get hurt and I'll never get anything. I could be a nice little boy and shut up and things might be all right for everybody else. But Sam's paid millions to players who never done a thing and now a player who has done a lot is just askin' for all that's due him."

I called Schulman in Palm Springs. His response was, "He said *what?*" He went on to say, "I don't understand this. No, I don't have anything to say on the matter right now. Thanks for calling." I don't think I helped make his Saturday evening's relaxation.

It made a bold story—a top of the newspaper headline deluxe. It was fascination. The little guy, the one who made three hundred public appearances a year and gave every ounce of sweat in his skinny body every time he went on the court, the guy who rose from unqualified nobodyness to national acclaim, was sticking his hand out for more money. That had been so much his appearance—his folksy lucky-to-be-here-but-I'm-as-happy-as-you-are-that-I-am stature.

For some reason the outburst didn't surprise me. I was more captivated, though, by the thing that had happened inside Watts' head. His sense of invincibility had been shattered by that injury. He had been built into a bigger-than-life spirit. The house in the suburbs and the three cars and the people celebrating him and the women wanting him and the statistics praising him and the national media saluting him, all sent him into delightful overdrive. He was young and everything was just on the *grow*. Great and sweet Jesus, I might be governor by the time I get through, if I want it. I'm already more popular than Bill Russell—how much higher can I go?

It's the thing of fame. If you have 2 million eyes on you, it is like fuel. They put in an energy of adulation, they pump you up. Your chemistry changes, you become something greater than the world around you. They say that with their cheers and their letters and their money and their crawling at you. You are pumped into an image of immortality, the self-perspective and the outward one. Then something happens. There is a flicker of change. Maybe you wake up one morning and suddenly think it can't go on forever or that you really are only held up by a most fragile formula. Suddenly you realize you can't control it—they have given it to you by celebrating what you have accomplished. But they might celebrate something else tomorrow. It's as if there is a squirt of mortality injected into that chemistry and you're changing. Maybe they don't see it for a while. But the magic is broken within you. It was a painful knee injury which broke Watts' chemical magic. He suddenly realized he could get hurt and never sign for anything more than he already was scheduled for on his present contract. It could all blow up and go away. It's a minuscule thing, the way it happens inside a man, a superstar, but once the change starts, he likely panics. Some quietly inside of themselves. Some out in the middle of the public, screaming—like Watts.

Watts had gone from just over the minimum, $20,000, in his rookie year to a new contract calling for $40,000 and $45,000 the next two seasons. He had signed his present contract early in his third year—before going on to win the steals and assists titles and being awarded the citizenship award. Before blooming. He had gone to the bargaining table asking for $145,000 for each of the next five years. Brown was getting $200,000, Oleynick $100,000. His demands were not out of line. But Russell as coach held a leverage (the way he could use him, or not use him) because he was Russell the G.M. Watts was intimidated, he claims, into signing for three years at $80,000, $90,000 and $100,000, with $10,000 deferred in each of the seasons.

I was in a tavern (you're right, I'm always in a tavern) the evening Watts' Pay-Me-or-Trade-Me piece broke. A couple of guys were discussing, or mainly cussing, the greed of pro sports. They agreed over a pitcher that they were sick and tired of forking over nine bucks to make Russell and his friends rich. Their words prompted me to agree that prices were out of line, but that the blame didn't so much belong with the players for their greed as with the fans for their unflinching support at the turnstiles. I knew that Watts was crippling his image with his demands, but that was only because the fans had established him as the knight in peasant's frock—a guy who knew humility and gratitude. Sure he was violating the romanticism ring. This was not the behavior they wanted from Watts. Damn the rationality, we want our little champion of the poor. By threatening trade, he was breaking up their bond with him. He was no longer the fans' partner through tough times and good till death do 'em in. But to expect him to be selfless was to expect someone who had won a five-minute grab-all-you-can spree in a supermarket to move about casually so as not to seem overly greedy. I had no doubt that he was the single biggest drawing factor the Sonics had going for them. He was guaranteed showtime, even on bad nights of production.

I put together a sports editorial. I wasn't contending he was actually the only draw, but that if fans paid large sums to see Seattle, they owed plenty to Watts. The morality of contracts honored seemed a moot point in view of Schulman's past performances in court. The piece was headlined: "If Fans Still Go, Give Slick The Dough." I contended:

> Here workaday values don't apply, because pro sports long ago entered into the realm of socioeconomic absurdity. As Harry Truman once reflected, "If you've got too much money too soon, it ruins you by setting you too far apart from most of the human race." There is no way pro athletes should be getting the moon-shot salaries they are receiving. But there's also no reason fans should be putting so much emphasis on sports that they will pay the seat prices they do to support the show. Yet, if the fans are willing to pay the freight and are so dependent on sports and athletes that they have to make these participants bigger than life—then the players deserve everything they can grab.

The most interesting aspect of the editorial was that each side seemed to see what they wanted in it and continued to blame the others. Players thought it said: "If the fans give up the money, it belongs to us, not the owners." Fans responded by saying: "Yeah, those athletes are spoiled and full of greed." Sonics management doubted that "Watts was worth any particular number of fans per game." But it must have hit a nerve, because the letters and phone calls came in on a strong wave— supporting Watts, chastising him, supporting my stand, challenging it. The piece had been written as much out of an attempt at provocation as an expression of opinion. The response said it was worthwhile.

Two days after the editorial, the Sonics were in Kansas City to wrap up the road trip. Mussehl, Watts' lawyer, called and said he had the terms of Watts' demand: a four-year no-cut with a minimum of $200,000. If Schulman doesn't want to comply with that, Watts wants to be traded to one of three clubs, the Knicks, the 76ers or the Lakers. There was no mention of the Spurs or the Nets, who apparently had dropped out of the running somewhere during the past half week. Watts wanted to enter into talks with Schulman within the next ten days, with the new contract or trade to take effect in the off-season.

Zollie Volchok said Watts' contract had been "torn up and re-negotiated." Mussehl said that wasn't true, that Watts had played out the second year and the new contract hadn't taken effect until the current season, even though he was signed at the start of the previous one. Mussehl said Watts had built-in bonuses of $5,000 if the club made the playoffs and another $5,000 if the team won the Western Conference title.

This is one of the areas that gets difficult for a reporter. The legal interpretation almost always has to come through people you have to just assume are telling the truth. But Volchok's statement had been believed until subsequent research proved it inaccurate. Even when you get a copy of documents, the language and the dates are sometimes so obscure to the novice reader that the reporter is still at the mercy of someone else's interpretation. And there was more legal-eagle flying by Watts. Earlier in the month, in a move that drew only passing attention, he had filed a $100,000 lawsuit against a lumber firm for using his name on their reader board. Mussehl said a letter had been written to the company asking that the sign be removed, but the company had ignored the request. The message read: "Look Watts New, Slick Super Spruce Paneling 24 Cents Lineal."

Now on the same day he was demanding the four-year no-cut, Watts' lawyer was filing still another suit, this time against an automobile agency for using Watts's name in a radio spot. The jingle went: "Why is Subaru a good car for the Northwest? Well, we have Slick roads, I think, we have Slick Watts, and if you're going to drive on his head, you'll need good traction." (Well, maybe it sounded better with music.) The spot, according to the complaint, was degrading to Watts and was exploitive of his advertising value without remuneration. It seemed petty to the nonparticipant, to be suing over something like this. Why, it seemed a guy ought to be damn happy somebody even *wanted* to use his name.

Of course, from a commercial standpoint, an athlete has every right to use his popularity for promotional gain. Players' pictures can't be used in commercial ventures without permission, other than in the presentation of news. At the same time he was suing for unauthorized use of his name, Watts was under contract with Pro-Keds sports shoes for $6,000 a year and was about to sign a contract to serve as national spokesman for Uniroyal. He also was close to putting his endorsement powers behind a national shampoo. His name was worth money and to expect him to give it away was to expect your neighbor, the doctor, to give you a free examination or your other neighbor, the barber, to give you a free haircut. All the while, Watts was tearing up that storybook reputation.

Just to keep all four burners on high, Brown had decided to speak out that day in the *Times*, telling Heberlein he would be happier playing elsewhere and commenting: "Every trade bothers me. All those cats are good cats. But it's just like the old war movie where the sergeant tells you not to get too close to the guy next to you." I called Watts to check on Mussehl's figures, to make sure they were what he had in mind, and I mentioned the Brown article of that afternoon.

"Freddy's got strong ideas," Watts said, laughing, "but you know ol' Fred. Soon as somebody pins him down on that and he gets some pressure, he'll say he was misquoted. I love Fred, I really do, but you know he ain't got the heart to hang it out there like I do."

That evening, on the pregame show for the televised coverage of the game, Brown said, "Well, I haven't seen the article, of course, because it just came out today and I'm back here, but I think I must have been misquoted. The newspapers have a tendency to exaggerate. I didn't tell anybody that I wanted to be traded. I just said it was hard on me here. . . ." One thing you can say about Watts, he knows his teammate.

Seattle held on for a one-point win and wound up the road trip two and four. The club was half a step ahead of Kansas City for the sixth and final playoff berth in the Western Conference. There still were two months to go in the season. And Schulman had finally stated there would be no renegotiating of contracts—Watts' or anybody else's.

The letters continued to come in regarding the Watts issue: "Thought I'd write to applaud your editorial on Watts. I've been a Sonic fan for years, but I'll be damned if I'll go see another major sporting event until the public as a whole begins to see what pro athletics are costing the average working man. . . . There's something to be said about the excitement of the crowd, but you're right when you said until we realize how stupid we are for supporting pro sports at the box office, we're going to become victims of the 'Slick Watts syndrome.' " (Well, that's not exactly how I worded it, but you've got the point.) "Have you ever noticed that when Slick is out of the lineup how much more movement the five men on the court have? Do you suppose Philly would enjoy Slick playing with the ball as Erving, McGinnis and Collins stand and wait? . . . As for Mr. Brown, who in their right mind would honor the no-cut contract that he carries around? . . . Yes both just might be unemployed if they don't stay with Mr. Russell." (They were attacking from all sides, now the rear.) "Are you saying professional athletes are spoiled brats or are you saying that the man in the bleachers is confused? I get the impression it's the former. If not, why didn't you set them straight? I know many professional athletes and very few of whom I would describe as spoiled brats or runaway colts full of ego and greed. Even though the human society has many important and unmet needs, entertainment is always going to be rated very high in our society. What do the fans get in a professional sports event? Besides the opportunity to get together as a social activity, they get several hours of the impossible. Yes, impossible. The things done by professional athletes are literally feats of the impossible for 99 percent of the fans . . . certainly they should be paid as professionals. The training required to become a pro athlete is certainly as rigorous as the law or medical professions, if not more so." (I suspect that wasn't written by a doctor or a lawyer.) "So Sam Schulman thinks it's time contracts are honored? Is this the same Sam Schulman who enticed Haywood, Brisker and McDaniels into leaving ABA contracts—against the terms of the NBA franchise contract Schulman signed? Is this the same Sam Schulman who pulled out of Brisker's and McDaniels' contracts when they bombed out? It's good to know that with Schulman, a contract is as strong as the honor of the individuals who sign it. Good luck Slick!" (And this):

> Hooray for the Green/Hooray for the Gold
> Buy yourself a ticket/And watch the Sonics fold
> Slick's all upset/'Cause he wants more money
> I guess that I should sympathize/But I just think it's funny
> Schulman's let us know that/He can't afford Bill Russell
> (He who has the money,/Also has the muscle)
> I get all depressed/When the Sonics don't hustle
> Maybe I'll feel better/When they get rid of Russell
> We've waited half a season/For Tommy to get tough
> I guess the fact that he's alive/Will have to be enough
> I used to be a Sonics' fan/I swore I'd never quit
> But they hit the bottom/And I don't give a shit
> Burma Shave
> Signed, Lisa Remted.

The Sonics were back home for three and then it would be back out for seventeen days of the high road. Boston was the first visitor after all the statements in the media. Watts heard a good sprinkling of boos—the first of his pro career in the Coliseum. Brown was booed. Russell was booed. The P.A. announcer completely forgot about Schulman sitting across from him at courtside and overlooked, for the first time in the club's history, introducing him. No point in risking a Boo Poll with Watts. The whole cast looked like it would get gonged off the stage at any minute.

27

Mid-March Madness

Rain worked relentlessly against the windshield wipers, city lights alternating between smears of color and polka dots of glare. I couldn't help but feel, as I drove from the Coliseum to the office, that I had made a mistake sentencing the Sonics to death so early, as I had done in my Atlanta game lead nearly a month earlier. It wasn't that they had revived. On the contrary. And I was running out of ways to analogously bury them ever deeper as their quality continued to decompose.

Cleveland, in a twenty-point hammering, had just handed Seattle its seventh loss in nine outings and third straight at home. All this was leading up to a seventeen-day road trip, the longest anyone would take in the league this year. The *P-I* hadn't planned to send me, but I protested this was the most dramatic chapter in Sonic history about to unfold. Russell and his team were going out into the desert and one of them would return—there was going to be bloodshed and glory dispelled. There was no doubt, considering the way the Sonics were playing and reacting to their problems, that they would lose all ten and the blame that would be tossed around would be headlines every morning.

Russell seemed crestfallen in the postgame interview that evening. He conveyed the feeling that he was losing control of his ship, that the crew was out on deck ready to man their lifeboats and putting a hole in the bottom of his. "I don't think anyone is consciously trying to fight me. But there seems to be a difference of opinion of what we're trying to get done out there. We're not waving the white flag, but it's almost reached that point. No, I don't think it's a defeatist attitude although you'd almost think that at times. We're just not paying the price for winning. It's a last resort, but I think I'll come up with something." I had pursued those last words during the unusually long postgame session. I wanted something more than the likes of "I've got an idea." I was letting visions of all those time-outs where nothing was said, and all those practices where I understood nothing was accomplished, point an ever more critical attitude toward Russell.

Still, he had said, "We took a time-out and I diagrammed a play. I even told every player where he was supposed to be and where he was supposed to go. When they can't even step over the line and execute a play this late in the season you've got problems." Who was causing them? When he said, "We have to win at least six of these games on the road. It's not impossible. There's always the thought that maybe we've bottomed out," I refrained from laughing in his face only out of respect for his contribution to basketball and his physical threat to my body.

In the first of ten games on the road spread over the seventeen-day span, Seattle dropped its eighth of ten and fourth straight by a 134–104 measure at Portland. Walton didn't play, due to a sprained ankle. Seattle didn't play for reasons not yet determined. An autopsy was being ordered. Russell kept the team in the locker room for over twenty minutes, sufficient to blow any chance I had to get any interviews against Saturday night's earlier deadline. The team flew out while Hopkins and I stayed over—off to the NAIA national basketball tournament in Kansas City the next day.

I wanted an outburst from Hopkins and he "outbursted" all the way to Kansas City, all right. But when I asked him what I could use he almost spilled his whiskey sour. "We was just talkin'. Don't use none of that, now. Oh, no." So I sat there with a head full of his fuming and frustration over how Russell wasn't organized and didn't demand anything at practices and how he threatened the players one minute and pleaded with them the next and how if he'd just spend more time on the buses and holding meetings things would be a helluva lot better. I contemplated a commentary and then decided just to let the inevitable disaster unfold over the next two weeks.

The Jazz were horrible enough, two nights later, to allow Seattle a sloppy victory at New Orleans. The next day, at the Atlanta airport, an hour and a half went slowly. Oleynick and Wilkerson were sitting side by side on benches, both clad in carpenter's overalls. Wilkerson said he used to install carpets and plaster ceilings to warrant his workman's clothes. "Frank, Frank?" I called to Oleynick, his ears covered by headphones which were connected to a tape player in an athletic bag. "Frank." He looked up. "You ever build anything?" He looked at me with a tough-guy curled lip and talked too loudly, not being able to hear himself over his headphones. "Are you kidding? The only thing I do with boards is dribble a ball off 'em."

The tape decks were just one of the relaxations in Russell's regimentation over the past month. He had also allowed players to drink on the planes this year and recently, to allow players to take separate rooms if they wanted to pay the extra rate. None of this was allowed during the first three years of his regime. Russell adjusting, but what were the results?

We hit Boston, enjoying a sparkling chilly and fresh day, at 2:30 P.M. I grabbed all three Boston papers and jumped on the bus. There was an article headlined: "Bill Russell's Days with the Sonics Numbered." It read: "Rumors are snowballing that the man, Bill Russell, is making a farewell swing through the NBA cities as coach of the Seattle Sonics even though he has a year left on a lucrative five-year pact. . . ." It went on to say that Russell was upset that Schulman had made his statement when he did and that he had become, in effect, a lame-duck coach. The article documented Watts' and Brown's uprisings in the media. It said Schulman had confided to friends that he made a mistake in speaking out when he did.

Russell's *last* swing through the league? Well, now, that seemed a little presumptuous.

At the hotel I was standing in the hallway waiting for the luggage cart to make its way down to my duffle bag. I had finally tired of packing sports jackets and dress shirts and trying to fold everything so safely every time we stopped. I finally had gotten tired, too, of nice luggage getting ground into a punching bag. So I had stuffed a couple pairs of slacks, all my Levi's and a couple sweaters into a duffle bag and that was the way we were going to see America this time. My bag was on the bottom of seventy-five suitcases, medicine bags and ultra-sound kits, squashed into the shape of a pillow. What's a mother to do?

Dr. Marty Kushner, the Sonics' doctor, who was in Boston on personal matters, came down the hall. He asked if I had seen that article on Russell. He added, "Russ has got to go. It's up to the press. Sam wants to make the move, but is afraid of public opinion. It's up to the press to support Sam."

Not three minutes later, I was in Furtado's room checking out a pair of socks. Watts was ranting and raving about Russell. I hadn't heard the first part of the conversation. He was saying, " . . . I told Sam, Russ treats us like niggers." He addressed me as I came across the room. "I told you what was going to happen way back at the start of the season, didn't I, B.J.? Told you it was gonna be some heavy shit. He treats us like niggers, man. But you know, you can't keep a good man down. Unless you lay down with him—and I ain't gonna let him make me do that."

The last time we had been here, I had been springing into the McAdoo talks with Schulman. I wanted to check a couple of things with him now on a guy named Russell. Was there really a chance he might not be back *next year*? I called Los Angeles. He was in Palm Springs. I called Palm Springs. He wasn't there.

That night Seattle took the Celtics apart limb, shirt and shoe sole, 114–86. The Sonics played powerfully, from what inspiration no one knew.

When we hit Philly the next afternoon, Burleson and I walked through the airport toward the baggage claim. No sooner had he commented, "You can always tell the people who don't travel much because they're the ones who get talked into buying the flowers," than a woman in her twenties blocked our path with a big smile, an arm full of flowers and her pitch. "Hi, how are you gentlemen today? Would you like to have a flower to celebrate spring?" She was starting to pin one on Burleson. He stepped back and patiently brushed her hand away. "We are accepting donations for our mission . . ." We shook our heads and started to walk away. "No thank you," we called in unison. "Don't you love God today?" she snorted loudly and stormed off.

"Those people are the worst pests we run into," said Burleson. "They think because they are from some religion they can intimidate you into buying their flowers. Like you'll be afraid to say no." I nodded in agreement and wondered how many flowers we could collect over a season's worth of airports.

We barely pulled to a halt in front of the baggage claim when Burleson was confronted with another form of social assault he never could escape.

"Why, how tall are you, anyway?" called a middle-aged lady, clucking forward with two similarly aged companions.

"Seven-two, ma'am," he said patiently, turning away as politely as possible, and right into a middle-aged man who hit him with, "Boy, are you ever tall. I'll bet you're seven-six. How tall are you, anyway?"

"Seven-two," Burleson replied, his voice taking on a forced laugh. "How 'bout you? How short are you? How's the weather down there anyway? Been short all your life? Must be tough to get a place in the front row of a parade."

The guy smiled back. But he somehow hadn't gotten the message. "Come on now, how tall are you really. You're more than seven-two."

Burleson shook his head and started to walk away. Wilkerson, half sharing Burleson's sarcasm, and also trying to smooth things over, said, "He's really eight-three. Tallest man in the world, no kidding."

The guy turned to his wife and they were trying to decide if he was really eight-three when a toothy cannonball bus driver came bouncing in. He probably killed to get these assignments, because he was always our man in Philly. He came up to Watts. They greeted each other warmly.

"Say, Slick, how do ya think I'd look bald," he chortled, running his stubby fingers over the dozen oily hairs which went straight back on his pate.

"Ya gotta have a round head and a cute face," Watts replied, hugging the guy.

I had a gift certificate for a restaurant in downtown Philly, courtesy of the 76ers broadcaster who had interviewed me at halftime of the club's recent visit to Seattle. They had wanted to know what to make of Schulman's words on Russell. I interpreted them as indicating it looked like Schulman was trying to lay the foundation to get rid of Russell when his contract expired. Didn't he really mean it when he said he wanted Russell to stay on as coach? I didn't think so. Was there any chance he would be back next year? I was pretty sure he would be.

The restaurant wasn't bad, a deluxe hamburger house—fancy ways with beer, beef and a bun. The atmosphere went the way of a baby's bib when a waitress slipped coming out of the kitchen. Her legs went up in the air, the huge metal platter she was carrying with maybe a dozen plates of burgers and salads went up in the air. She came down, falling backward through the swinging door. The platter came down sounding like someone had just caused an eight-car crash in the room. Come to think of it, THAT'S what Russell's full bore laugh sounds like. The burgers went everywhere. The waitress started out crying and evolved into hysterical laughter. A good act, but all the spilled food told me it ought to be booked into a Weight Watchers' convention.

Green was on the taping table when I walked into the Sonics' locker room at the Spectrum the next evening. He interrupted whatever he was telling Furtado and said to me, in a voice singsong street sweet, "Hey, man, where's my money?" He didn't smile.

"What do I owe you?" I asked, thinking that not only has he got me for the Nuggets winning their division, but he'll probably get San Antonio into the playoffs as well. And it has hardly been an issue that has created great communication between us during the year. He rolled his head and told any of the others in the room who cared to listen, "Oh, that's right. Now he gets amnesia."

I told him I'd figure it out and give him his due when everything was decided. He just went on with his singsong, talking his rap. Didn't matter what he was saying. Just talking, filling time.

The locker room didn't smell foul tonight. Just of Baumodine, an analgesic balm that Norwood was using to rub into his knees and the coconut scent of the body oil used by many of the players. There was no fox loose in there tonight, as Gilliam used to say on nights when there hadn't been a chance to wash out uniforms—when, instead, they had just been tossed into a bag, zipped shut and then hauled out damp and ripe the next evening.

To sit in a locker room for an hour before a game and see the little ailments and the not so little that needed to be attended to is to marvel at the wear and tear the NBA body takes. The blood blisters, the boils, the infections under a callus, the ingrown toenails, the sprained ankle, sprained fingers, a case of the clap. Patch 'em up and send 'em out. The good trainer tries to keep ahead of boils and calluses and so forth by looking a player over as he's taping him. There isn't much even the best trainer in the league can do about preventing a case of clap.

Seattle got down by twenty-five by the half and then came storming back to miss by only a hoop. It was a loss, but the momentum had been with the Sonics when the horn sounded. The next night, McAdoo went four-for-fifteen against the Sonics. The Knicks fell by three. Seattle had won three of four out here. Any more of this nonsense and I was going to ask for blood tests. I asked Russell if Weatherspoon deserved special credit for sitting in McAdoo's jock all night. "Do we play them again?" Russell asked. "Nope." "Yeah, he was it," Russell cackled. Green was in good spirits too, having shaken off a couple of weeks worth of 0-1,000 shooting. "My shot has come back from Hawaii. It caught a good tan and came back. We were tired, but they seemed worse. Man, this trip ain't even half over—we'll be old men by the time we get back." McAdoo wasn't at all happy with the evening's outcome, nor, it seemed, with his rapport with his teammates. "I hope we don't come back with the same personnel next year, because the same things will happen. Coaches don't win games, players do." He hadn't signed a contract with the Knicks yet. He was asked if he had any second thoughts about having come to New York. He didn't answer. It could have been Schulman's worry.

Haywood was still sidelined with a leg injury and had disappeared by the time I got to the Knicks' locker room. But the man I wanted was Bradley—there was a big red-faced memory in my head from the last visit here. I decided to leave behind December's aborted question pertaining to reporters asking intelligent questions, and pursue another matter. Bradley's legs were spread wide enough to hold his pants at midthigh while he buttoned a white shirt that looked like it hadn't seen an iron the last two times through the washer. Maybe it was the fact he was only a dozen games shy of his announced retirement from pro ball that gave him unusual patience—almost an interest—in his postgame discussion.

"Bill, you once described Russell as the most intelligent player in the game. What exactly did he have that gave him that distinction?" I asked after introducing myself without being dealt any acknowledgment of the previous encounter at the Knicks' bench. He continued to dress as he talked, purposefully, phrasing his sentences in thoughts that carried momentary pauses to allow their maximum reception.

"His ability to sense an opponent's weakness, his ability to create uncertainty in the mind of an opponent, his ability to embarrass a player who would be thrown off his game and his ability to avoid angering a player who would therefore be more effective made Russell the greatest player to ever play the game," he explained, tucking in his shirt. "I think it was absolutely essential for his self-esteem and personal makeup for Bill to go out every night and prove again who he was." Bradley pulled on a camel-colored sweater and closed his locker. "That's my own armchair analysis. But to me there's no one playing today combining his physical skills, emotional makeup and his keen intelligence for the game."

I asked, "Wouldn't Walton be the closest thing today, what with his aggressive pursuit of excellence, enthusiasm and physical ability?"

"I think the game is fun to Walton, but I don't think it was for Russell. When Walton is out there making things happen and the team is playing well, he's having fun. I think Russell was trying to prove things to himself that were so intense he couldn't have fun."

Food, as they say, for thought. And helpful inasmuch as I was still having a hard time drawing a real bead on Russell. I wanted to shine a light on that Russell mystique—not to bring him down, but to know what was there and what wasn't there. Oh me, oh my, this man is such a contradiction. Is he truth or is he fiction? There was no way I could bring another season to a close without making some assessment of Russell, especially in light of this season's trials.

Trying to interpret this latest trend of road success was beyond any conclusive answers from me. I was glad to flee to South Carolina for four days of that special escape one achieves with a fine buddy— especially when the sun shines on a seacoast town. Green used one of the off days to be cleared of his drug charge.

I finally made connections with Schulman. He asked what was going on with the club. I told him I couldn't figure it out. I told him about the Boston article stating this was Russell's last go-round. He asked me how I felt the media would feel about Russell not returning. I said I didn't know what the stand would be overall. Some would maybe look at it as another Schulman escapade, there were bound to be some of those sentiments, especially with his holding firm against Watts on the same stand. Others would be anxious to see Russell bounced and support the move. I didn't tell him where I stood and he didn't ask.

Truth was, I really didn't know. To bring the Great One down would make heavy headlines. I wasn't real pleased with the growth our relationship had taken, as in, seemingly no growth. It would be more fun to cover a team that was not at war with itself and it would be more enjoyable to hopefully have a coach who you could call without feeling as if you'd just gotten him out of the sauna. It would be nice to have a guy you could hang out with, have a few belts, share some stories. But, at that hour, I didn't think it was even fifty-fifty that Russell would not be back. After all, his team was tearing up the league—on the road.

In Philadelphia, Kirkpatrick had commented, "All the coaches around the league say, 'Don't bother to scout Seattle—they just run around like crazy. You can't figure out their system, because they don't have one.'" Mayhem has its pluses. Watts was the leader of the pack and one thing you had to say for him, even though he was complaining to every reporter who would listen to him all across the country, he was putting out everything he had on the court.

Seattle picked off another at the expense of Washington, winning by four. Reporters crowded around Russell, who seemed to be enjoying the stir his group was causing, having now won four of its past five. Asked what had turned the club around, Russell just kept saying, "I had some ideas and they seem to be working. No, I'm not surprised." At first I was curious. But when he wouldn't discuss the particulars, I found myself moving toward furious. Most of the media had moved into the locker room when I kept at Russell, "You can't just say 'I had some ideas.' What were they? When were they implemented?" We went around and around. It became obvious, after a while, that I didn't think he had a damn thing to do with what was happening. I was unfair to him, maybe, not to accept that there had been a dramatic turnabout in the verdicts being acquired by the Sonics. But through conversations with players and watching them on the court, I didn't see where Russell was doing anything special. I just couldn't stand to see him hauling in all that credit behind a screen of mystique. Maybe he deserved it, but he'd have to convince me.

The next morning we were bound for Detroit. I wound up sitting across the aisle from Russell. He was in a good mood. Had he not sensed my contempt for his words last night? He's smart, sensitive. Of course he had. Does he like people who stand up to him? Why does he send people down the road? Why does he refuse to talk to a Wayne Cody? Why did he ask me why I was so negative? Maybe there's a system to his thoughts and behavior. Maybe.

We stumbled onto the subject of officials and tough calls. He said Richie Powers made the gutsy call of all time in the final game of the 1963 playoffs at Los Angeles. "They had all these balloons up there in nets," Russell said, framing the play. "They thought they finally had us. And they almost did. Baylor got loose for a fast break right at the end of the game. I was the only guy back. I knew he always went to his right, so I stunted and then stepped in front of him as he made his move to the hoop. He ran right over me. The ball went in. If Powers calls it my foul, they've got it tied and Baylor's on the line for the winner. If it's a charge, it's our championship. The whole place is screaming. And Powers called the charge. Greatest show of guts I ever saw from an official. They didn't get to drop all those balloons, either," he added with a solid laugh.

One play. One minute, or maybe just a second in a man's life. There are crucial crossroads for every man somewhere along his road—maybe in battle, in love, in some time frame there will be those frozen moments of action and thought. They often happen in a blitz, but are left to be rerun for all the rest of one's life. In sports, where one of the main appeals of competition is the study of individuals under pressure, those frozen moments may last in the memory of millions. The way you handled that one play may make your reputation for life, regardless of what else you have accomplished or failed to attain.

Now Russell, his career wrapped up in a big glossy image of glory, was leading a loose-goose band of players into Detroit. Sometimes, if you let yourself get caught up in the image of the all-conquering gladiator, Russell didn't seem like the same flesh that had accomplished all that.

He was in a good mood as we landed in Detroit, calling to an attractive stewardess in the baggage claim area, "Carry your bag? Walk your dog? Shoot your husband?" It's familiar to us. Almost always merited at least a smile from them. And we could use a smile—the weather had gone from summery spring in the East to nasty winter in the Midwest. Sleet drove out of a gray and cold sky. I parked myself in the Ponchatrain Hotel and planned to stay there until the next day. Detroit has never been known for its hospitality.

The weather was still miserable the next day. I decided I had to get out of that room and do something. I finally decided to hell with Russell's ban and went over to Cobo Hall across the street where the Sonics were having shooting practice. The team was floating around on the court, involved in games of 21. Russell sat on the sideline reading a long letter and looking at some pictures which were enclosed. I started to look at them, then decided that would be rude. He wore a long coat and his Greek fisherman's cap. I decided I wouldn't be evasive and headed right up to him, sat down and said hello. He murmured a greeting. I asked him what he thought of UCLA getting beat by Idaho State the night before. He expressed surprise, but looked as though he would prefer to read without me making a big deal out of being there. I headed up into the stands and ran around until most everyone had left. Brown cast a long bomb that missed the backboard and bounced into the end seats. He put on his coat and departed—leaving Furtado to play Easter egg hunt in the seats.

Eventually Wilkerson and I were left to be challenged by a couple of guys who appeared out of the woodwork in basketball gear. We split up and I was checking Wilkerson. I was surprised at his strength. Watching a game, you forget the power of these people. You see the contact, but you don't remember just what it is until you lean on one of the performers yourself. There is all that grace and all that muscle. Strong, run-you-over strong. But I kept flipping in little scoop hooks to counteract his drives and he kept saying, "Where'd you learn that hook?" and he kept laughing every time it went in. I told him I developed it in New York when all them leapin' bastards would put my jumper in the benches. He kept laughing and trying to block it—until he finally got a hold of one and put it in the seats.

Then I was all alone in Cobo. The lights had been turned down so that it reminded me of dusk, just before dinnertime, shootin' at the hoop in the alley. I shot and shot and dribbled, stopped, jumped and shot until my arm began to ache. But I didn't want to quit. I imagined all the great games and great plays that had been made at these baskets. I thought of all the celebration that surrounded everything on a court such as this when the spotlights were on and the stands were packed. Now it was just another hoop for a man to indulge his love of a game. The ball made such a nice sound off the court in the empty arena. It felt so nice, coming up with whatever spin I put down on the dribble. The shot felt even better. The ball felt so delicate as it left the fingers and did whatever I asked, off the glass, up and under, over and through. What a satisfying sight, that lacy dance of the net. I know of nothing so simple and still satisfying as just shooting a leather basketball over an orange rim and down through, making the net dance. I ran the court, dribbling for a layup, taking it out of the net and going the other way. Back and forth, getting tired. Bring the sweat till it burns the eyes, runs in the mouth. Go until the chest aches for oxygen. Stop and shoot two free throws with no time left on the clock, down one. Then back and forth some more. Drive and score, jump and score, a boy and his ball. Basketball is indeed poetry when taken to its heart of boy, ball and net. And I say "boy" because it all becomes too complicated when approached by men.

Ask Tolson. We were sitting in the coffee shop an hour after I had finally thrown myself out of the gym. Here was a man who could dunk a basketball on a par with the very best in the league. He played a game that was wild, but somehow graceful—like a huge swan taking off from a lake. He didn't have the control nor the discipline nor the all-around skills to make it big in the NBA. But he was there and he was presently enraged at the way he was being treated by his coach. "I don't want him to embarrass me like that anymore. In Washington he put me in for twenty-seven seconds, Blaine. Twenty-seven seconds. He humiliated me. What am I supposed to do in twenty-seven seconds? I'd rather sit there with Frank Oleynick. Don't do that to me. I know I can play, but he won't give me a chance," Tolson rolled on, his face sad and angry all at one time. "He uses you thirty minutes one time against a team and then not at all the next time against the same team. Don't make sense, man." Tolson kicked a long leg out from under the table and slapped a large hand on a thigh. I pictured the body strutting around the campus at Arkansas. On top of his game. Somebody. Now humiliation, despair flowing out of frustration. He'd worked so hard to get back into the NBA. Now he was getting all that bool-sheeeet again. "Russ told me after I went twelve minutes in the first half against Boston then none in the second half, 'It wasn't that you didn't play well—I just got what I wanted from you tonight.' What's he want from me? Just tell me. I can play."

He never got off the bench that evening. But the Sonics went on and had their fun—at least in the first half as they bolted to a sixteen-point lead. Watts had seventeen points and four steals, Burleson thirteen points, three steals and nine rebounds. Still, Russell was burned at his troops, and let them know it with a halftime lashing. He said they should have been up by twenty or twenty-five. Detroit had been there willing to give more, he told them. Take it. The Sonics sulked, instead, and let Detroit get back within one before losing—even though Seattle threw the ball away three times in the final thirty seconds. Five of six on the road. Seattle was still two behind K.C., who had lost at Chicago the same evening. The Bulls trailed Seattle by half a game. The Bulls had won eleven of twelve. The Bulls would host the Sonics tomorrow night.

Heberlein and I picked up the rental car and parked across the street from the Chicago Stadium. It was fifty yards from the arena door—forty-nine yards more than we would have preferred to have to handle by the time we were through working. More than one media person has had a gun stuck in the ribs or just found his or her car broken into, stolen, or maybe just up on blocks with the tires gone, when they came out at midnight.

What was unfolding in the Chicago Stadium during the final month should be forever savored by those who experienced it as the ultimate in what sports escapism can create. Lunging for the playoffs after a two and fourteen season's start, the Bulls inspired an emotional orgy with their closing rush that totally captivated the Windy City. It had been a bitter winter served up on the shores of Lake Michigan. There had been a terrible el crash and beloved Mayor Richard Daley had passed away. People needed a release and they found it by tying themselves to the Bulls.

The stirring outpouring that developed was tremendously enhanced by the design of Chicago Stadium—it being of the old school among basketball arenas with steeply banked tiers stacked from court level to hawk's-perch ceiling. Boston Garden is the only other NBA arena still serving basketball in such an atmosphere. Even the most remote seats are close to the sides of the court, creating what amounts to four tall walls of people when the place is packed. The acoustics may lack the latest in equipment, but for concentrated feedback the volume level is probably second only to that attainable with headphones. Whoever felt the need to buy the stadium's organ—surely the largest one to be found outside the Mormon Tabernacle—also must love to listen to jet planes take off. The place seems loud even when it is empty with each of the 17,374 seats sporting a glossy coat of bright red paint. The whole interior looks as though a giant hooker spilled her nail polish.

When the tide of support reached its peak, as many as three thousand fans in excess of the seating capacity were crammed into corners and poured across the aisles. No one thought to invite the fire marshal. This was the setting the night Seattle rolled in.

There was a commendable offering of boos as the Sonics were introduced, each starter trotting out to the free-throw line to stand and fidget and rock on his heels until protocol was served.

Then they turned the lights off—all of them. And P.A. announcer Tom Edwards and some healthy hands on the organ went to work on the last of any inhibitions that might be left among the crowd, which had risen en masse as the lights went out. Each Bull, starting at the bottom of the bench, was escorted out of the darkness to midcourt in a spotlight. Once it started, Edwards' voice could only be heard in pieces, like the words of a sailor on deck in a storm. The organist rammed her enthusiasm into the fury, but mainly there was the crowd's roar—an incredible roar of nearly twenty thousand throats coming down out of the blackness. It started that way. Sitting at courtside, at the bottom of this well of noise, tingles of excitement covered the skin like goose bumps. By the time they got to the starters—Van Lier, May, Johnson—it had become almost scary. The roar felt as if it was moving the body, as if you were riding a huge wave—full of the glorious rush of power, but also frightened by where it might take you. When 7'2" Artis Gilmore ambled out under the spotlight to complete the string of Bulls stretched across the court there were no longer separate parts to Edwards' voice, the organ or the crowd. If Lake Michigan had crashed through the roof at that moment no one packed in that howling blackness would have heard it—or cared.

It would have been the biggie and the Sonics had neither the poise nor the presence of pointsmanship to equal the challenge. The Sonics fell by twelve, but it could have been thirty. Seattle's best offensive move of the night was delivered by Burleson. Slickered into his fourth foul by Artis Gilmore just ten minutes into the game, Burleson came to the sideline and kicked his chair five feet into a fan's lap. "The guy was upset at first, but later he accepted my apology. He was cool."

It would have been comforting to have about fifteen thousand of those bodies around when we finished our chores and headed for the parking lot. A couple inches of mushy snow had fallen to coat our trek to Milwaukee. As we trotted across the street and down the block to the car I kept looking over my shoulder and wondering what I would throw first if a gang of local residents should appear out of the darkness. I probably would have just thrown up my hands and prayed for a press pass to heaven. There were no cops around. No guards. Nobody, including the bad guys. We didn't even wipe the snow off the car. Just jumped in and gunned it for the freeway. I was either in a masochistic mood or didn't want to have to blame Heberlein when we ended up in a ditch or maybe I felt that having made it to the car, nothing could stop us now. I volunteered to drive. It wasn't quite the relaxing drive we had undertaken in those jaunts from Philly to New York City.

Squinting into the snow for the road, swerving and skidding as bare patches traded the path with frozen yuk, we made Milwaukee shortly after 3 A.M. Furtado was walking down the street, heading for a snack. We joined him. We had been up at 5:45 Milwaukee time to leave Detroit. Checked into the hotel at Chicago at 10 A.M., and out at 5:30 P.M. Now it's 4 A.M. as we finish eating—eight hours until tipoff.

When Brown went down in the second half, clutching his ankle and rolling around, Green caught my eye and rolled his. He wandered by the press table as they were helping Brown off the court. "Be out the rest of the year," Green said, curling his upper lip in a sneer. Seattle had already lost Weatherspoon and Johnson with injuries and looked out of luck with twenty-eight seconds to go. Then Watts stabbed the ball out of rookie Quinn Buckner's hands, outraced him for possession and laid it in for what turned out to be the winning points. Russell had his sixth win. I couldn't stand it any longer. I told him, "I've got a confession to make. I thought you were full of shit when you said that you could win six out here." He laughed and said, "I know you did."

The next morning, in the Marc Plaza coffee shop, Watts bounced around like he had fleas. He was up and out into the lobby and back. He wore a Sherlock Holmes two-billed cap, a capelike leather coat. He blew mercilessly on a harmonica.

"B.J., what's happenin'?" Blast, blast on the mouth organ. "Man, I ain't never gonna commit no crime 'cause I can't even stand lookin' at hotel walls this many days. To be in jail would drive me insane."

"I wouldn't want to be your cellmate, I'll tell you that," I said against the blast-wail of his mouthpiece.

Green strolled in. Looked around. Sat down next to me. Love came in, pretended he didn't want to see us, walked over. Joined us. Everybody was loose. I was at a loss for words that Green and Love would sit down at my table, let alone go out of their way to say good morning. Being on the road for what seemed like forever could either turn you into bitter enemies or bring you close, as though you've shared a war together. Of course, the team that is winning seems to get a great improvement in attitude.

"I'm so tired of lookin' at all these same faces," Green drawled, "no matter when I see them again, it's gonna be too soon."

"I wouldn't want to ever look at yo' face again if I could avoid it," Watts shot back.

There is no telling where that verbal trail would have led had Spoon not come jerkin-shufflin' in, leanin' on a cane for his injured leg. He wasn't leaning. He was leanin'—like just kind of doin' it *with* the cane, rather than using it for support.

"Look at that jive nigger," said Watts. "Walk for me, Spoon." Weatherspoon, who seemed to have rubber bands for every joint, grinned and strutted his cool walk over to the table and sat down.

"Gentlemen, are you ready for a visit to Cleve-lan'?" Weatherspoon said in his soft voice, still grinning.

"I am ready for *home*, man," said Green.

The bus was loaded, waiting in front of the Marc Plaza. "Where's Fred?" Tolson called out. "Sent him home to get his ankle treated," Furtado answered. "Sheeeeit," five voices answered. "Where's Spoon?"

asked Watts. Weatherspoon stepped onto the bus at that moment, walked halfway down the aisle, turned around, held up a hand in a wave without saying anything. Furtado told the driver to hold it. Weatherspoon disappeared into the hotel and returned five minutes later. He climbed back on, this time with his cane.

"Sheeeeit, Spoon. You oughta get yo' crippled ass on the same Red Cross plane with Fred. You ain't doin' us no good here, boy. Just holdin' up the bus." Weatherspoon just grinned and took it from his teammates, who were full of tired energy. As we motored to the airport, a trio tangled in the middle of the bus in gleeful jive:

Say Shrimp
Awwww, you Kansas City mother-fucker
Come on, say shrimp
Ass-howl
Say asshole then.
Sheeeeit, you can't talk boy. You can't play no d and you can't talk.
Shit, I don't play at all.
You wanna play guard tonight, boy, run the show?
I ain't gonna play at all. Come on say shrimps.
I don't feel like it.
AWWWWWWWW come on say it. Say shrimps so my man here can hear what Ahm talkin' about.
You get out of my face. You oughta have to take a number to set up an appointment to talk to me, you jive nigger.
Appointment?
Yeah, an appointment.
Hey, take that suit off and get it to the cleaners in Cleveland.
Naw, I wore it this whole trip and I'm gonna wear it all the way home.
Sheeit, it's machine-washable and drip-dry.
Fuck you.
Man, that shirt looks like a sheet you fucked somebody twice on.
It's drip-dried.
Well, you better go wash it, but don't put no Clorox on it.
Where'd you get that hat, mother-fucker?
That's a famous hat, been through some shit.
It looks like shit.
Hey, give me back my hat. Aw you General Custer looking mother-fucker.
Wait a minute, looks good on you, need a haircut though.
I'm gonna make this hat look famous. I see Russ wearing that fuckin' little leather pillbox he's got, I can wear this.
I hear that.
Hey, how long's the flight to Cleveland?

An hour.

An hour in the wrong direction.

What you mean?

He means that fuckin' Cleveland is east, you dumb ignorant midwestern mother-fucker. We wanna go west, dumbshit.

Cleveland's west, you asshole.

West of New York, east of Milwaukee, you wire-faced motherfucker.

Fuck you, you can't even say shrimps.

Shreeemps. There, ass-howl.

Awwwwghahahaha. You can't even talk, you fuck head.

Hey, fuck you. Give me my hat back.

Hey——, hey you ignorant bear fucker.

HA HA HA HA, he got on that teddy bear bitch, didn't he?

Sheeeit, we couldn't a fought him for the little bitch, she was round as a bear, just a little round bear.

Hey ——, she have any fur on her?

Fuck you, she wasn't bad.

She have claws. She scratch your ass? You animal mother-fucker?

Hey, leave my shirt alone. Hey, don't tear it, you mother-fucker you.

Ah hhhhhahahahah, he's got a scratch there man, ha ah hahah, you ol' lady gonna shoot you bear fuckin' ass.

Hey, give me my hat, you mother-fucker, we're here.

Hey, get my suit bag back there. Hey ——, hey, come on, you mother-fucker, hand me my bag.

You owe me five dollars and ten cents for the phone, motherfucker. You buyin' my burger.

Fuck you, teddy bear fucker, ha ah ha.

What time the plane leave, Frank?

There was nearly an hour to kill before the flight to Cleveland. The Bucks were heading off to New York at the same time. Green, Oleynick, Norwood and Milwaukee's Kevin Restani were spread along both sides of me at the lunch counter. Oleynick and Restani talked about the old days of their careers, two years back when they were playing in the WCAC—Oleynick at Seattle U and Restani at USF. Oleynick bought a couple of rounds of beer.

"Frank, you are a very generous man," I told him. "What are you going to do when you go broke? I don't think it'll all come back."

"Hey man, I'd rather live good now and have a few laughs than live like a monk and be old before I know what hit me. You take it now, B.J. That's the way it is on the streets, man."

Green picked up the conversation when the topic became trades. "I

221

know I won't be back. I'm just a gypsy man. Don't matter where they send me. I'm just a gypsy-playin' basketballer. Yeah, just a gypsy." He didn't seem so much lonely as simply a man with a lonely road to travel—a jump shot for hire.

Cleveland is one place most players, gypsies and the rest, don't long to be stationed. Toots Shor pegged Cleveland one night when a customer in Shor's New York restaurant complained about the cost of his steak. "I could get the same steak for half this price in Cleveland," the customer alleged. "Yes," Shor agreed, "but when you finished you'd still be in Cleveland." It's true Cleveland may not be the end of the NBA trail, or as some have suggested, the world, but you can see it from there. Cleveland isn't completely a mess, they just moved the home of the Cavaliers thirty-five miles away in the middle of a cornfield so that people could make it to their cars after a game. Or so they'd have cars to make it to. I don't care to go anywhere in Cleveland. Anywhere.

As we checked into our hotel, Oleynick was pumped and ready to roll. I sensed another New Orleans in the making and while there were no hurricanes to contend with, I begged off in clear conscience. Besides, since he saw the movie *Rocky*, Oleynick had developed an annoying habit of sparring on other people. The one they used to call "Magic" has become "The Italian Stallion" in Sonicville.

Midevening I headed down the hall and came across Watts' room. His door was open. He was eating dinner on a room service cart—two pieces of apple pie à la mode and a bottle of his beloved white wine. Probably not that bad a combination at that. "You know after all this we been through this year, we gonna make the playoffs. Ain't that a gas?" Watts laughed as he picked a piece of pie off his bathrobe. "And we gonna save Russ's job so we can go through all this again next year."

That's a real gas.

The next evening, as we walked off the bus at the Coliseum in Ridgefield Township, I pulled alongside Russell. We walked into the arena and as players filed past and disappeared into the locker room, we stood and talked. It was conversational. I told him I just couldn't figure out the team and how they could go out and put together a trip like this in the wake of all that had occurred earlier.

"There are things that I could see. I've been in this business twenty-five years. You should come to understand some things in that time," he commented, arms folded across his chest, casual, not in a hurry to leave. We looked down the corridor and out onto the court where a few Cavs were shooting. The bouncing balls sounded like popcorn popping.

I referred to that early-season conversation we had in another

222

corridor. Why didn't the guys ever feel comfortable coming to you and talking?

"They would if they were coming to talk straight. But they know I don't want to hear any bullshit. Let me tell you something. Twenty years ago everyone had eight Bobby Wilkersons, guys who dedicated themselves to being the best they possibly could be with their abilities. With expansion the character was defused. We were so close at Boston. We played jokes on each other and would mimic each other. We loved each other. That gave us something that carried us. I don't see that kind of attitude and interest in each other now. Maybe it's that the players aren't together very long. But I see it more as character. And character is something you can't hand to someone. It's just like you can't go out and take the shot for him with two seconds to go."

I told him of my conversation with Havlicek and how money had been an incentive to pursue success. He discounted money as having made that much of a difference.

"Cous and I never participated in the playoff shares because it made so little difference in our salaries. I was making $22,500 to start. You got $2,000 for going all the way. Money is the same today, relatively. Salaries have always been out of perspective with the rest of society. I'm getting paid a ridiculously large amount for the position I have, but I feel very sincerely that for every dollar I've been paid I've earned it five times. I can't be a coach and leave myself at the mercy of some other general manager. So I won't do that. I could take the money for next year—but I've given my word on a five-year contract and that's what I plan to live up to. I don't care what the public thinks. Boos don't bother me any more than cheers affect me. Fans are fickle."

It was a nice visit, one that reminded me of the pleasure one could get from Russell—when he let you.

Seattle played poorly enough to lose and did so by four. For all that had been accomplished out here, the Sonics were heading home having lost ground to K.C. and Chicago. But at least they were heading home.

As we broke through clouds over the Cascades and spotted Seattle in early-spring greenery, I felt as though we had been out on a safari with experiences those down below could never possibly imagine. We had been in some strange world and, even though the stories had come back each day, it didn't seem like we had been any part of this city—no connection. It was as though we were coming out of a movie and all the action of that movie was still going on somewhere even though the characters were right here, ready to become partners again with familiar beds and familiar faces.

28

Down the Drain to Dispatch the Dictator

If there is a greater form of rejection in sports than boos, it is to have the crowd simply get up and walk out. The Sonics were fortunate that was the worst their fans did as they blew by twenty-one to Phoenix on the first game back from the road trip. The Suns hadn't won on the road in thirty-seven days. They were missing four of their standout players. A mystifying note rose in the wake of the humiliating loss—Seattle hadn't practiced in the four days since returning from the east. Russell offered no explanation.

Following a loss at Los Angeles and a victory at home against Houston, Seattle sauntered to Oakland for the last road game of the regular season. The flight down gave me an opportunity to hand over $30 to Green for our little preseason wager on the ABA teams. Denver had won the Midwest Division, costing me $20. Denver and San Antonio were both playoff bound, another $10. Green contended it should be $10 for each team. I explained why that wasn't so, and kept trying to forget the fact he was making $200,000 against my $20,000. He stuffed the bills in his shirt and asked if I had any other matters worth wagering upon. At least he was smiling. In fact, we finally had a pleasant, prolonged rap. Why couldn't it stay at this level? Why? Why?

The morning of the game, Art Spander of the San Francisco *Chronicle* had a piece on Walton along with the game story of the Warriors' loss the previous night at Portland. He had attempted an interview and had been confronted with a Walton who wasn't in a talking mood. Spander had approached Walton in the Blazer locker room after shooting practice. He kept asking questions, trying to bring a comment on just about anything Walton might be interested in discussing. Walton kept saying, "I don't like to give interviews before a game." I could sympathize with Spander for the feeling of professional—and it becomes personal—rejection. All you want to do is ask a couple of questions. But I also felt a smugness that I had broken through where other accomplished journalists failed.

It was one of those menthol fresh days in the Bay Area. In fact that was what a companion kept smoking all day as we drove down the coast and toured the spring green hills south of San Francisco. Salems, I think they were.

While we were cavorting in the hills, a startling pageantry was being performed on the floor of the Oakland Coliseum where the

Sonics were going through shooting practice. You have to suspect it was no more than a coincidence, it happening in the Bay Area and all. But, with Russell, who knows for sure? He might have picked up some special breeze coming in under the door—a scent of whatever it was that entered his psyche twenty-five years earlier on the playgrounds of Oakland and compelled him toward basketball immortality.

It was the final road practice of the season. Maybe Russell had heard some of the comments made by players as they became increasingly disenchanted with him during the season. Maybe he had heard them say, "He wasn't that great. He just stood out in his day when the league was different." As the incident was related, Watts had slithered in through a forest of arms and tossed up another of those physics-mocking scoop shots that went around a corner, came off the glass and in.

"If you ever brought that shit in on me, I'd make you eat it," was about what Russell said.

"Don't be so sure," Watts replied.

Russell moved out onto the court, a pair of sneakers conveniently adorned at the bottom of his flared Levi's. Watts drove on him. He scooped up a running flip. Russell put it into the chairs at courtside. Watts wanted another chance. He drove again, flipping a quick shot as Russell trailed. Russell rose and swatted it away—possibly fouling Watts, but no more so than the way he used to defend the heartland for Boston. There are many who claim he fouled all the time, but that the officials were so much in awe of him that they wouldn't call it. Not quite fair respect for the game's greatest shot blocker, according to those who were there.

"Anyone else?" Russell asked after stopping Watts the second time.

Johnson, born in 1954 within months of Russell's first of two-straight NCAA championships at USF, wanted to try him. Johnson drove, stopped, faked Russell into the air, stepped around and leaned up a little five-footer. Russell, who had pivoted in midair after being faked, slammed the ball off the glass with his right hand and caught it. Johnson's mouth dropped open.

Why, he didn't say, but Weatherspoon wanted to challenge The Man after Johnson. This was playground—check The Man out, try him. Spoon drooped forward, holding the ball inches above the floor, rocking back and forth. He took a couple of dribbles, driving right, stooped low and then rose, lofting a high-arching fallaway from fifteen feet. Russell was on the ball before it was six inches out of Spoon's hands. Russell turned with the ball, took a couple steps toward the hoop, rose and stuffed it. He was cackling before the ball hit the floor. He had enough, he said. It may be the last time he'll ever touch a basketball.

That evening I made it to the arena just in time to wolf down some quiche Lorraine, dried banana chips and handfuls of raisins and nuts—a little Mother Earthiness by the Warriors' owner, Franklin Mieuli. The Sonics hammered away at the lead and with fifteen seconds left kept alive the faintest of playoff hopes as Tolson flew into the stands after a wild pass. He somehow got it back onto the court where Green controlled it and flipped to Seals under the basket for a stuffer to produce his evening's thirty-eighth point. Barry kicked the floor in disgust. Four hours later I paid a hotel clerk twenty dollars for a ride to the San Francisco airport. Not only did I get there on time, but he gave me a free sermon on the glory of football over other sports because NFL teams have prayer meetings. "You don't see any of that in the NBA," he lamented. Not so you'd notice.

I arrived home after 4 A.M. and was at the Coliseum just before the 1:45 tipoff against the Blazers. Portland left Seattle with both feet in the grave, but it wasn't until two days later that the long-ago predicted playoff elimination was made official. And it couldn't have come in a more humiliating fashion—against the Nets.

There were little signs—well, some that weren't even that little—of insurrection among the Sonics. Players seemed to be making mistakes that didn't fit into their abilities. Just little things like losing control of the ball and stepping on the sideline and getting treated like a turnstile on defense. Green had developed a routine of slovenliness along the way, calling for hand powder as he walked toward the scorer's table whenever he was to report in, spilling the powder along the sideline, leaving a trail of gum wrappers and sometimes a towel for Furtado to scoop up in his wake. Late in this game Russell called for him. He took forever to get his warm-ups off. Having missed the scheduled chance to get into the game, Green sauntered by Russell and mumbled, "I'll hurry more next time." Russell, with chin in hands, mumbled back, "No, you won't." It wasn't that the club was purposefully trying to blow games—the players just didn't give a damn about anything but the season being over. They had let their feelings of animosity for Russell take over any other goals and personal pride.

Still, as lousy as Seattle played, it couldn't help but keep up with the Nets. As the game came down to the wire, Loughery called out to Strom, "You can't handle this, Earl. I'd hate to see you in a big game." With twenty-one seconds left and Seattle huddled during a time-out, trying to come up with a plan for the tying basket, Strom toweled off his face and muttered to no one in particular, "Can you imagine putting the fans through five more minutes of this?" Seattle wasn't up to overtime, though, and as I followed Russell down the corridor to the locker room, I wondered if he could sense the media perched for the kill.

Before the game I had asked him how he was doing. He had

226

replied, "I'll tell you, it's so good right now it scares me." Now, as he entered the interview room, he tried to dredge up a smile. The question line was obvious: The team is officially out of contention, are you coming back? No one spoke for a pregnant five or six seconds.

"What's this leave you with?" I asked.

"Out of the playoffs," he laughed, hoping others might pick up the lighter mood. "The waiting is over." There was another pause.

"What else?" I asked, wondering why I couldn't just jump out and ask if he was quitting.

"Just have to finish out the schedule like a few other teams," he said matter-of-factly.

Five more seconds passed.

"And then?" I tried again.

He laughed. "Then comes summer."

"What happens then?" I persisted, feeling caught in a slow-moving gait, unable to break loose and sprint, unable to ask the question that was on everyone's mind. No one else was saying anything, just writing and watching.

"I don't know," Russell replied, his face getting serious, his voice dropping.

"Are you planning on coming back next year?" I finally got it out.

There was another five-second pause. I wondered what counter-punch he would deliver.

"I don't know," he answered quietly.

"If it's up to you?" I asked.

"I wouldn't want to get into that now. I don't think it's the right time," he stated in a tone that said let's drop it.

Another reporter jumped in. "Do you see any basic player needs on this club for next year?"

"I don't want to talk about that either."

He's as bad as Walton, someone whispered. There was a momentary pause. Russell continued: "I'm very disappointed right now and I don't think that's the right time to talk about things. I don't want to say anything rash. It's easy enough to see what we need in players, but it's much tougher to get somebody who can do a better job in those spots."

He went on to state that Dennis Johnson was the only player he felt had exceeded what Russell had expected of him. He said Burleson obviously wasn't on schedule toward developing into a dominating center.

"What's wrong with him?" someone asked.

"I don't know. It's inside of him."

"You couldn't bring it out?" the reporter continued.

"There's only so much a coach can do with a player or a team."

"Do you have anything to prove by fulfilling the final year on your contract?"

"I don't have anything to prove to anyone. I always do the best I can and don't worry about the results. After two years as a player there wasn't anything to prove—except a curiosity to find out how good I could be. I can guarantee you there are some things that happened this year that will never happen to me again. For example, I will never again have a team that plays like that on the road."

He refused to say if he would guarantee that by not having a team next year.

As I sat down to compose my final column of the season, I didn't know for sure what his future would be, nor was I certain of mine. I would bet that I would be covering the Sonics, despite some nibbling thoughts of disenchantment. I was of the inclination that he wouldn't be back. There was, in one realm, a soap opera scenario: Will Bill Russell make a stand against Sam Schulman? Who will lose face? Which side will the media take? There was a more serious, from my personal perspective, side to all this. The NBA dance wouldn't be very comfortable for me next year if Russell returned and I wrote what was in my head. But I had looked upon him in two basic ways the past two years. One, in pursuit of some sort of a meaningful rapport. Two, as a project to study and try to determine what this guy was really all about. Perhaps my frustrations at the former influenced my determinations of the latter. It developed into a piece that was headlined: "Why Russell Won't Return."

Bill Russell is complex enough to keep you forever fascinated if you don't become frustrated along the way.

That makes for a man of intriguing study in the spotlight focused by the media and a nation's sports fans. However, it does not wear particularly well in the execution of his present duties as coach and general manager of the Seattle Sonics.

In two years spent weighing his words, watching his actions and thereby trying to paint a picture of this long-legged legend, I've found he just doesn't fit onto the canvas.

A two-hour plane ride conversation leaves you convinced of his sensitivity and broad knowledge of the world's affairs. While he tends to dominate the conversation, his wit can leave you parting with tears of laughter rolling off your cheeks.

Yet, when you run into him a few hours later, you may encounter a moody glower that should never be directed at anything less despicable than a child molester. That doesn't make for endearing relationships.

His personality dominates his role with the Sonics. That personality reads a flat "okay" or "nay" to the majority of folks who are at long distance range.

But as you wade in closer, there is a man of deep pride, apparent honesty and an unwavering code that Bill Russell will never be ruled by anyone or anything. You never forget the well-muscled ego flexed inside the man.

It seems somehow obscene to dissect a personality in public, yet he makes a celebrated living as a public figure—something that is not as comfortable to his nature as most suppose.

It's my feeling that Bill Russell is generally a very inward person who may enjoy the chance to bestow his humor and cleverness through the media on occasion, but basically wishes the public wasn't such an overbearing part of the world in which he can best make his living.

He frequently makes light of all the hoopla that is made of himself and the Sonics and pro sports in general. He's right, of course, that the public's obsession with sports heroes and the local clubs is a mishandling of reality. He's right that inflation and starvation are more important than whether the Sonics make the playoffs.

But, the interest, even if misplaced or overdone, packs plenty of green-backed support and that is why Russell can make a quarter of a million dollars a year supervising young men as they play a child's game.

At first glance, it seems bewildering that Russell could have put so much into his role as a player and yet seemingly be so casual about his present duties.

He once told me, "there isn't a job in the world that can't be done in four hours a day if a person is organized." I'm sure he meant managerial positions and would be willing to admit to a few exceptions—but, he doesn't rate being a coach and general manager among them.

Research into the performance of chores by other coaches around the NBA reveals that Russell simply does not put in as many hours as his colleagues. He doesn't scout, he doesn't review video tapes, he doesn't work extensively in developing individuals or the team.

Of course, he would be allowed his unorthodox approach IF they produced competitive results. They haven't.

He hired his assistant, Bob Hopkins, to provide most of the technical input into the program, but he does not allow Hoppy the total control over that facet. So, what is produced is a placing of parts into a gear box that does not always mesh.

Russell knows the game of basketball, but probably not to the extent that many of his coaching counterparts who have read the books and attended the clinics since he quit playing in 1969.

His advice to individuals seems correct at times during a game. His direction during a timeout may have merit. But, the ideas and the systems haven't been drilled in thoroughly so that they are virtually second nature by the time the team steps on the court.

Russell is the only coach in the NBA who bars reporters from his practices, so only spying eyes and the game-time product convinces me that the club does not have a well-drilled foundation.

Perhaps he has forgotten how many hours went into refining the Celtics' disciplined attack. Earlier this year Boston guard JoJo White lamented that the present-day Celtics won't work hard to polish their fastbreak. "You've got to do it and do it and do it until you are filling the lanes and cutting through in your sleep," White said.

I'm convinced Russell's not all that interested in the game. He never planned to coach again after he left the Celtics. The only reason he came back was because Sam Schulman gave him an incredible offer which he literally could not refuse.

When Schulman first asked him to take the reins of the Sonic runaways, Russell thought of everything a man could possibly ask for without breaking into shamed laughter and told Sam that's what it would take to land him. When Schulman said "you've got it," Russell had to take it.

His name filled the seats in the Coliseum for the first time in the franchise's history. That's part of what Russell means when he says, "I've earned five dollars for every dollar I've been paid here."

His stature impressed most of the players and allowed him to run off those he couldn't get to march in line. He hauled the club into the playoffs at the end of the second year—and that was the peak of the production, at least competitively.

Under Russell the club never has been disciplined either on or off the court. He says, "A good player can find 100 reasons to play well and not-so-good players can find 100 reasons NOT to play well."

He has sifted through dozens of personalities looking for a group that will show up every night ready to work hard and provide self-motivation.

When the club was squashed by a better-prepared and more disciplined Phoenix contingent last spring in the playoffs, a lot of the Sonic players privately expressed resentment that they had been "humiliated."

Russell is not totally to blame, but Seattle never really recovered from that. A number of players let what had been an eroding confidence and rapport with Russell crumble into total disenchantment this season.

Throughout this campaign, players bitched about not knowing in advance if they were going to play 30 minutes or 30 seconds. There were occasions where a player wouldn't know he was starting until the announcer called out his name. There were occasions where the team walked out for the opening tip frantically trying to determine defensive assignments. There were timeouts called when an opponent had just run off 10 straight points and nothing would be corrected by the coach while the players might chatter about an adjustment among themselves or simply drink Gatorade until the horn blew and then go back into action.

A coach cannot pull puppet strings and there are some personalities among the Sonics who do not contribute as much as they could. But, a coach is being paid for the sole task of making sure his team is competitive and if the players don't believe in his program—you've got a problem.

Russell cares about winning—but not enough to work himself into glue over it. Unfortunately for him, there are many coaches around the league who do. It's not a conscious thing, but he's just not as hungry as most of his counterparts. He's already had enough glory to last a man 10 lifetimes.

He's competing against coaches with similar tools of intellect and personnel who are hungrier and therefore put in much more time and determination. They may not spend more hours on the practice court, but the pre-practice preparation makes them more productive.

Schulman sees that now. He knows that nothing major can change next year. He knows that Russell has already admitted publicly he has nothing to prove as coach—other than to "do the best I can and let the results take care of themselves."

Sonic fans seem like they would rally around a dead horse in 100-degree weather as long as it wore the green and white. But, Schulman has to be worried about their patience when it comes time to buy season tickets for next year.

The Sonics have stunk up the Coliseum pretty well in the last month and that scent is going to linger.

The majority of the players want Russell gone. They don't believe in the way he deals with them. They claim his personality is "overbearing," that "he's just on a head trip."

It's possible they would perform better under a new personality dealing a new program. It's possible they would better respond to tighter rules and more relaxed personality ties. The pressure would then be on the players to prove they can give 100 percent to anyone. As long as Russell is there, they have a handy excuse not to.

Late-season losses to the weakest teams in the league drove the issue right out into the sunlight. There are no excuses of key injuries or unconquerable schedule obstacles. The team has hit the rocks.

That situation leaves Schulman with little choice but to seek to buy up Russell's final year. The maximum payoff would be about $300,000 when all the little odds and ends are accounted for. The stockholders may consider that another botching of the bankbook and take action against Schulman.

But, they'll be wise to remember what Russell has done for the franchise and what kind of a mess it was when "The Dictator" rolled into town on the heels of a 26-56 campaign and half-empty seating.

The Sonics haven't slipped all the way back to where Russell came in, but they could approximate such disaster next year if the players won't respond to their leader.

Russell knows that and when he ponders another long, long season of being embarrassed by what is happening on the court and facing the same tireless questions of his club's demise as he visits 21 other major cities, he has to feel a desire to step away.

He may ponder coming back and really showing he can build a winner. But, it's such a long grind with so much more work required and there are simply more important things in Russell's life—such as enjoying it—that it's not worth it to him.

That's why it is this writer's guess he will be willing to accept some sort of a settlement on his final year's dues and move on to new adventures more suitable to his personality and interests.

There's no doubt Bill Russell will be a fascinating study wherever he goes and that he has been the biggest individual to ever perform in Seattle sports. His character is not diminished—he has just run his course with the Sonics.

The piece was subsequently selected as the best feature of the year by the Pro Basketball Writers Association. I was proud to have been so definitive, but I also felt that I had somehow betrayed him. It seemed distasteful to be laying into someone for public consumption when so much of my observation had been in near privacy.

I had written my piece in midweek and encountered Russell before it ran. I felt a need to say something, but I couldn't define what it was. I wanted to say that I thought he was a dynamic, sometimes profound individual. I was sorry that we didn't agree on some of his philosophies of coaching and operating a team. I felt I was sitting in judgment based purely on personal tastes. I wanted to tell him I was sorry I had to dissect him in public, but it was a job that I had to do. All I really could get out was, "I'm sorry our roles don't allow us to have a freer communication." I also sent him a card, quoting Andy Warhol: "In the future everybody will be famous for fifteen minutes." I meant it to mean, you're just getting what's coming because you're Bill Russell the public commodity, not because you're Bill Russell the person. Of course, I was foolish to try to separate the two.

Meyers had written a column in the *Times*, which also ran that morning of the season's final game. He had said, "I do not believe Russell will return. I hope I am wrong." His contention was that the personality and the national stature made for good copy. We were lucky to have him in Seattle. I agreed to the extent that Meyers' role did not require wading the same involved waters as Heberlein or I faced covering the Sonics. Meyers wanted him around to make his job of writing columns more interesting. I wanted him gone, I finally discovered, in hopes of making my job as a beat reporter more convenient.

There was national attention focused on what his decision would be. United Press moved a story combining the observations of both Meyers and myself. It was well played around the country.

That afternoon of the final game, he walked out to take his seat, splendid in a deep blue suit. He made an effort not to look at me. All during the game, during time-outs, he would not make eye contact with me as there had been occasion to do in any other game over the past two years. I hadn't written his ticket out of town, but I hadn't made it easy for him to stay on. I felt good as people stopped by my press seat to congratulate me on the article. I felt that I had taken something evasive and pinned it down on paper, something people were interested in. And yet I felt in a way that I had betrayed Russell—picked him open. There was plently left of his mystique, but I had carved a little off the surface.

With the media, at least part of it, having committed itself with critical sentiments, all that was left was to hear from the fans and the players. One man doesn't make a mandate, of course, but there was a good round of approving laughs when a fan yelled out during the game: "Hey, Russell, when you leave don't forget to take Burleson with you." Five minutes remained in the season when Russell called Green back off the bench to replace Burleson. Green waltzed by the bench en route to the scorer's table, asking, demanding his usual ritual of "gum, powder, towel" from Furtado. Then he turned and started something with Russell. Looking down at Russell, he was saying something inaudible from where I was sitting. Russell kept answering, "Yeah, go for Tommy." The horn blew for Green to enter the game. He took a long stride right at Russell and said in a plain voice, "You're a motherfucker, that's for sure." Russell just looked at him, emotionless. Two minutes later there was a time-out. Green came over to the bench, fuming. He sat down, but before the group could close in, he jumped up and yelled at Furtado that his knee hurt. He spit something like, "Fuckin' joke," toward Russell and walked to the end of the bench where he grabbed his warm-up jacket, put it on his shoulders, sat down and stared straight ahead. Russell sent in a sub. Then Brown came over to Furtado before the time-out had ended and said his foot hurt. Furtado said, "Now you're using the trainer." Brown was pissed, but didn't say any more.

I asked Green, after the game in the locker room, what was going on. "That mother-fucker sees Jabbar beating on his boy and sends me in to take the whippin'. Fuck the man. Fuck him. Fuck this place. Shit, can you believe him. He just uses people as if they was junk. . . ."

Furtado was in the laundry room pounding his fist on the wash machine to keep back the tears. This wasn't the way it was supposed to be with people who had to share so much over all these months. This wasn't the way people were supposed to treat each other.

Meanwhile, more than two dozen newspaper, TV and radio reporters were jammed into the interview room. The Lakers had sealed the season with a dreary defeat of the Sonics. Now, what would Russell's announcement be? It seemed as though all the media was poised against this man who sat on the couch stroking his beard. When there were just a few of the regulars, or even just myself going one-to-one, even when challenging him, it didn't seem the same as this. It seemed as though we were dogs backing a lamb into a corner. But Russell is no lamb, of course. He held everyone at bay. "I haven't reached a determination yet. I can't give you any insight into it. This isn't the proper time to discuss it." He turned things back on the hounds. "I think all this attention is kind of funny. What I do just isn't that important. Like everyone else, I work for a living and whatever I do won't stop it from raining here next week."

Valid in principle. But when a personality commands $250,000 a year for a job, it is because people have decided to make the job subject to public consumption. After all, if he was being paid for being a personality (not for coaching or general managing), he was then cheating the Sonics. How could you look at all the little things that added up to the sort of job he was doing and not agree? Things like: The Sonics step on the court for the opening tip and Bantom calls out to Russell, "What we got for a match?" As Russell looks around at who is on the court, he's saying, "Ah, ah, er, you take . . ." and the ball goes up without the Sonics even knowing who they are checking. Like a team running off ten straight points and Russell not calling time-out, explaining: "There's no point in calling a time-out unless you have something to say." And all those time-outs when nothing was said.

His employer wasn't satisfied. "I censored Bill repeatedly in private for making concessions to athletes on their contracts. I could have blown up twenty times. But this being a business so exposed to the public eye, I don't want to get the reputation as the hatchet guy, made to look like the ogre all the time. Even if you win you lose. I don't want that image nationally. If I was to sue Russell I would be on the front pages of every newspaper in the country and having to drag out all the gritty details."

Here was Schulman trying to defend his investment and looking like the loser again. It is the media that decides that owners aren't supposed to play with their teams—making trades and suggestions as to how the club should be run. Why not? It's his investment. It's his toy. But Schulman, even though he was doing what the majority of fans apparently wanted—judging by their mailed opinions—was losing face again. He wouldn't honor Russell's contract, but he wouldn't re-negotiate Watts, claiming, "A contract is a contract."

So the season was over, but there was a whole new watch to stand. Rumors were loose near and far that Russell would be replaced. Costello, Hopkins, Bill Sharman, who would the new coach be? Jerry Tarkanian's name kept coming up. No one knew for sure that Russell was leaving, yet the news interest was off to the next step—anticipation sells news. The Nevada–Las Vegas coach, who had just finished third in the NCAA finals, was on the brink of incurring probation. He'd be glad to get out, the rumor millers said. Schulman would say only that he hadn't met with Russell, yet. Any other discussion was premature.

A story arose that Schulman had been to Las Vegas to meet with Tarkanian. Schulman would neither confirm it nor deny it. He said he hadn't heard from Russell. The season had been over less than a week, not a day had gone by without some kind of speculative story in either paper—and the principals weren't even in communication. A phone call to Russell's home provided the message, "He left town and won't be back for a while." Some claimed he was golfing in California, others claimed he was camping in Canada. Two days later, a week since the end of the season, Schulman said he couldn't find Russell. I knew he would be foxy, but this was just great—we would be chasing this all summer.

Nine days after the season's conclusion, Schulman said he had talked with Russell and a meeting was planned in the near future. "I've talked with Bill on the phone and we plan to meet. Bill's a very classy guy and I think he wants to do what's best for the Sonics. I just plan to have a very open discussion of what has happened over the past four years and especially last year, and we'll just have to reassess the future. We have a very good rapport and we will remain good friends whatever we decide."

Ten days after the season's end, Schulman finally admitted he had talked with Tarkanian, but said he had also made an offer to Russell that would allow him to remain for the next season. I finally got hold of Tarkanian and he said that the Sonics had made him an offer through his agent. Schulman flatly denied that. And, the next day, Watts called from Los Angeles to say he was meeting with Schulman. Schulman said he hadn't heard from Watts, but he wasn't going to renegotiate anybody's contract. He said, too, that he had met with Russell. No decision yet.

The night I went to Portland to take in a Blazers versus Denver Western Conference semifinal playoff game, my editor came up with the story that Tarkanian had been offered the Sonic job and it was his to take or turn down. The report had come from one of Tarkanian's coaching friends. I called Schulman the next day and he said that was pure bunk. Oh, who do we believe? Why does everyone so well deceive?

Three weeks after the season's finale, I came out with the report that Russell would take a settlement of roughly half his $250,000 due salary and depart. I didn't think it was such a profound observation, but apparently more people were uncertain as to what Russell would do than I thought. At a sportswriter's luncheon that afternoon, a prominent radio sportscaster called my story "totally irresponsible journalism." He was upset that I had quoted a "reliable source" as the perpetrator of the news. He didn't want to credit me if he used the story on the air and he couldn't very well say it was a reliable source if he didn't know who it was. He couldn't possibly know it was a good friend of Russell's.

Two days later I was sitting in Russell's office with Hopkins and Furtado. It felt as if there was a ghost in the room. His face loomed from pictures on every wall, but where was Russell? Why didn't he come around or answer the phone? Walsh walked in and said that he had just been fired. The purge was starting. The next day Schulman walked out of Russell's office where he had been on the phone. Newsmen, who had been camped around the office for the past two days since Schulman arrived in town, came to attention. He cleared his throat and proclaimed: "Gentlemen, we've got an agreement. We've reached a settlement on the final year of Bill's contract." I looked at my watch. It was 12:10, May 4. Bill Russell was officially back out of basketball.

It seemed fitting that Russell did not show for the wake. A man who was reluctant to share himself with the public, whose private-stock humor and philosophy were always delivered from a station of aloofness, Russell knew better than to let anyone have a clear shot at him now that he had finally been handed a loss. They said he was "released." It was too much to say "fired"—Russell always had the image of being in control. He had come to town celebrated as "The Dictator." He had addressed the media that day with a command and a style that were unquestionably overwhelming. Roaring his laugh, making promises, giving one and all the dream that the next dynasty in pro basketball would be Celtics-West. He hadn't promised a dynasty exactly, just an NBA title. Now he was checking out, dreams shy and at least a year short of the plan. Russell couldn't come forth to say, "I have failed." He didn't see it that way. He submitted a written message care of his lawyer: ". . . I have mixed emotions about leaving the Sonics, but I feel I have reached a point in my career where I want to pursue other activities. . . ."

Later, after Hopkins had been named Russell's successor, we had a conversation. Hopkins commented, "He told me he was almost on the verge of quitting when Sam said he was too expensive. He was insulted. He's a very proud man. He's also very sensitive to what people think. He tells you he doesn't pay any attention, but he is very sensitive to everything that is written about him. He thought about coming back for his final season, but he would have had to make a lot of changes in personnel. It wasn't worth all that."

Russell, who hadn't said "good morning" to some of the Sonic office crew twice in four years, appeared at a going-away party held by the staff. He told one, "I haven't been very communicative because I don't like to talk to new people. When I was younger I listened to people and what they said hurt me." That sounds unacceptable, yet why was he now bothering to explain himself to even a person he would probably never see again? If he was indeed so sensitive, which I believe to be true, then why could he be so terribly cold to others?

It was all part of the Russell Mystique. One must give his due to a man who can drive himself to the peak of accomplishment that Russell achieved in an arena where thousands challenged. Who can say what voice drove him on and on? Who can say what voice refused to let him fail? The thing one has to marvel at isn't just that he heard such a compelling inner voice, but that he could make himself follow it in a way few ever approximate. I am speaking of him in this regard as a player. Yet the drive goes on—not in the sports arena, obviously, for he did not put in all the time and effort he knew was necessary to manufacture a champion as a coach and general manager. But he never could quite understand players who would not motivate themselves to an all-out effort. He gave that as a player and apparently the Celtics as he knew them were people full of pride and dedication to excellence. He probably had a difficult time respecting those who were on his Sonics' roster when he knew he was so much better as a player than they were—maybe even now—and they weren't trying to be as good as they could be.

But he still answers inner needs to be in control of his life and has the discipline to carry them out. He knows the public will take a man of his stature and play with him and the media will fondle until there is only a myth in the mirror. He once said, "If you lose that fine, competitive edge, mentally or physically, you're dead." Even though he would repeatedly say, "You can't be a good sportswriter or a good anything if you take it all too seriously," he never lets up against the world. He never lets anyone get too close. As a player he *willed* his body to make the play that required supreme effort out of sheer mental determination to prove he was the best man. In his life today, he *wills* himself to be in control, to be superior.

Maybe it was true, what Watts and Haywood claimed, that Russell couldn't stand a rival for popularity. I tend to think that inaccurate. Yet why did he lay such a devastating blow to Chamberlain—his only possible rival in the cage world at the time of Russell's retirement? In the 1969 playoffs, Russell's finale, Chamberlain hurt his knee in the late stages of the championship game. He took himself out of the game. He asked to come back in a few minutes later, but Bill Van Bredakolff told him to sit. The Celtics went on to win the title, Russell's eleventh in thirteen years. Soon after he retired and while speaking at a college he suddenly offered: "Wilt copped out in the last game. Any injury short of a broken leg or a broken back isn't good enough. When he took himself out of that game, when he hurt his knee, well, I wouldn't have put him back in the game either."

Chamberlain reflected in his autobiography, *Wilt*: "When friends told me what Bill had said, I was shocked—and hurt. Other people had been saying the same thing, but I hadn't let them bother me. They were just ignorant fans who either had a hard-on for me or were disappointed because the Lakers had lost another championship. Bill was different. Or, at least, I thought he was. He was a friend. He knew me, and he knew the game. He'd hurt his ankle, and had to come out of the game and St. Louis had beat Boston for the championship. I sure as shit wouldn't say he copped out then, and he shouldn't have said I copped out in 1969. . . ."

I don't believe it was a slip of the tongue or an emotional outburst. That's not Russell. He calculated that public opinion was leaning his way and pulled everyone into his camp—cementing for history his stature as king of basketball's mountain. He has the tools of intelligence, humor and cunning to make himself dynamic. Answering an obsession that he control his life on every front, Russell will remain one of the true Superstars of our time.

29

Fanfare and a Fundamental Frustration

A piece of birthday cake covered with a slice of ice cream came across the living room on a small plate, passed hand to hand through the crowded gathering. I couldn't tell whose birthday it was—apparently one of the children sitting next to Walton at a large round oak table in the far corner. It seemed many of the others in the room, sitting on chairs and on the floor, standing in doorways, didn't know whose party it was either. There was no music, but the room was alive with sound, clusters of chattering conversation, little outbreaks of children's laughter. There were others in the room who didn't seem to know anyone but Walton. I didn't. No one seemed nervous, in need of forced conversation. Tan bodies in running shorts, thin faces peeking out from under long hair—men and women—all seemed to add up to a peacefulness. Some were Walton's neighbors, some friends from San Diego and Detroit and other points who had come to Portland to take in the championship series against the 76ers. Walton's head could be seen bobbing in conversation with the children. He was happy. He was with people who could carry on without having to react to him. The cake was quite good.

Three hours earlier he had led the Blazers to their first win of the series. I had found him in the trainer's room, icing his knees. He wanted to keep the rest of the media away. Bob Robinson of the Portland *Oregonian* and myself were the only ones in the room with him. Finally, the trainer, Ron Culp, came in and said he really should go out and talk to the press. He told me to stop over at his house later as he strolled out to meet the press, wearing only an old T-shirt. He sat in a stuffed chair, and, as Ellie Kossack of *Sport Magazine* described it, "scratched his nuts and said he didn't want to discuss anything."

Two hours earlier I had been sitting in the NBA hospitality room with writers from the Philadelphia papers, plus New York, Los Angeles, Washington, Chicago and less media centers. "He's an asshole. Hell, I don't care if he wants to talk. Fuck 'em," a Washington writer was spouting. "All he says is, 'You win and you lose as a team.' What kind of shit is that? I said, 'I understand you're a student of the game. Don't you want to discuss it?' He says, 'I'm not a teacher.' Fuck 'em. Fuck all those Portland guys. All they talk about is 'team, team, team.' There isn't one of them worth quoting." Another writer adds, "You see that jerk Lucas go over and shake hands with Dawkins? What a bunch of hype. I wish Dawkins had decked him."

There was no way I could tell them where I was going as I excused myself.

As the birthday party broke up, Walton sat on the front steps of his old Victorian house in an old and worn-out Victorian neighborhood. He was talking about how he felt the TV coverage of the Western Conference finals against the Lakers had been biased in favor of Los Angeles, how they catered to the major metropolitan audience. He was disgusted that when Lucas had gone down to shake hands with Dawkins during the introductions, TV had been showing a replay of the fight the two had the previous game in Philadelphia. He said he had told CBS sportscaster Brent Musburger he hoped they wouldn't be biased in favor of Philadelphia in this series. He also told him to quit calling him "Mountain Man." I told Walton I had used that in my story this afternoon. I thought it had a nice regional ring to it. He said he didn't like nicknames. He said they were degrading. A neighbor came by and told Walton he had just finished *Being There*, by Jerzy Kosinski. They enthused about that. He told of other books by this author I had yet to read. Two young ladies walking up the other side of the street called over to see if anyone was interested in buying a canary they had in a box. Walton shook his head.

"Aren't you Bill Walton?" one of them called.

"Nope," he answered.

I asked why they were selling the bird. Actually I wanted to get a closer look at them. One had a gold star pierced through a nostril. Walton gave me a bit of a glare for encouraging them as they crossed the street.

"You sure look like Walton," Gold Star said.

"Hey, you are Bill Walton," the other chimed in. I couldn't bear to look at him. "You guys sure looked great today on TV. Do you live here?"

"I just like my privacy," he said quietly.

"Sure," they agreed and departed.

Later that evening Jack Scott, who was living with Walton, told stories about reporters who kept trying to talk their way into the house. He said he was getting interviewed more now by guys trying to get at Walton then he had when he was in the headlines for his political activism.

The evening's offering of philosophies put me a little farther down a strange road which I had found myself traveling since late in the season. My early-season enthusiasm had been bounced off course several times during the season, but when I actually changed directions, I don't exactly know. Somewhere along the way, late in the season when every front seemed to be a battleground, I started asking myself questions about the role I was living. Until then, it had been questions about how to function in that role. I could recall the start of the season and

240

the bubbling enthusiasm I felt, how I wanted to cover pro basketball until I retired. I still did, but I was beginning to have thoughts, doubts at this point, of how comfortable I could ever be in the role of reporter.

A week before the end of the season, Brown had sauntered out to the Sonics' bench in street clothes, still ailing from that sprained ankle suffered at Milwaukee. Heberlein popped up and scooted over to ask of his condition and when he would be back in action. As Heberlein leaned down, Brown looked at me over Heberlein's shoulder and rolled his eyes as if to say, "See the chipmunk come to eat out of my hand." Heberlein was just doing his job, a thorough job, but he looked to the player as being so inferior. An innocent incident, but another one that made me think of all the times a reporter must respond to players and coaches. They pick their nose and we ask what they mined.

There had been some mail. The article quoting "a reliable source" had upset others besides the local radio reporter. Russell's coach at USF, who was now living in Washington, had even lettered his criticism: "Dear John Owen: . . . Blaine Johnson must have better things to do than to quote an 'informed source' and a 'reliable source' as the basis for his recent story re the Sonic coaching situation. His lack of preparation coupled with his bold but unsubstantiated (to date) predictions are unprofessional. . . . Signed, Phil Woolpert." Owen had answered: ". . . Johnson tries to 'tell it like it is' even if he has to protect sources of stories like the one headlined, 'Russell Won't Return,' which preceded Russell's resignation by two days."

There was another letter, written the final day of the season, the day of the "Why Russell Won't Return" commentary. It, too, was addressed to Owen. It read in part: "Why don't you fire this turkey, Blaine Johnson? Besides being a poor writer it's obvious he just doesn't like sports. Just because Russell and the Sonics are lousy is no reason for Johnson to degrade sports in general and basketball in particular. The jerk is a very misguided 'intellectual' with very little real intellect, if any, who is completely out of his realm. He belongs in a hippy protest march! Sports, and basketball in particular, are an IMPORTANT, wonderful, and enjoyable activity, pasttime and outlet in a tense, problematic world. It's very obvious that Johnson cannot appreciate this. His attitude towards sports is disgusting and contemptible. I don't know why he even bothers to be in the sports dept. of the *P-I*. His rotten attitude and employment are his problem, but why foist his drivel on your readers. That is your problem John. All you are doing is advertising to the public that Johnson is an ass and that you are one also for keeping him. . . ."

What disturbed me more than those letters was an editorial that Owen then wrote defending me: " 'What's really going on with the Sonics?' That phrase, involving a variety of subjects, is heard frequently by the sportswriters who cover any beat. And nothing should infuriate them more. Because the question implies that you can't read the real truth in your newspaper. If the reporters and editors are doing the job for which they are paid, the question should never have to be asked. That's the kind of job *P-I* pro basketball writer Blaine Johnson did, in chronicling the departure of Bill Russell from the Sonics. The season hadn't even ended when he predicted Russell would step down as coach of our NBA team, and he explained why at some length in an exclusive *P-I* article. When he learned Sonic President Sam Schulman was trying to buy up the final year of Russell's contract, it was printed in the *P-I*. When Johnson learned from sources that Russell would not contest the naming of a new coach and general manager and in fact was cooperating fully in the negotiations, Johnson wrote that his departure was now imminent. That same day a TV reporter asked Schulman what chances Russell had of returning to the team and was told, 'about 50-50.' At that time there was no chance Russell would return, as Johnson had learned. Schulman wasn't trying to deceive the TV reporter. He was just being overly cautious, since the final 'i' had not been dotted, the final 't' had not been crossed in the legal settlement. When our reporters find out 'what is really happening' they will try to tell you. They might have to guard their sources, sometimes they must observe legal safeguards. But they feel you are entitled to know what is happening with your team, the players you support and cheer, and the men who guide these franchises. And they aren't going to wait for handouts or press conferences. We're not, after all, dealing with national security. These are games that people play. But they are also teams you support with your interest and your money. Hopefully the next time you see one of us on the street, you won't have to ask: 'What's REALLY happening?' "

Applause, that's the way I should have read that. Instead, it made me feel guilty. I had hung it out on the line down the stretch. I had done some good reporting and some solid commentary and analysis throughout the season. But there had also been so many things that hadn't been written—because of privacy respected or communication protection—but, nonetheless, not written.

Signs of fatigue and frustration at the end of a long and involved season, I told myself.

But days like this rainy one in Portland were bearing further momentum toward some tough decisions. The morning after the birthday party at Walton's, the Blazers were working out in the Portland Coliseum. The Blazers were working on a backdoor play. Lucas cut across the key, Gross was too late with the pass. Ramsay, standing beyond the top of the key, slapped his hands sharply. "Come on. This is what we can get. Let's work at it. We're just walkin'. Let's go." The pace accelerated. There was a little more quickness, a little more contact, sharper cuts as they went through it again. Gross popped loose from the opposite side of the ball, took the pass and laid it in. "Good. Let's run the turnout. Let's run the turnout. Backdoor this on the other forward whenever it's necessary. Let's be sharp." The Blazers shifted into high, springing through the next sequence of plays. There was media plastered throughout the lower seating area. Those who had been covering the 76ers all year confessed to varying degrees of shock that a team would be this disciplined in practice.

A while later, when the 76ers took the court, I could see why. They were looser than that day I had seen them practice in Seattle way back in November. Jones wore a visor on backward. Free had a baseball cap on sideways. Dawkins wore a floppy beach hat and the string on his sweat pants was drawn up around his thick neck. No one shot a layup without putting something crazy on it. They juked and jived up and down the court. McGinnis, who was in a late-season shooting slump, received a chorus of "Brick, brick" from his teammates every time he took a shot. Carefree or crazy?

I found myself thinking, this team doesn't deserve to win anything. They don't work hard. They aren't disciplined. Yet they were the free spirits of the court that I professed to enjoy. I believed players should work hard and be regimented, yet I loved the free-wheeling show time. I'm reviewing something for which I don't even have a fixed standard, after all. Entertain, yes. But now it's the playoffs. Win, too. What's the difference from emphasizing winning in December? Well, it's a . . . let's see, there's a message there somewhere.

While the 76ers cavorted on the practice court, a small band of writers went into the Blazer locker room to interview Lucas.

"Just three minutes, Luke," they persisted as Lucas tried to duck out. "We won't hold you up. Just give us three minutes."

"All you'll want to do is talk about the fight," Lucas replied in a voice deep, softened by a drawl.

"No, we don't. You're a very vital player in this series, we just want to get your feelings on what is going on. We don't have to talk about the fight if you don't want."

"Okay, but just three minutes."

"How would you describe your temperament?" came the first question. "Do you have a quick temper?"

"No, I don't have a quick temper."

"Wouldn't you say that you become angry when things don't go your way on the court?"

"No. I don't go around inciting fights. I don't start things, if that's what you mean."

"Do you think you can intimidate somebody at this level of basketball?"

"I don't try to intimidate. I just play hard and try to help my team win."

"But you have a reputation for intimidation."

"I get more publicity on my intimidation than on my game. I've had a good year of basketball and I get more publicity out of one fight."

"Is that the press's fault?"

"The press likes to harp on issues of violence."

"Don't you think that is what fans want to read?"

"I think violence is overplayed by the press."

"What about the handshake yesterday. When you went down and shook hands with Dawkins, was that an Al McGuire tactic—psych a guy out?"

"I did that just to let him know everything was cool."

"Is Dawkins still pissed off at you?"

"I don't know. The guy is twenty years old. He's still young. He's going to be around another fourteen years."

"Would you say you duck publicity and shy away from the superstar image?"

"I prefer dealing with people more on a personal level than on a star level."

"Wouldn't it make you more effective with young people if you developed a superstar image?"

"I get along with them just fine."

"Do you think there's a chance you and Dawkins will get into it again before the series is over?"

"I'm not planning on it."

"What if one of your teammates was in a fight. Would you be anxious to help?"

"Hey, I thought we weren't going to talk about the fighting."

"There's a lot of griping among the 76ers. Do you think this hurts their chances of winning?"

"I don't know. I just worry about my team and what we have to do to win."

"Why is Portland so reluctant to talk with the press and discuss the series? Do you think the 76ers are going to read something and get inspired?"

"I can only speak for myself. I enjoy a lot of privacy."

And they went on, for over fifteen minutes before Lucas finally moved toward the door. One of the writers said, "See, that wasn't so bad, was it?" Lucas just shrugged. I hadn't needed a story, so I was able to watch. I found myself in Lucas' corner and resenting the press for pushing, crowding, tantalizing—like kids poking a stick through the zoo cage, trying to get the lion to roar. What disturbed me most was that the reporters were just doing their job—trying to come up with a big headline on an off-day of the finals. Trying to come up with something like, "Lucas says, 'I'll Fight the Whole City of Philadelphia if I Feel Like It.' "

That afternoon, as the rain punished the evergreens outside my hotel room, I wondered if I wasn't overanalyzing everything. I felt I had become, over the course of this NBA season, obsessed with a search for meaning to every turnover and locker room quote. I was caught up in the sixties significance scene—trying to make things fall into orderly profiles and to make my role in the whole thing productive, rather than simply responsive. I didn't want to just follow in the image of a thousand other reporters interviewing and reviewing a thousand athletes. Yet, what was I accomplishing by trying so intensely to be unique? Headaches. Why couldn't I just be like Bob Logan? Why couldn't I just wade in, ask questions, take my shots?

I had dinner that evening with Logan, who had covered the Chicago Bulls for eleven years on behalf of the Chicago *Tribune*. As we bounced in and out of Chicago en route to points everywhere else, I was always attracted to his hard-hitting style. I had no idea there had been an interruption to his beat assignment. Logan has a wit that leaves you wincing, but at the same time, chuckling. He's always tossing a pun at you, something like: "Speaking of the Celtics, when you fly from Boston to Chicago you get the Auerbach." With the Scotch going down, we talked of the league we covered. It felt like veterans of a foreign experience that few, even in our profession, could know about. We talked of the constant tension that you experience, fearing you will miss something, be it a trade breaking across the country or something breaking on the court. "You're writing down a foul shot when Awtrey hits Kareem in the head. You never relax," Logan said, adding he got along well with most of the players in the league and had developed a workable rapport in most locker rooms as he became known over the years. We agreed Maravich was among the worst interviews. Cowens was tough. I told him of my frustrations with Russell. "He was without a question the toughest interview I ever dealt with in the NBA," Logan commented. "He was the one coach I never had a meaningful discussion with. He'd stand there and say his bit after a game, but after a certain period the curtain would drop again and he's not there even though he's still standing there. You couldn't get inside."

As the evening progressed we were discussing pressure from management on newspapers to make their reporters support the franchise. I said I had never had that pressure from Owen, he was honest-John journalism all the way down the line. Logan said he used to think he was safe, too. Until two years earlier he had written a piece headlined: "Bulls Inept on Floor, in Office." He said he had been called in by his editor. "I asked him what I had done. He said, 'You're off the beat—editorializing too much.' They felt I was too negative in my coverage of the Bulls. I was as low as I've ever been in twenty-four years of this racket. The '75 recession was deep and there were no jobs anywhere. Well, I served my time in the penalty box that year, working on the copy desk. When the playoffs came around they said, 'Go now and sin no more.' I was back on the beat. But I don't have any doubt who is more important when push comes to shove. I'm not going hunting for heads anymore. I just tell what happens on the court and remember that I'm more important than the paper—they decided that."

I'm not sure why, maybe I was applying more of the romanticism to my colleagues, but when Logan related that, I felt as though I had just been thrown for a twenty-yard loss. It wasn't that I was worried about my paper not backing me. On the contrary, they expected me to go full blast. But here was a master of the locker room telling me there was no way to handle this job without weighing and worrying and constantly contemplating the future—yours.

As Portland once again destroyed Philadelphia the next evening in the series' fourth game, I found myself riding that grand wave of emotion super-psyched fans can create. The Portland Coliseum was pure pandemonium throughout the game. They crooned "Luuuuuuuuke" in that mournful, haunting sound which accompanied the emergence of the Monolith in the movie *2001*. Jammed into every supportable space of the place, they produced a noise that seemed to mix with my blood and make me simmer with pure pleasure. The Portland Coliseum didn't hold as many patrons, but this was the same atmosphere as there had been at Chicago Stadium—scream your head off, get carried away. I didn't need to join in the yelling. I was enjoying the events that took place on the floor for their basketball focus, as well. But I wondered if some of the pleasure wasn't enhanced because I was watching two teams that I had no direct involvement with? There was no one out there with whom I had battled over an interview or bickered with over some statement I had written or tired of after two weeks on the road. I was back, at least one step, toward the fan's perspective—and I liked it.

I was struck by the comments of a few of the writers. All they cared about was Philly winning so they could wrap it up at home the next game and no one would then have to troop all the way back across the country to sit around in rainy, boring Portland for another session. No sooner did I find myself condemning them for their self-centered, no-sense-of-fun attitudes, when I realized that was the way some Sonics' fans looked upon my negativism in the late stages of the season. They had gone to those games expecting to be entertained, to enjoy the noise and the commotion and the crazy things on the court. Also to win, of course, if possible. But I was telling them every morning what a lousy show it was and while they might even have agreed as they went out the door booing, many of them didn't want to be reminded of the sad state of their team the next day. And they certainly didn't want to listen to me harp about how the team didn't deserve to be going to any playoffs after they had stunk up the league for most of the season. Rally around, be loose, be optimistic, have fun.

Following the second game, which allowed Portland to equalize the series on a thirty-two-point runaway, I was on another swing through the locker rooms. There was at least a feeling of purpose in all the questions during the playoffs. There were match-ups and trends and themes to explore. There was meaningful analysis of players performing under the ultimate in pressure and breakdowns in execution which had worked all year. Again, I was the only one to invade Walton's hideout cubicle in the locker room. Once again Erving provided the ultimate in patience in the other locker room, having faced thirty minutes of the same questions by the time I got to him. I found myself approaching him with, "Julius, I know you've discussed it all forty times, but I'd appreciate it if you could tell me . . ." Why the fuck was I so meek? Because I couldn't stand to shove myself in some guy's face without at least acknowledging that I was asking something of him, taking from him.

I was back at Walton's that evening. The conversations and the food and the interplay among those present would have made a very attractive feature. Here I was, sitting in the living room with the man who—because of the spotlight on the playoffs—was becoming the talk of the country. He was on the way to being named MVP of the whole show. A lot of people would have liked to be sitting where I was that night. He was saying things that he probably wouldn't have minded my using, like: "Once you get into a game you don't remember the last one or who is ahead in the series. You're just doing whatever you can to win this one," and "I love big, roaring crowds, even when they're against you. Like in Chicago. That crowd back there was the trip of all time. I've never experienced anything like it in all of basketball. That makes you want to play—I love it." He talked about opposing centers and how, on a little pregame show he did for each Blazer broadcast, he had laid into the press for derogatory nicknames. "It's racist the way they call Dawkins 'King Kong' and say, 'That's a gorilla dunk.' They look at him in an apelike sense, not as a human being."

There were other things that were discussed and experienced that would have been captivating copy. I felt irresponsible, frustrated as a reporter and a writer that I couldn't impart them. But I was there as a person, not as a journalist. I came away flattered that I could be accepted into someone's house and be trusted. But I again felt that sense of self-deception. The functionalism was working against the egoism. I was a spy if I did my job. But where do you turn it off? You can't sit there and say, "Can I use *that*?" The guy is at home, relaxing. And is that any different than Russell on a plane at 6 A.M.? Doesn't he have the right to say something that I won't write or weigh against him? Doesn't he have the right to just be in a grouchy mood? Doesn't any player have the right to stay out all night and smoke dope and make love with a lady without me standing on a sanctimonious perch telling the public that he's junk on the court because he hangs all night? But I want to write it all, tell everybody "What's Happenin'." What to do?

Driving back to Seattle I found myself moving faster down that road of challenging my role as a reporter. I was finding fault with each phase. It wasn't just one set of values or a code of behavior that I found unattractive, I was finding something disconcerting each way I turned. I was now looking at my job as a handful of incompatible parts. I laughed at the seriousness applied to sport, yet I was now wound tight, as in uptight.

I recalled the night we had walked off the court in the Coliseum and a fan reached out to touch the player exiting in front of me. Not to shake his hand, nor to get an autograph, just to touch his fingers against sweat-glossed skin. The fan wasn't a kid, he was in his thirties. And he turned to his wife and said, "I touched him." The guy didn't realize this player would screw his wife if the fan went out for a cup of coffee.

Hero worship. I despised it, yet did I have the right to bring it down? After we had returned from that mid-March marathon on the road, Watts was scheduled to appear at an elementary school carnival. The school happened to be the one that my son, Aaron, attended. Watts had coincidentally blown the only two other scheduled school appearances I happened to be involved in with him. Throughout the trip I had reminded him that he had a date at that school on that first Saturday night back. If I was going to be there, he'd better be, too. They had scheduled an auction, over which he was to preside. He was late. They started without him. They tried to save the best items for last, hoping he would show to promote things like a ceramic lamp figurine in the likeness of Watts. It was cute, well made and went for forty-five dollars even though Watts was still tardy. A rubber basketball with all the Sonics' autographs went for thirty-five dollars. Finally, people started to leave. A balmy spring wind was blowing the banner that a group of kids held out front, still hoping their hero would show. Each headlighted car that came down the street was greeted with squeals and cheers only to prove a false alarm. Finally, the banner, which read, "Hi, Slick, Welcome to Briarcliff," was left to rustle along the gutter in the wind. Watts said the next day that he had fallen asleep. That should have been reported right along with all the applaudable things. Right? But after a while you begin to feel you are living with more concern for their lives than your own. Watchdog, when do you go off duty?

Early in the off-season *P-I* columnist Steve Rudman had contacted Haywood for a column. Woody told him in the sort of criticism he had used during his first trip back two years earlier that Seattle was racist and not worth his time. Mussehl, his lawyer, called the next day, after Rudman had written his column quoting all the comments, and said those were off the record and had only been intended as an explanation why he didn't want to do a column. Now Haywood wanted to set the record straight and, in effect, call Rudman a liar. Here is my desk mate versus a man who has turned me around and hassled me in the pursuit of my duties. Journalistically, I owed Haywood an audience and an opportunity to express himself. We did a feature the next day. I felt I had betrayed Rudman.

I couldn't take Heberlein's stand that you ask a question and you write what they give you for an answer. But I had to do that, in effect, in this latest Haywood piece. It bothered Heberlein that a player might be deceitful, but that was the player's fault. He finally decided to ride in coach class. He didn't want to hear all the jive and bickering up front. He wanted to maintain his sanity, to survive in the job he was paid to do. He wanted to keep as much emotionalism out of his approach to the job as he could. I wanted to take his attitude, but it wasn't my nature. The past season had been a masterpiece of social interplay and personality upheaval. A watcher of people couldn't have wanted more. The trouble was, I felt as though I were watching instead of doing. Even my crackerjack psychoanalysis trip was one of reacting to the lives of others, more than making things happen in mine.

Something else was happening with my attitude. What had been, through my career in journalism, a lust to get stories in the paper was becoming a contemplation of convenience. There had been countless times I stumbled across some little story and would feel compelled to write it up and see it in the paper the next day. I need a feeling of accomplishment with my time. Seeing an article in the paper made me feel I had done something the day before. Now, it wasn't to the extent of boredom, but I was experiencing feelings of futility. What difference did it make if the story proved invalid a week later? It didn't matter at all, earlier. Now I was beginning to wonder. After all his headline harangues about wanting more dough or to be let go, Watts had dropped his claim, saying, "I don't want anyone to think I'm giving in as a man or sayin' Sam's right. But I guess Sam knows he's got me in a corner." Then, a few days later Watts says he wants a "piece of the rock" after all. Then he says he's going to "shut up and let Sam win." Back and forth. After a while I begin to feel like an elevator. Push a button and we'll go up. Push another and we'll go down. All the while there are stories in the paper. But I'm beginning to wonder if I care.

There had been a couple of major press conferences, one to announce the trade of Burleson and another to announce the Sonics were moving to the Kingdome two seasons later. Both stories appeared in the *Times* before the press conference announcement. Alerted by the publicity director that there would be a press conference, the *Times* had jumped on the stories and they had beaten the competition by coming out prematurely. After the second round of this, I told the Sonics publicity staff they had better make sure I got the next story or I would never cooperate with them again. It was my feeling that if neither side had come up with the story on its own, then both should honor the club's release. "I have never gone against my word with anyone in this organization. I want to work together, as much as possible. I'm not here to flack for you. But if there is something coming, I appreciate knowing about it as early as possible so that I will have more time to work on it. I have always honored every release date on anything you have given me. It's ridiculous to be working twenty hours a day to break every story. We're both going to be pitching for what we can get. But if we don't have it in advance, let's just work out the releases fairly." The *Times* doesn't want to go along with that. My first inclination is to say, "I *will* work twenty hours a day to bury the *Times* and the Sonics." But my real thought is—why is everything so competitive, so necessarily aggressive?

I remember Russell's words: "When you lose that fine, competitive edge, mentally or physically, you're dead." In this business, you are.

I was moving to keep from being embarrassed, rather than really interested in the events, really anxious to call someone and dig for a story. There is nothing on the line but my ego, to beat somebody with a story, to dig up a good feature. But is that enough to justify so much time and thought and aggression toward subjects—as in people? I was tired of dissecting personalities and reducing games to fine-line analysis. It wasn't just basketball—my love for the game was at least working there. I found myself not interested in tearing into the meat of any game or any athlete. I just wanted to watch the action. Something was wrong in me. I wondered if I could get it back again.

The day Portland finished off Philly for the championship, I wasn't able to return to Portland. The *P-I* needed another body in the office that day. I was insulted, angry. The paper expected 100 percent from the reporter in the devotion to his duties. But when it came time for them to make some adjustments to acknowledge the reporter's emotions, that was different. Professionally they had a right to expect that I turn it on and off. Emotionally, it doesn't work. Foremost, the game warranted coverage. If we had covered the previous two, why not the grand finale? From that perspective, I was embarrassed among my colleagues in other cities. Personally, what was toughest to swallow was not to be at an event that would be more of a happening than a technical test. I wanted to be challenged to put it into words so that a colorful chapter in the history of Pacific Northwest sports would be written in my observation. I wanted, too, to share a special time with a person who had become a friend before there were people mobbing him in celebration. It was what should have been my climax to a season. Too, there was the romanticism, the rah-rah fan in me that wanted to feel part of that crowd going crazy.

Walton had told me what he really wanted was a close, exciting game. He got that in the final one. It was the connoisseur seeking the ultimate. I felt the same way as a journalist. There were many things distracting my enthusiasm these days, but I wanted the chance to write a great story as a finale to the season. Walton had made his mark as a pro—even if he never gained another title, he proved he could do it once. But I was left to ponder what I really thought of my job. What do I love about sports? The action, but above everything else, the unpredictability. Unlike even the most suspensive play or motion picture, *nobody* in the world knows what's going to happen at a sports event. What do I love about writing? Capturing an event with my observations and putting them into meaningful and, if appropriate, entertaining prose. As a writer, trying to comprehend a Russell or a whole NBA way of life can be a great challenge. It is as though you catch a scent of something—then the harder you try to inhale more of it, the more it fades away. It comes back and you work at it some more. It's fun, an exercise. Yet it is something you can come to resent, if you feel you are giving more to the challenge than can be rewarded by what you discover. If the game isn't fun for its own involvement, it's probably not worth pursuing the answers.

As summer moved across July, I felt like a candidate for characterization in a Feiffer cartoon. I think about things to make sure I'm not being lazy or careless with my life. Being lazy on life is bad because you won't be happy if you don't work hard and challenge yourself. But the more I work at trying to think about things, the less I enjoy life. So why don't I just be lazy and careless and enjoy life?

Being a beat reporter is more than a job. It becomes a way of life—in the time it consumes and in the involvement required of the journalist's thoughts and behavior. As someone once commented, it's a good way of life, but it's no way to live. It is a very good way to live if you are able to approach it with the proper set of expectations and concessions. One person's tastes in life will allow that, while another's will fight it, just as one person enjoys a full day on the golf course and others, such as myself, would rather be home making my yard look attractive.

A month before the start of training camp, as I contemplated the gearing up for the next season, I discovered I couldn't get geared up. What was initially suspected as being fatigue and frustration off the previous campaign, stayed on as unrelenting challenges to discover just what I wanted from my job. Maybe the most crucial thing that happened to me over the summer was the loss of curiosity concerning the personalities and activities of the NBA. For a journalist to lose his curiosity is as crippling as a symphony conductor becoming tone deaf. It was true that I often felt myself a pest in pushing for provocative material from individuals. And I did often feel myself in the role of a pimp as I cruised the locker rooms for postgame comments. But in retrospect, much of my discomfort in pursuing the role of a reporter was caused by the fact I really didn't care about the issues being discussed. I wouldn't want to read it if someone else was writing it. It often was making too big a matter of things not that important. They were important to me as a journalist for my stories, but not any longer to me as a person.

It was clear there was a conflict in me between my role as a reporter, the functionalism, and myself, the egoism. It had been ego-satisfying to get tight with a Walton. But at that point he was still an object—something that others were not able to touch. Once I became involved with him as a person, the role of the reporter seemed awkward, sometimes an insult. I didn't want to pursue individuals to see if I could gain a certain status with them. I wanted meaningful relationships in my life. Not everyone shall become a true friend, but each person should know he can trust me. When would I come across a story while sitting in the living room of a Walton that was so dynamic I couldn't let it pass?

I discovered as the new season approached, I couldn't devote myself to the type of writing I found satisfying nor to my love for the sport I was covering in the role of sportswriter. I didn't want to analyze every game, every opinion, every trade, every move executed by the Sonics. I didn't want to stand in a locker room and exchange ideas with a superstar. I didn't care who was making how much money or who was going to be traded where or what kind of a good or bad job a coach was doing. I didn't care if someone was setting a league record in offensive rebounds. There are fans who do care about all these things and there are dynamic, dedicated sportswriters who enjoy providing the information. But, for me, I had become someone who just wanted a good show when I sat down in my seat at eight o'clock.

Two weeks before the start of the next NBA cycle, I decided to leave sportswriting in pursuit of new adventures—ones in literary and construction fields where I could create with my plans and ideas, rather than being in a position of having to respond to the actions of others. I told Owen I was leaving. He asked if I was sure I wanted to give up what I had attained. I told him there was no way a person could step away from a position of this stature and be really sure. But I felt sure that I had crossed a line that left me unable to commit full enthusiasm and attention to my responsibilities. I called my son, Aaron, and told him I was giving up sportswriting.

"Does that mean you won't be sitting down on the court anymore?"

"Yep."

"Are there a lot of people mad at you?"

"Nooooo. Why?"

"Well, that guy who said 'fire that hippie' will be happy."

"Oh, you mean 'fire that turkey.' "

"Yeah . . . er, Dad, what's he mean, 'turkey'?"

"I guess in this case it was a guy who either took his job too seriously or not seriously enough."

"Oh."

EPILOGUE

Geese, at least that's what I supposed them to be, formed ragged chevrons across the face of the sunset above the eastern Nebraska plain. Dull-blue puffy clouds cluttered the copper sky as the sun faded over the flat horizon. It was November 12—six months and eight days after Russell's dismissal by the Sonics, six weeks after my resignation from the *P-I*. I was churning out the miles, homeward bound from more than a month of bouncing around the country to see friends and absorb nature's loveliness.

I twisted the radio dial across islands of static and country and western songs before finding WOAI, where Terry Stembridge, voice of the San Antonio Spurs, was launching his pregame show. " ... Of course, the big news in the Spurs camp today is the acquisition of Mike Green from Seattle for two second-round draft choices. We'll be back after this word from our sponsors to visit with Mike ... ."

My God, I thought, I won't know anyone in the Sonic locker room. There were only four left, Watts, Brown, Seals and Johnson, of the 12 players who had finished the previous season. Since Hopkins had been named coach and Lenny Wilkens had been hired as director of player personnel, the Sonics had dealt Burleson to Kansas City and Wilkerson to Denver to end up with Marvin Webster and Paul Silas. They had waived Bob Love, Norwood, Oleynick, Weatherspoon, Tolson, and now Green was gone.

There had been another chapter of training camp optimism. New regime, new conviction to reach the mountaintop. The Man was gone, long live the Man. The absence of Russell's dominating influence was as obvious as if they had erased the Space Needle from the Seattle skyline. Brown had gone public immediately with his sentiments on what it felt like to be out from under Russell's thumb: "Russell worked his first year, but then he began playing with the team as if it was a toy. No work was being done. There was no system. No organization. The only things that happened to us were out of the kindness of God. Then he began putting himself up against the players and I wanted nothing to do with it."

Maybe that was why so many of the players had been so difficult to deal with and why their efforts and behavior had been subject to criticism as being less than their full potential. Maybe the only way their egos could defend themselves against Russell's was to drag their feet, to balk and sulk—or to simply step out and challenge him as Gray had, with the inevitable walk down the road as the result. Maybe it was mostly Russell's fault. Maybe they would all come through now that he

255

was out of their way. Hopkins promised to work his troops into glue if it took that to build a winner. Watts beamed his bald dome out of a newspaper ad proclaiming: "If we don't win this year, Hoppy's gonna scalp us all."

But now eight of them were gone already. The Sonics must look like Kojak and eleven doorknobs about now, I mused, as I drove westward into the Nebraskan night. The club was losing three out of four games after not quite a month of league play. Maybe it hadn't been Russell's fault at all.

A few nights later I was in the Sonic locker room following another dreary Seattle loss. The hangdog look of the previous season was still there, but on so many new faces. Johnson and I sat in a corner of the room as he quietly dressed. He wasn't getting much playing time. He was thoroughly dejected and was eager to pour his troubles into an ear that had heard this sort of story before. "This isn't for me, man. I gotta get out of here. My career is going down the drain. They don't have no use for me here and you know I can play. I'm gonna demand to be traded or just walk out of here."

I told him he'd be joining Oleynick in the Eastern League if he got pushy. "You haven't had a chance to show the league what you can do, DJ, and if you get to making demands to be traded or if you sit at the end of the bench and sulk, they'll never give you a chance. They'll weed you out, man, and never know what they missed. You've gotta forget the humiliation and give it everything you've got when you get called on." I didn't dare agree with him that he was being wasted on the bench.

He didn't have much of a chance to react to my advice under those dire conditions, though, because not even two weeks later, on November 30, the captain of the Sonic ship walked the plank. Wilkens was named to replace Hopkins as coach. The club's record was 5-17. Johnson replaced Watts in the starting lineup, rounding out the backcourt with Gus Williams, who had been acquired earlier from Golden State. Webster was in the hole. A blond rookie named Jack Sikma was at forward along with veteran John Johnson. Only one starter, DJ, had been a Sonic at the end of the previous year.

Schulman had executed his ultimate in a long series of Scramble Acts. He booted Hopkins after barely a month of the regular season. Question: If he could justify hiring a man for a job, how could he be satisfied that hiring was an error after that short time? Question: If he ran Wilkens down the road in 1972, first forcing him to give up the coaching half of the player-coach role he had held while leading Seattle to its winningest season (47) and then trading him to Cleveland amid the most overt protest ever mounted by Sonic fans, how could he then reinstate him as coach in 1978? In fact, the turmoil created in the wake of Wilkens' dismissal in 1972 left the franchise in such a mess it drove

Schulman to spend all that money to beg Russell to come aboard and bail out the club a year later.

Schulman avoided having to answer such embarrassing questions because his team immediately launched what became probably the most dramatic turnaround in the history of the NBA. The seeds of such a fable, planted in those first days of Wilkens' takeover, tell a lot about the influence of emotions in the NBA. Seattle turned into an instant winner—reeling off victories at an 80 percent clip during the next month. What had happened? The club caught that magical scent of confidence, built out of a great big whiff of r-e-l-i-e-f.

Hopkins had been even more domineering than Russell, according to those who had performed in both regimes. While Russell had been accused of not devoting enough time to his coaching responsibilities, Hopkins was accused of working too hard—sometimes interrupting the flow of a practice with a 20-minute dissertation on various options for a certain play. Besides, Hopkins was also one of the most candid in criticism of his players in the media. That caused a reaction. "He was telling us too much. We couldn't keep up with him. He is a nice guy, but he didn't know how to relate to us. He was always putting us down, asking for more and more. He was never satisfied. I've got to say that being with Lenny is like gettin' out of jail," was the assessment of one Sonic observer shortly after Wilkens took the controls.

If it could be simplified to this extent, the three keys to success in the NBA must be: 1) health, 2) happiness and 3) a hero in the hole. They may not come in exactly that order, but Seattle came up with all three under Wilkens. He made some changes, but the key was that Seattle got some victories—immediate feedback for effort extended. The Sonics were on the road when Wilkens first took over. If the club had been playing even good basketball, it still shouldn't have expected to win half its games. But it played superior ball and it did win, home and away. And, the club was suddenly high on itself. The framework of a champion was built, fragile as a house of cards initially, but then the bottom ones became stable and the structure of momentum grew.

Tensions lifted and the embarrassing dread to take the court now became fun. "Kickin' ass feels awfully nice after all we been through," DJ offered one night as the days became sunnier. Brown, who had been out with a knee injury at the time of Hopkins' firing, became the sixth man, coming off the bench with his patented firepower. He was suddenly playing with more dedication and leadership than he had shown in those six previous seasons as a pro. He was making dazzling passes on the fastbreak. He was even taking an occasional charge on defense.

Of course, it happens in the hole and Webster began to bloom. His rookie year at Denver had been batted apart by illness and he hadn't seen much playing time the next year. Denver got rid of a question mark when he was traded. He had been awkward, turnover prone and offensively ineffective during the season's opening month. It didn't seem Denver had given away anything other than a 7'2" shot-blocker who could vacuum the boards on some nights against some centers. Now he started to blend into the offense. He started to stay down more on defense and consistently came up with double-figure boards. He started to get confidence and his wealth of natural athletic ability started to break out like the sun through rain clouds. He developed game by game. He became a good journeyman and then a darn solid center and, by season's end, maybe the third best postman in the league.

DJ got better and better. The team smoothed out and smothered people. How much credit did Wilkens deserve? How big a role does happiness play?

Amid the spectacle of the Sonics' rise, a poignant subplot was written. Watts was being allowed virtually no part of the developing glory. His playing time diminished to nothing. He sat on the bench in humiliation, grumbling with the also-benched Seals. It began to seem as though Watts was the fall guy for not only Hopkins' woes, but Russell's too.

"Slick wanted to be Mr. Clutch, tryin' to get all the headlines in the last quarter. The guy was costing us games because he kept goin' off," Hopkins explained to me one night after having been fired. "I wanted to bench him, but Lenny said we should keep playin' him so that his market value wouldn't drop. We had benched Green and then couldn't make much of a deal when we finally decided to let him go. I kept tryin' to tell Slick he had to get his head together. I been followin' him since high school. I know him. I told him he had it made in Seattle and he better settle for the role he was bein' given. I told him no black ballplayer is gonna make any public relations money on the side with any of the southern teams. Shut up, stay put and count your blessin's. I told him that. But he wouldn't listen. Said he had to make it now. If I'd gotten Slick out of the way, I would have been okay. But I didn't know Sam was so restless. He and Lenny were so worried about the fans turnin' on us if we traded Slick."

Wilkens made the move that seemed completely unimaginable a few months earlier as he traded Watts to New Orleans on January 4, for a first-round draft choice in 1981.

Up to that point, through the terrible start and the immediate turnaround in the win column, I had felt no emotional involvement regarding the Sonics. I felt quite removed, in fact, and content to enjoy the games and even more content to be heading out the door of the Coliseum when it was over—not having to digest, interpret nor recreate any of what had taken place on the court or in the locker room. I felt bad for Hoppy when he was sent packing. I sympathized with his hurt when he told me: "Sam never said one word to me after that first game of the season. I never knew where I stood. I guess I didn't understand all the politics. I thought it was just a coaching job."

When Watts was traded I felt a genuine ache inside. I felt bitterness toward the fans because they took it without a peep of protest. I felt there had been an injustice. What was worse was that Watts had apparently brought it down on himself. Dear ol' Slickeroo, the guy who saved all of us from so many nights of boredom, who was, in fact, the Franchise, but who made the mistake of thinking that allowed him to run the whole show—including Sam's and Lenny's.

Wilkens said Watts would not adjust to the role they wanted him to play. "He wanted thirty minutes a game. I didn't see how I could promise him that. So he wanted to go elsewhere." The willpower and ego which had carried him from walk-on to local saint had also brought him down.

He came back to haunt the Sonics when they visited New Orleans shortly after the trade. At his mayhem-making best, Watts ripped the Sonics apart. It was his last hurrah. He was awkwardly ineffective on the return to Seattle, where he received warm ovations. He rode the bench at season's end in New Orleans. KIRO-TV hired him to handle the commentary for some of the early playoff games after he came home to Seattle. He had broadcast two games before the complaints that his "colorful jargon" was incomprehensible caused his relief from TV duties.

Following that, as the playoff games moved into the next rounds, fewer people gathered around Watts at the Coliseum. Instead fans seemed awkward and some tried to slip away, trying to avoid eye contact. It finally dawned on me, they were uncomfortable with Watts because he was a reminder of the price that had been paid to achieve the euphoria the club was now providing. Not only was he not part of it, it wouldn't be happening if he were still there. Hopkins and Russell were never around, so no one had to think about their plight.

Watts continued to grin and bear it, promising himself and those who would listen: "I just gotta get me a club that will let me run the ball and things'll be all right. I just gotta go somewhere else to get my ring."

But Seattle was making its Run for the Ring, right now. I had pondered trying to chronicle the details of the club's steady rise from despair to dignity and then decided that wasn't the intent of this book nor the fascination of what was really happening. I was preoccupied with flashbacks and comparisons with what had taken place when it had been other players and teams in seasonal drives.

The sight of Sikma, knees high, head down, arms pumping, as he raced back on defense reminded me of the gutty determination of Dave Debusschere when he was the heart of the Knicks' run at a championship. The Coliseum crowd ripping its throat out reminded me that it was now Seattle's turn to ride that grand wave of pandemonium, to turn the Sonics' court into a Bowl of Howl, as it had been Chicago's turn the previous spring and Portland's during last summer's playoffs. Here was the nation finally discovering the unmatchable marksmanship of Brown. He was being called Downtown Freddy Brown. He was having his turn as the prototype for playground long-range bombers. It was now the national media's turn to try to wade through his verbal games, the con and the dodge amid the sincere and the astute. I was reminded how Watts and Norwood had once sat in the locker room and said, as they pointed at Brown's locker, "We'll never have a championship team with him around." Now Brown was headed for the finals. Here was Dennis Johnson, only a bundle of weeks after telling me he was ready to walk out, becoming a national star. Puffing his cheeks as he roared up and down the court, making unimaginable blocks as he neutralized David Thompson in the Western Conference finals.

It was Seattle's turn. The Sonics took care of Kareem Abdul-Jabbar and the rest of the Lakers two-to-one and moved into a best-of-seven series against defending champion Portland. The Blazers had been in a class by themselves during the regular season, mowing aside everyone and looking very much like dynasty material before Walton and just about everyone else went down with injuries. Walton came back just in time for the Seattle series. He was still suffering from a foot injury. He did something he swore he would never do. After hobbling through the first game, which Seattle stunningly won at Portland, he took a painkiller to endure the second game. In the second half he broke a bone in his foot—he was through. An unusual reaction developed in the sentiments of Seattle fans. Everywhere people were heard commenting: "It's sad he can't play. He's so good. I almost would rather have him in there and us have less chance to win than see him go out this way." They wouldn't have said that about Abdul-Jabbar or Elvin Hayes. Is that because of racism? Or had Walton somehow gotten across the impression that his desire and competitive spirit are more pronounced than that of the other two? Whatever, even though Walton was named MVP for the season, it wasn't his turn this spring.

The time belonged to people like Lenny Wilkens. Fired by Portland the year before Ramsay brought the Blazers their title, Wilkens was gaining revenge with each passing day. Seattle put away the hobbled Blazers in six games. Although his quiet manner, composure, dignity, class, call it what you will, made him seem above things like revenge. "Lenny makes you feel good about yourself. He makes you want to give him all your attention and effort," commented the same observer who earlier compared being with Wilkens after Hopkins as "like being out of jail." What did Wilkens have that Russell and Hopkins lacked? Maybe more determination than Russell but certainly not more than Hopkins. Maybe more status among the players than Hopkins but certainly not more than Russell had initially. Maybe more organization, maybe more communication, maybe he wound up with the right blend of personalities. One thing is certain, he put all the necessary ingredients into the pot at the right time.

I couldn't help but wonder why all those who had been an integral part of the Sonic family a year earlier now seemed not to be the right ingredients when things were bubbling. How that family had disintegrated! Watts' fate was the most overt, but the rest provided their share of melodrama. Burleson's campaign with Kansas City seemed to cement his destiny to not be a great center, but rather, as one KC writer said, "he's the Great White Heap." He capped the season six games short of its scheduled finish when he tore his knee up in a motorcycle accident in Phoenix. Oleynick was given trials with Milwaukee and Indiana before the season began and was left to duty in the Eastern League. Weatherspoon was picked up and subsequently released by Chicago. Norwood was picked up by Detroit where he started for a few weeks, then was released. He played in a mid-Atlantic pro league before it folded, and resurfaced for emergency duty with the crippled Blazers late in the season. Green worked as a backup center for San Antonio as the Spurs won the Central Division title, but were bounced out of the playoffs by Washington. Bantom had a commendable campaign as a starting forward with Indiana. Tolson played for Anchorage in the Eastern League.

Wilkerson started at guard for Denver, facing the Sonics in the Western Conference finals—and going from status as a popular ex-Sonic to a booed enemy as he turned his rough-and-rumble style on his old mates before the Sonics won the series in six. Changes, changes. Gray injured a knee playing tennis during the summer and his career thereby ended. Furtado finally had a chance to perform his duties as a trainer in the environment of dedication and pride that had troubled him so deeply by its absence the previous years. Even though Seals was still in the midst of the Sonics' success, he saw the bright lights fade as he dropped from starting forward to minimal reserve duty over the season. Bob Walsh, bounced as assistant GM in the Russell purge, became a talent agent in Seattle. His roster of clients included Russell. Hopkins disappeared into the scouting trail after being fired and never showed again in the Coliseum. Russell, who also never showed in the Coliseum, seemed content to enjoy his new marriage—to Didi Anstett, Miss USA in 1968—various TV appearances and the composition of a weekly general interest column in the Seattle *Times*.

Always I was hearing the question, "Don't you miss covering the Sonics, especially now that they're going so great?" Always I gave an honest "No, I don't miss it at all. In truth, win or lose, there is still the competitiveness, the tension of squeezing the players to talk, still the jealousies over who is getting quoted. The pressure and responsibilities don't change, just the issues and the faces." Pete Vecsey, NBA columnist for the New York *Post*, asked a different question as we sat side-by-side during game No. 1 of the championship series against the Bullets. The Sonics had just rallied from 19 down with 14 minutes left to pull out a spectacular victory. Over the roar of the crowd, which Watts described as being so loud "you can't hear your ears," Vecsey said, "You've got to miss being able to write something like that for tomorrow's paper." I had to admit that much was frustrating.

The Sonics went up 2-1 after a one-point victory at Washington. They suffered a stunning setback by losing in overtime before a record crowd of nearly 40,000 in the Kingdome, but came back two days later to go up 3-2 with a victory in the Coliseum. The Sonics were on the doorstep of a dream come true. Dennis Johnson was holding a slight edge over Brown or Webster in the race for MVP of the championship series. Schulman could not contain his glee as he told a reporter: "This whole season has been a miracle and I deserve that it has happened to me."

And then it all came apart. Washington destroyed the Sonics by a playoff record 35 points at Washington to even the series. Those tandem intangibles—fate and momentum—were never in the Sonic camp in the showdown seventh game, although Seattle still had a faint chance with 1:30 remaining. The Sonics had rallied from far back to pull to within four points when the season, with all its on-court drama and human triumph and tragedy, came down to one play. A jumper by Bullet guard Charles Johnson dropped off the bottom side of the rim and stayed low on the floor. Webster, Sikma and Silas reached for it, fumbled it, failed to come up with it. Tom Henderson dove into the scramble of arms and legs, popped the ball loose to teammate Mitch Kupchak. The latter sucked it up for a layin, getting fouled by Webster in the process. His accompanying free throw put the spread at seven instead of a possible two. The look of anguish on the face of Silas, a veteran of two NBA titles at Boston, told you it was the big play of the sort men rerun for a summer or a lifetime. It was the sort of play that broke the magical spell which had been created six months and seven days earlier when Wilkens became coach.

Brown wore a tear on his cheek as he came off the court. He knew that all those plans and dreams of training camp had come so hauntingly close to being fulfilled, even after the tortured start. "You don't get this far very often," he said softly in a postgame visit completely void of any of the customary sparring. "There are a lot of things that can happen that will keep you from ever getting back this close to that ring."

Could all this have happened with the cast that was assembled the previous year under Russell?

"The potential for all this was here initially with Russell, maybe even more so because we all had such respect for him and his accomplishments when he came to the Sonics," Brown answered. "You have to respect a coach and what he is trying to do. The more we came to see of Russell, the more that disappeared. Things might fall apart with Lenny, but it won't be due to a lack of communication. Lenny has the personality plus the skills the job requires plus the dedication. Russ wasn't that hungry and Hoppy couldn't get it across. They didn't fit the role."

As I walked out of the locker room, there stood Leonard Gray. His smile was warm, his hand quick to come forward for the cup-slip-and-grip. His words and manner denied that this could be the same man who had raised so much friction in this very locker room. We talked casually as we walked down the corridor. Bantom showed up and joined us. I found myself saying, "It's interesting that after all the tension and adversity we can finally be real enough to talk to each other like human beings."

"My coach and your editor might have had something to do with our tension," Gray answered with a smile. "I'm just a country farmer enjoying the good life now and you're building your houses and writing your books. We don't have to be what somebody else needs us to be."

I looked past Bantom, down the hallway. Talvin Skinner, Tolson and Watts were mingling with some friends. "Guess we've heard from just about everyone but the Big Fella," I said in reference to Russell's absence.

"That tells you something," answered Gray. "That tells you a whole lot about where we were all comin' from."

A week later, as the season fast faded into another bound and filed set of memories, I asked Hopkins how Russell felt about all this.

"He's happy. We play golf every day. He has no regrets. He just didn't believe there wasn't more pride in the league. But he learned. There's no way you could get him back in that again. Oh, maybe if you offered him half a million a year."

I was tempted to call Russell, but I feared he would feel none too warmly toward me considering my parting shots at his career as a coach. I was content to savor the good there was of our relationship and, besides, I knew that if he said he would indeed take half a million a year to return to coaching I would have to call Schulman to see how soon he would be making the offer.

There's no doubt in my mind someone else deserves that story.